TOP FEDERAL TAX
ISSUES FOR 2009
CPE COURSE

CCH Editorial Staff Publication

.CCH
a Wolters Kluwer business

Contributors

Editor.. George G. Jones, J.D., LL.M
Contributing Editors................................... Torie D. Cole, J.D.
Hilary Goehausen, J.D.
Brant Goldwyn, J.D.
Chandra Walker, MPIA, J.D.
George L. Yaksick, Jr., J.D.
Production Coordinator............................. Gabriel E. Santana
Design/Layout......................................Laila Gaidulis
Production ....Lynn J. Brown

This publication is designed to provide accurate and authoritative information in regard to the subject matter covered. It is sold with the understanding
that the publisher is not engaged in rendering legal, accounting, or other
professional service. If legal advice or other expert assistance is required,
the services of a competent professional person should be sought.

ISBN 978-0-8080-1883-4

© 2008, CCH INCORPORATED
4025 W. Peterson Ave.
Chicago, IL 60646-6085
1 800 248 3248
www.CCHGroup.com

TOP FEDERAL TAX ISSUES FOR 2009 CPE COURSE

Introduction

Each year, a handful of tax issues typically requires special attention by tax practitioners. The reasons vary, from a particularly complicated new provision in the Internal Revenue Code, to a planning technique opened up by a new regulation or ruling, or the availability of a significant tax benefit with a short window of opportunity. Sometimes a developing business need creates a new set of tax problems, or pressure exerted by Congress or the Administration puts more heat on some taxpayers while giving others more slack. All these share in creating a unique mix that in turn creates special opportunities and pitfalls in the coming year. The past year has seen more than its share of these developments.

CCH's *Top Federal Tax Issues for 2009 CPE Course* identifies the events of the past year that have developed into "hot" issues. These tax issues have been selected as particularly relevant to tax practice in 2009. They have been selected not only because of their impact on return preparation during the 2008 tax season but also because of the important role they play in developing effective tax strategies for 2009. Some issues are outgrowths of several years of developments; others have burst onto the tax scene unexpectedly. Among the latter are issues directly related to the recent economic downturn. Some have been emphasized in IRS publications and notices; others are too new or too controversial to be noted by the IRS either in depth or at all.

This course is designed to help reassure the tax practitioner that he or she is not missing out on advising clients about a hot, new tax opportunity or is not susceptible to being blindsided by a brewing controversy. In short, it is designed to give the tax practitioner a closer look into the opportunities and pitfalls presented by the changes. Among the topics examined in the *Top Federal Tax Issues for 2009 CPE Course* are:

- This Year's Tax News and Legislation
- Mortgage Workouts and Foreclosures: Tax Alternatives and Consequences
- Tax Relief for a Business in Distress
- Limited Liability Companies: Traps and Opportunities
- Retirement Savings for Small Businesses
- Revised Form 990 and Instructions Create New Compliance Challenges for Tax-Exempt Organizations
- Worker Classification
- New Preparer Penalty Standards

Throughout the Course you will find Study Questions to help you test your knowledge, and comments that are vital to understanding a particular strategy or idea. Answers to the Study Questions with feedback on both correct and incorrect responses are provided in a special section beginning on page 9.1.

To assist you in your later reference and research, a detailed topical index has been included for this Course beginning on page 10.1.

This Course is divided into three Modules. Take your time and review all Course Modules. When you feel confident that you thoroughly understand the material, turn to the CPE Quizzer. Complete one, or all, Module Quizzers for continuing professional education credit. Further information is provided in the CPE Quizzer instructions on page 11.1.

October 2008

COURSE OBJECTIVES

This course was prepared to provide the participant with an overview of specific tax issues that impact 2008 tax return preparation and tax planning in 2009. These are the issues that "everyone is talking about;" each impacts a significant number of taxpayers in significant ways.

Upon course completion, you will be able to:

- Describe the terms and scope of new tax breaks given by Congress to individuals and businesses under the umbrella of "economic stimulus;"
- Compare the different tax consequences among a mortgage workout, foreclosure, a deed in lieu of foreclosure, a short sale, and a sale by a bankruptcy court;
- Determine in what ways Congress's latest attempt at helping struggling businesses, the *Emergency Economic Stabilization Act of 2008*, has altered the rules;
- Determine how traditional rules involving business losses are being used advantageously in current, multi-year planning techniques;
- Recognize the current drawbacks and pitfalls associated with LLCs, including self-employment tax issues, conversion issues, and disregarded entity issues;
- List the basic steps in establishing a qualified retirement plan;
- Identify the components of the revised Form 990 as they apply to a variety of tax exempt organizations;
- Understand the employment tax obligations of employers vis-à-vis employees and independent contractors; and
- Explain the changes made by the *Emergency Economic Stabilization Act of 2008;*

CCH'S PLEDGE TO QUALITY

Thank you for choosing this CCH Continuing Education product. We will continue to produce high quality products that challenge your intellect and give you the best option for your Continuing Education requirements. Should you have a concern about this or any other CCH CPE product, please call our Customer Service Department at 1-800-248-3248.

NEW ONLINE GRADING gives you immediate 24/7 grading with instant results and no Express Grading Fee.

The **CCH Testing Center** website gives you and others in your firm easy, free access to CCH print courses and allows you to complete your CPE exams online for immediate results. Plus, the **My Courses** feature provides convenient storage for your CPE course certificates and completed exams.

Go to **www.cchtestingcenter.com** to complete your exam online.

One **complimentary copy** of this course is provided with certain CCH Federal Taxation publications. Additional copies of this course may be ordered for $31.00 each by calling 1-800-248-3248 (ask for product 0-0982-200).

TOP FEDERAL TAX ISSUES FOR 2009 CPE COURSE

Contents

MODULE 2: SMALL BUSINESS PLANNING

MODULE 3: TAX REPORTING IN TRANSITION

7 Worker Classification

8 New Preparer Penalty Standards

This Year's Tax News and Legislation

In 2008, Congress enacted five major tax bills: the *Economic Stimulus Act of 2008;* the *Housing and Economic Recovery Act of 2008;* the *Heroes Earnings Assistance and Relief Tax Act of 2008;* the *Heartland, Habitat, Harvest, and Horticulture Act of 2008,* and the *Emergency Economic Stabilization Act of 2008.* The new laws include many tax incentives targeted to individuals, businesses of all sizes, military personnel, veterans, senior citizens, and many others. This course explores some of the more widely applicable tax breaks, especially those impacting individuals and businesses. The chapter also looks at the *Mortgage Forgiveness Debt Relief Act of 2007,* which Congress passed in December of 2007.

LEARNING OBJECTIVES

Upon completion of this course, you will be able to:
- Identify the recent tax acts enacted by Congress;
- Describe the terms and amounts of the economic stimulus payments issued in 2008 to qualifying taxpayers;
- Identify tax incentives designed to shore up the housing industry and help first-time homebuyers;
- List tax incentives for military personnel;
- Describe tax breaks for farmers and ranchers; and
- Project the impact of tax extenders and the alternative minimum tax (AMT) patch.

INTRODUCTION

In recent years, Congress has been using the Internal Revenue Code to stimulate the economy, and 2008 is no exception. The four major tax acts passed by Congress in 2008 all include tax incentives to encourage consumer and business spending and investment. The *Economic Stimulus Act of 2008* gave many qualifying individuals one-time payments of between $300 and $600 (and more if the taxpayer had children). The *Heroes Earnings Assistance and Relief Tax Act of 2008* includes tax incentives for military personnel who are receiving combat pay and saving for retirement. The *Housing and Economic Recovery Act of 2008* gives qualifying first-time homebuyers a tax credit and provides an additional standard deduction for state and local taxes for nonitemizers. The *Heartland, Habitat, Harvest, and Horticulture*

Act targets more than $1 billion in tax relief to farmers and ranchers. Many of the tax breaks are targeted to narrow groups of taxpayers. The *Mortgage Forgiveness Debt Relief Act of 2007* is part of a multibillion-dollar relief package for homeowners, builders, and banks caught in the current mortgage meltdown. Finally, Congress passed an alternative minimum tax (AMT) "patch" and package of extenders, energy incentives, and disaster relief in October 2008 in the *Emergency Economic Stabilization Act of 2008.*

ECONOMIC STIMULUS ACT OF 2008

In January 2008, Congress passed the *Economic Stimulus Act of 2008* to help jump-start the U.S. economy. Congress authorized more than $100 billion in economic stimulus payments (also known as *tax rebates*) to encourage consumer spending along with two business incentives: enhanced Code Sec. 179 expensing and bonus depreciation.

Economic Stimulus Payments

Between April and July of 2008, nearly 100 million Americans received a total of roughly $100 billion in economic stimulus payments. At the time this CPE course is being prepared, the Treasury Department and the IRS are continuing to distribute payments to eligible taxpayers. The IRS expects to distribute more than 130 million payments by the end of 2008.

Calculating the payment. The economic stimulus payments are technically a refundable credit against tax. They are calculated as the greater of:
- Net income tax liability, not to exceed $600 ($1,200 for married couples filing jointly); or
- $300 ($600 for joint filers) if the individual has either
  - At least $3,000 of any combination of earned income, Social Security benefits, and certain veterans' benefits (including survivors of disabled veterans), or
  - Net income tax liability of at least $1 and gross income greater than the sum of the applicable basic standard deduction amount and one personal exemption (two if a joint return).

Income phaseouts. Congress imposed income limits on recipients. The payment amounts start to phase out when a single taxpayer's AGI is greater than $75,000 ($150,000 for married couples filing jointly). The payments phase out at 5 percent of the amount exceeding the applicable AGI threshold. The $600 credit for individuals, therefore, phases out completely at $87,000 AGI, and the $1,200 credit for married couples filing jointly phases out completely at $174,000 AGI.

Retirees and disabled individuals. Individuals must file a 2007 return to receive an economic stimulus payment. There is no other method of securing a payment if a person qualifies. Many retirees and individuals on disability do not file returns because they have no taxable income. However, the *Economic Stimulus Act* treats Social Security, Railroad Retirement, and VA disability benefits as income for purposes of the payments. The IRS undertook a massive public education campaign in 2008 to remind retirees and individuals on disability to file a return and receive a payment.

CAUTION

Supplemental security income (SSI) payments are not considered income for purposes of the economic stimulus payments.

Filers on extension. Individuals who received a filing extension and who do not file their 2007 return until the extended October 15, 2008, deadline will not receive their economic stimulus payments until after they file. However, the IRS has indicated that no payments will be mailed or direct deposited to taxpayers after December 31, 2008.

Child payments. Besides the economic stimulus payments, taxpayers with children are eligible for $300 payments per child. To qualify, a child must have been younger than age 17 as of December 31, 2007. In other words, if a child was 16 or younger at the end of 2007 and meets the other eligibility requirements, the child will qualify for the $300 stimulus payment.

Reduced payments. The IRS is treating the economic stimulus payments like refunds if an individual has an unpaid tax debt. The IRS can apply all or part of the payment to pay past-due pay past-due federal or state income taxes as well as nontax federal debt such as student loans and child support.

ITINs. Millions of individuals file their federal returns using individual taxpayer identification numbers (ITINs). However, Congress prohibited the IRS from issuing economic stimulus payments to individuals lacking Social Security numbers. There is only one exception: If the taxpayer or his or her spouse is a member of the U.S. military, and one spouse does not have a Social Security number, the couple will still receive an economic stimulus payment. The HEART Act (discussed below) created this exception.

Distribution. The U.S. Treasury and the IRS distributed the payments based on the last two digits of the recipient's Social Security number. The bulk of the payments were made by direct deposit and mailing of paper checks between late April and mid-July.

Common questions. One of the most commonly asked questions of the IRS—and many tax professionals—by individuals is, "Why was my payment less than what my friends and neighbors received?" A payment may be less than the maximum ($600 for single individuals and $1,200 for married couples filing jointly) if any of the following applies:

- The taxpayer is single and his or her net income tax liability is less than $600;
- The taxpayer is married and the couple's net income tax liability is less than $1,200;
- The taxpayer is single and his or her AGI is more than $75,000;
- The taxpayer is married and the couple is filing a joint return reflecting AGI of more than $150,000;
- The taxpayer owes back taxes; or
- The taxpayer has nontax federal debts such as unpaid student loans or child-support obligations.

> **PLANNING POINTER**
>
> The IRS has indicated that 2008 returns (Form 1040s) will include a line to claim an economic stimulus payment for individuals who qualified in 2008 for a payment but did not receive one before the end of 2008.

Code Sec. 179 Expensing

The *Economic Stimulus Act of 2008* also enhanced Code Sec. 179 expensing. Under Code Sec. 179, taxpayers can elect to recover all or part of the cost of qualifying property, up to a limit, by deducting it in the year it is placed in service. The Code Sec. 179 small business expensing deduction enables many businesses to deduct the entire cost of their depreciable property during the tax year in which it is purchased and placed in service.

Dollar limits. Before the *Economic Stimulus Act of 2008,* taxpayers could expense up to $128,000 for 2008. The new law raises the dollar limit to $250,000 for 2008 (and only for 2008). After 2008, the ceiling drops to $125,000 for 2009 and 2010, indexed for inflation, and $25,000 for 2011 and beyond, with no inflation adjustments.

Expensing phaseout. The ceiling begins to phase out when the business's investment in other eligible property hits certain stated levels. When the expensing cap was $128,000, it began to phase out dollar-for-dollar at $510,000. Under the new law, the new investment ceiling limitation (the phaseout threshold) is $800,000; writeoffs can be taken until business purchases reach $1,050,000.

Property. The property must be purchased for use in a trade or business. It cannot be held for investment or the production of income. Property that is purchased for personal use and then converted to business use does not qualify for expensing.

Election. Taxpayers make a Code Sec. 179 expensing election on an amended return without the IRS' consent for any tax year beginning in the period from January 1, 2008, to December 31, 2010.

Bonus Depreciation

Congress has used *bonus depreciation* several times in recent years to help struggling businesses. The *Economic Stimulus Act of 2008* allows a business to depreciate 50 percent of the adjusted basis of certain qualified property during the year the property is placed in service.

Bonus depreciation can be claimed for both regular tax and alternative minimum tax (AMT) liability unless the taxpayer makes an election out. Once made, an election out cannot be revoked without IRS consent.

> **COMMENT**
>
> The IRS provided guidance on 2008 bonus depreciation and expensing under the *Economic Stimulus Act of 2008* in Rev. Proc. 2008-54 issued in August 2008. The IRS indicated that except for the amounts and dates, the act had not changed the rules for bonus depreciation under Code Sec. 168(k). The IRS instructed taxpayers to apply Treasury Reg. Sec. 1.168(k)-1 for bonus depreciation under the *Economic Stimulus Act of 2008*.

> **EXAMPLE**
>
> A taxpayer purchases new depreciable property in 2008 and places it in service in the same year. The property costs $100,000 and is five-year property, subject to a half-year convention. The taxpayer can take 50-percent bonus depreciation of $50,000 in the first year. This reduces the property's basis to $50,000. The taxpayer can also take one-half of a full-year's depreciation ($10,000) in the first year. Thus, for 2008, the taxpayer can deduct depreciation of $60,000; in this case, 60 percent of the property's basis. The remaining $40,000 is deducted throughout the remaining four years of the property's term, using either the general depreciation schedule under MACRS or the alternative depreciation schedule (straight-line depreciation).

Bonus depreciation is available for every item of tangible personal property except inventory. However, the bonus is not available for intangibles, except for certain computer software. Additionally, bonus depreciation cannot be taken for tangible personal property used outside the U.S. or for property depreciated under the alternative depreciation system.

The taxpayer must place the property in service during 2008. The placed-in-service date is extended through 2009 for property with a recovery period of 10 years or longer, transportation property (property used to transport people or property), and for certain aircraft. The property must have an estimated production period exceeding one year and an estimated cost exceeding $1 million.

Luxury automobiles. The *Economic Stimulus Act of 2008* also raised the Code Sec. 280F limitations on "luxury" automobile depreciation. Ordinarily, first-year depreciation for passenger automobiles is capped at $3,060 (inflation adjusted). However, in the past, when 30-percent depreciation was available, the limit was increased by $4,600, and when 50-percent bonus depreciation was available, the limit was increased by $7,650. The new law raises the cap once again, this time by $8,000 for 50-percent bonus depreciation claimed for a new passenger automobile. The $8,000 is not adjusted for inflation. The amount yields a total first-year depreciation limit of $11,060. If the vehicle is not predominantly used for business in a subsequent year, the bonus depreciation must be recaptured.

STUDY QUESTIONS

1. Which of the following taxpayers received economic stimulus payments in 2008?
   a. Taxpayers owing back taxes or child support
   b. Individuals who received benefits from Social Security, Railroad Retirement, or VA disability
   c. Taxpayers who did not have Social Security numbers and were not military personnel
   d. Taxpayers who filed a return using an ITIN

2. The *Economic Stimulus Act of 2008* increased the first-year depreciation maximum of _____ for luxury automobiles by _____.
   a. $3,060; $8,000
   b. $2,500; $4,600
   c. $2,060; $7,650
   d. The *Economic Stimulus Act of 2008* did not change the first-year depreciation for luxury automobiles

HOUSING AND ECONOMIC RECOVERY ACT OF 2008

In July 2008, after months of negotiations between Congress and the White House over a comprehensive housing bill, Congress passed and President Bush signed the *Housing and Economic Recovery Act of 2008* (Housing Act). The massive bill overhauls government regulation of the mortgage industry and lenders, and also includes more than $15 billion in tax incentives. Three tax provisions of the 2008 Housing Act are especially important:

- The first-time homebuyer tax credit;
- An additional standard deduction for state and local real property taxes for nonitemizers; and
- A change in the treatment of the home sale gain exclusion.

First-Time Homebuyer Tax Credit

Congress authorized a refundable first-time homebuyer tax credit in the Housing Act to encourage home sales. The credit is temporary and actually operates more like a loan than a tax break. The credit can reach a maximum of $7,500 for qualifying taxpayers. It is also subject to income phaseouts.

PLANNING POINTER

The credit is only available for individuals who purchase a principal residence after April 8, 2008, and before July 1, 2009.

COMMENT

The IRS is expected to issue guidance in the near future on the Housing Act first-time homebuyer credit and it is likely to be similar to the District of Columbia first-time homebuyer credit. Individuals who reside in the District of Columbia have been eligible for a first-time homebuyer credit since 1997 (although it expired at the end of 2007). The District of Columbia homebuyer tax credit reaches $5,000 for qualifying taxpayers (or $2,500 if the taxpayer is married and filed a separate return). The credit phases out for individuals with incomes exceeding set thresholds.

CAUTION

An individual must not have owned a home during the past three years to qualify for the first-time homebuyer credit.

Amount of credit. The first-time homebuyer tax credit is equal to the lesser of:

- $7,500; or
- 10 percent of the purchase price of the home.

CAUTION

The credit is reduced to $3,750 for a married taxpayer who files a separate return.

PLANNING POINTER

The first-time homebuyer credit is available to two or more unmarried individuals (for example, a father and daughter or a same sex couple in a civil union) who purchase a home together. The IRS is expected to issue guidance in the near future on how the credit will be allocated among unmarried taxpayers.

EXAMPLE

Philip Malloy is age 24 and single. He purchases a home, his first-ever purchase of a home, in August 2008 for $75,000. Philip's modified AGI is $70,000, and he uses the home as his principal residence. Philip qualifies for a $7,500 credit on his 2008 return. Repayment will begin with his 2010 return when he must start repaying the credit by increasing his federal income tax by $500 each year ($7,500 × 6 2/3 percent) for the next 15 years.

Income phaseouts. Congress limited the credit to lower-income and moderate-income individuals. The credit phases out for taxpayers with modified adjusted gross income (AGI) in excess of $75,000 (or $150,000 for joint filers). The phaseout reduces the credit (but not below zero) by the amount that bears the same ratio to the unreduced amount of the credit, as the taxpayer's excess modified AGI exceeding $75,000 (or $150,000 for joint filers) bears to $20,000. No credit is available when a taxpayer's modified AGI reaches $95,000 (or $170,000 for joint filers).

Repayment. Unlike other tax credits, the first-time homebuyer tax credit must be repaid. Taxpayers who elect to take the first-time homebuyer credit must repay it in equal installments over 15 years. Repayment generally begins two years after the purchase by adding $500 to the homeowner's tax bill each year for 15 years. If the taxpayer sells the home before the end of the 15-year period, repayment is accelerated. However, if the taxpayer dies before the end of the 15-year period, repayment is excused. Special rules apply in the case of involuntary conversion or transfer incident to divorce.

PLANNING POINTER

The IRS has indicated that it will likely add a line to individual tax returns (Forms 1040) to report the amount of the first-time homebuyer tax credit that the taxpayer is repaying.

COMMENT

Some taxpayers may wish to accelerate repayment of the first-time home-buyer tax credit. The IRS may address this in future guidance.

CAUTION

The first-time homebuyer credit is not available to nonresident aliens, individuals who qualify for a similar District of Columbia credit, or individuals whose financing comes from tax-exempt mortgage revenue bonds.

Additional Standard Deduction for State and Local Property Taxes

Individuals who do not itemize their deductions on their federal income tax returns may claim an additional standard deduction for state and local real property taxes, up to $500 ($1,000 for joint returns). This temporary deduction was first created by the *Housing and Economic Recovery Act* and extended by the *Emergency Economic Stabilization Act of 2008*. The incentive is available in 2008 and 2009.

Amount. The additional standard deduction for state and local property taxes is the lesser of:

- The amount allowable as a deduction for state and local taxes if the taxpayer claimed itemized deductions; or
- $500 ($1,000 in the case of joint returns).

PLANNING POINTER

Mortgage interest is often the key to taking itemized deductions. With high interest payments, people are able to deduct additional items such as state and local taxes and charitable contributions. People who own their homes outright, or whose mortgage payments are low or consist mainly of principal rather than interest, may not qualify for itemizing. This provision allows such taxpayers a deduction to defray some of the costs of home ownership—but only for 2008.

Limitations. The additional standard deduction cannot be higher than what the taxpayer would have deducted if he or she claimed an itemized deduction for real property taxes.

The deduction is not allowed for real estate taxes that have been deducted elsewhere on the return. For example, a landlord will not be able to take a standard deduction for real estate taxes that he or she has deducted against rental income on Schedule E.

Revised Home Sale Gain Exclusion

Under the Housing Act, taxpayers who use their home as a vacation home or for rental for some of the time will no longer be able to exclude the portion of gain allocated to nonqualified use. The treatment effectively prevents taxpayers from converting a vacation home into a principal residence after 2008 and using the full home sale exclusion. The new treatment applies to sales and exchanges completed after December 31, 2008.

More Incentives

Besides these three tax-related provisions, the Housing Act also:
- Increases and simplifies the low-income housing tax credit
- Simplifies the rules for tax-exempt housing bonds;
- Temporarily expands the mortgage revenue bond program to allow the refinancing of existing subprime loans;
- Enacts a package of real estate investment trust (REIT) reforms (affecting income tests, the treatment of REIT subsidies and other technical aspects of the operation of REITs);
- Enhances the rehabilitation tax credit;
- Bans seller-funded down payment assistance programs (DAPs);
- Provides preforeclosure counseling for distressed homeowners; and
- Authorizes loans from the U.S. Treasury to Fannie Mae and Freddie Mac.

> **COMMENT**
>
> The Housing Act also authorized the Treasury Department to take control of Fannie Mae and Freddie Mac. In September, the Treasury Department announced that it will assume direct control over the operations of the two entities, which, combined, insure more than 50 percent of the nation's mortgages.

> **COMMENT**
>
> Although the Housing Act is primarily targeted at individuals, Congress included an important tax break for corporations in this act. The Housing Act allows corporations to temporarily claim a limited amount of unused alternative minimum tax (AMT) and research credits in lieu of taking bonus depreciation under the *Economic Stimulus Act of 2008*. The amount of the accelerated AMT or research credit is refundable, permitting corporations to receive a payment for the credit amount even if they have no tax liability for the tax year in which the accelerated credit is claimed.

Offsets

The tax incentives in the Housing Act all require *offsets*—that is, revenue raisers to counterbalance the loss of money to the U.S. Treasury. The Housing Act offsets its tax breaks by imposing information reporting requirements on credit card transactions, reducing the home sale exclusion (discussed above), a delay in worldwide allocation of interest rules, and accelerated corporate estimated tax payments.

Information Reporting

There is a direct correlation between information reporting and tax compliance. Reporting compliance is strongest in the presence of substantial information reporting. The Housing Act significantly expands information reporting to cover credit card companies and electronic payment processors. Under the Housing Act, credit card companies and electronic payment processors will be required to annually file aggregate transaction reports with the IRS listing their total annual payments to individual merchants who receive more than $20,000 and conduct more than 200 transactions each year. The new requirement is effective for sales made on or after January 1, 2011.

COMMENT

Electronic payment processors include the popular PayPal feature for online transactions. PayPal recently informed its customers that the first information reports under the Housing Act will go to the IRS in January 2012.

STUDY QUESTIONS

3. The first-time homebuyer tax credit is unique in that it:

  a. Must be repaid
  b. Must be claimed on an amended return
  c. Must be claimed across three equal installments
  d. Is not subject to phaseout based on the taxpayer's annual income

4. Which of the following is **not** included in the *Housing and Economic Recovery Act of 2008*?

  a. Increased low-income housing tax credit
  b. Expansion of the mortgage revenue bond program for homeowners refinancing subprime loans
  c. Banning of seller-assisted down payment programs
  d. All of the above included in the Housing Act

MORTGAGE FORGIVENESS DEBT RELIEF ACT OF 2007

Home mortgage delinquencies and foreclosures are at all-time highs in 2008 and the outlook for improvement is not good. Individuals who have mortgage debt forgiven in 2007, 2008, or 2009 may be able to claim special tax relief under the *Mortgage Forgiveness Debt Relief Act of 2007* (and in 2010, 2011, or 2012 under an extension by the *Emergency Economic Stabilization Act of 2008*). Normally, when a lender forecloses on property, sells the home for less than the borrower's outstanding mortgage, and forgives all or part of the mortgage debt, the Internal Revenue Code treats the cancelled debt as taxable income to the homeowner. However, the *Mortgage Forgiveness Debt Relief Act of 2007* excludes discharges involving up to $2 million of indebtedness ($1 million for a married taxpayer filing a separate return) secured by a principal residence and incurred in the acquisition, construction, or substantial improvement of the residence from federal tax. Congress made the new exclusion retroactive to January 1, 2007, to help as many homeowners as possible.

> **PLANNING POINTER**
>
> The exclusion is temporary. It was originally set to expire after 2009. The *Emergency Economic Stabilization Act of 2008* extended it through 2012.

Additionally, the *Mortgage Forgiveness Debt Relief Act of 2007* also helps homeowners whose mortgage debt may have been reduced through a *restructuring* (also known as a *mortgage workout*). In some cases, a lender may permit a homeowner to make partial payments for several months and then catch up in the future with additional payments. Other times, a lender may be willing to adjust the loan to carry a lower interest rate, either temporarily or permanently.

> **COMMENT**
>
> Homeowners who are approved for a mortgage workout may be responsible for some out-of-pocket expenses, such as recording fees.

> **EXAMPLE**
>
> Eve Wickam purchased her home in 2006 and has a $300,000 mortgage debt. Eve is unable to make her mortgage payments and her lender ultimately forecloses in early 2008. The lender sells the home for $240,000 in satisfaction of the debt later that year. Eve has $60,000 in income from the discharge of indebtedness. Under the *Mortgage Forgiveness Debt Relief Act of 2007*, Eve may exclude the $60,000 from income.

COMMENT

Debt used to refinance qualifying debt is eligible for the exclusion, but only up to the amount of the old mortgage principal, just before the refinancing.

CAUTION

Debt forgiven on second homes, rental property, business property, credit cards, or car loans does not qualify for the new tax-relief provision.

The Housing Act created a new program (HOPE for Homeowners) to help distressed homeowners refinance into government-insured mortgages. The new mortgages will be offered by FHA-approved lenders that will refinance the loans of individuals who are at risk of losing their homes to foreclosure. The program is open only to owner-occupants who are unable to afford their current mortgage payments. They must have a mortgage debt-to-income ratio greater than 31 percent as of March 31, 2008.

PLANNING POINTER

If the homeowner's mortgage is insured, a distressed homeowner may be able to secure a loan from the mortgage guarantor to bring the account current.

PLANNING POINTER

Another option for a distressed homeowner is called *deed in lieu of foreclosure.* Essentially, the homeowner vacates the residence and turns it over to the lender. The lender, in exchange, forgives the debt.

STUDY QUESTIONS

5. The *Housing and Economic Recovery Act of 2008* created a temporary additional standard deduction for individuals who do not itemize their deductions (*nonitemizers*) for:

   a. State and local real property taxes
   b. Business entertainment expenses
   c. Medical expenses
   d. Charitable contributions

---

6. To help homeowners refinance home loans into government-insured mortgages, the Housing Act created the program:

  a. Debt Forgiveness for Homeowners
  b. HOPE for Homeowners
  c. Mortgage Workout for Borrowers
  d. FHA Mortgage Restructuring

HEROES EARNINGS ASSISTANCE AND RELIEF TAX ACT OF 2008

The *Heroes Earnings Assistance and Relief Tax Act of 2008* (HEART Act) targets tax relief to individuals on active duty, reservists called to active duty, military families, and veterans. The HEART Act was enacted at the same time as the Farm Act (which is discussed later in this chapter) and it was overshadowed by the massive farm bill. The incentives are generous, totaling $1.2 billion, and help military personnel not only when they are called to active duty but also when they return home.

Combat Pay

Tens of thousands of U.S. troops are serving in combat zones around the world. Combat pay is tax-free. However, this tax-free treatment can cause some military families to lose eligibility for the earned income credit. The HEART Act treats combat pay as earned income for purposes of the earned income credit.

> **CAUTION**
>
> This treatment is permanent and is also retroactive to December 31, 2007.

> **PLANNING POINTER**
>
> Generally, the pay of members of the U.S. Armed Forces is included in gross income. However, the combat pay of enlisted personnel is not included. Commissioned officers may exclude part of their pay from gross income for any month and this part is limited to the maximum enlisted amount. This amount is equal to the highest rate of basic pay at the highest pay grade for enlisted personnel plus any special hostile fire or imminent danger pay that the officer receives.

Economic Stimulus Payments

The HEART Act extends the economic stimulus payments authorized in the *Economic Stimulus Act of 2008* to servicemen and women whose spouses lack Social Security numbers. The *Economic Stimulus Act of 2008* expressly prohibited the IRS from making economic stimulus payments to individuals who do not have a Social Security number, inadvertently denying the payments to their spouses. Congress corrected that oversight in the HEART Act.

Retirement Savings

When a reservist is called to active duty, he or she may want to make an early withdrawal from a 401(k) plan or other retirement arrangement. Generally, there is an early-withdraw penalty. The HEART Act permanently waives this penalty for reservists who are called to active duty for at least 179 days. The reservist generally has two years after the end of the active duty period to repay (in one or more contributions) the amount of the distribution and to avoid including the distribution in income.

COMMENT

The *Pension Protection Act of 2006* authorized similar treatment but it was temporary. The provision in the HEART ACT applies to individuals ordered or called to active duty on or after December 31, 2007.

EXAMPLE

Amy Jefferson is employed by XYZ Co. Amy is 35 years old and is a member of the U.S. Army Reserve. On November 2, 2008, Amy is called to active duty in Afghanistan. Before departing for Afghanistan, Amy withdraws $3,000 from her traditional IRA to pay down some debts. Her withdrawal is allowable and is not subject to the 10-percent penalty for early withdrawal. Furthermore, Amy has two years, after she has returned from active service, to repay these withdrawn funds.

Death Benefits

Survivors of servicemen and women who die in the line of duty (and in some other circumstances) receive tax-free death benefits. The HEART Act gives survivors more choices about where to invest these benefits. An individual who receives a military death gratuity or payment under the Servicemembers' Group Life Insurance (SGLI) program may contribute an amount up to the sum of the gratuity and SGLI payments received to a Roth IRA or Coverdell education savings account, notwithstanding other contribution limits that may apply.

Roth IRA. Under the HEART Act, the contribution to a Roth IRA of an amount received as a military death gratuity or SGLI payment will be considered a qualified rollover contribution for purposes of Code Sec. 408A if the contribution is made before the end of the one-year period beginning on the date on which the amount is received. The amount of the contribution must not exceed the sum of the gratuity and SGLI payments received, less the amount of gratuity and SGLI payments that were contributed to a Coverdell education savings account (ESA). Such rollovers will be disregarded for purposes of the rule in Code Sec. 408(d)(3)(B), which generally limits the number of rollovers to one per year.

Coverdell ESA. Under the HEART Act, the contribution of an amount received as a military death gratuity or SGLI payment to a Coverdell ESA will be considered a rollover contribution if the contribution is made before the end of the one-year period beginning on the date on which the amount is received, and the contribution does not exceed the sum of the gratuity and SGLI payments received, less the amount of such payments that were contributed to a Roth IRA or to another Coverdell ESA. The rule under Code Sec. 530(d)(5), which generally limits the number of tax-free rollovers to one per year, will not apply for purposes of rollovers under this provision.

Differential Pay

When a reservist is called to active duty, he or she has to leave their current employer. Some employers voluntarily pay the difference between the reservist's regular pay and his or her military pay (*differential pay*). The new law gives small employers a temporary tax credit for this differential pay. Small businesses having fewer than 50 employees can claim a new credit equal to 20 percent of differential wages paid to qualified workers called up for active military duty. Eligible differential wage payments are differential wage payments up to $20,000. The new law also treats differential pay as wages, which will make it easier for employers to contribute to the reservist's employer-sponsored retirement plans.

> **COMMENT**
>
> The employer's deduction for compensation paid is reduced by the amount of the differential wage credit.

> **CAUTION**
>
> The differential pay credit is temporary and does not apply to payments made after December 31, 2009.

PLANNING POINTER

Employers of disabled veterans can also take advantage of the work opportunity tax credit. The work opportunity tax credit encourages employers to hire individuals from various economically-challenged groups, such as disabled veterans, and, in exchange, employers receive a tax break.

Health Flexible Spending Arrangements

Generally, amounts left over in a health flexible spending arrangement (FSA) at the end of the year (plus a 2½-month grace period) must be forfeited. The HEART Act does away with this use-it-or-lose-it rule for qualifying individuals and allows them to receive all or a portion of the balance in the health FSA, provided the individual is called to active military duty for more than 179 days or for an indefinite period. The distribution must be made by the end of the reimbursement period for the tax year in which the call to active duty occurs.

REMINDER

Military personnel have special protections under the *Servicemembers Civil Relief Act*. That law limits the interest that may be charged on mortgages incurred (or acquired) by a service member (including debts incurred jointly with a spouse) before he or she entered into active military service. Mortgage lenders must, at the request of the service member, reduce the interest rate to no more than 6 percent per year during the period of active military service and recalculate the payments to reflect the lower rate. The Housing Act (discussed above) also prohibits mortgage lenders from foreclosing while a service member is on active duty or within 9 months (previously 90 days) after military service.

More Provisions

The HEART Act also:

- Extends the time period for filing claims for credits or refunds for retired military personnel who receive disability determinations from the Department of Veterans Affairs;
- Provides that state and local tax benefits and limited payments made to volunteer emergency response personnel and excludable from their gross income are not subject to social security taxes, unemployment taxes, or wage withholding for tax years beginning after 2007 and before 2011;
- Permanently extends an exception to the first-time homebuyer rule for qualified mortgage bonds for veterans; and
- Clarifies that state-paid veterans' bonuses are tax-free.

Offsets

To pay for the tax relief in the HEART Act, Congress closed some loopholes that allowed government contractors to avoid paying employment taxes along with tightening the rules on expatriation (individuals who renounce their U.S. citizenship for tax reasons).

Government contractors. Before the HEART Act, some government contractors were allegedly using offshore companies to avoid employment taxes. The HEART Act stops this practice by treating foreign subsidiaries of U.S. companies performing services under contract with the U.S. government as U.S. employers for Social Security, Medicare, and federal unemployment taxes. However, Congress made an exception if the subsidiary is located in a foreign country that has similar FICA taxes.

Expatriates. Every year, a few individuals renounce their U.S. citizenship for tax purposes. The HEART Act changes rules for taxing expatriates. Individuals having a net worth of at least $2 million who relinquish their U.S. citizenship or long-term residency would owe taxes on the appreciated value of their assets, as if the assets had been sold, subject to certain limitations. Additionally, a gift or bequest from an expatriate to a U.S. citizen or resident would be subject to a special transfer tax owed by the U.S. recipient at the rates for U.S. gift tax, currently 45 percent. The tax on gifts would apply to amounts that exceed the gift tax exclusion, which is currently $12,000.

> **COMMENT**
>
> The HEART Act also raises the minimum penalty for failure to file a federal tax return within 60 days of the due date (with extensions) to the lesser of $135 or 100 percent of the net amount of tax due.

FARM ACT

The *Heartland, Habitat, Harvest, and Horticulture Act* (the Farm Act) is one of the largest pieces of legislation in recent memory. It is a massive overhaul of government regulation of farming, including the contentious subject of farm subsidies. The $300 billion Farm Act includes roughly $1.7 billion in tax incentives. These incentives are, naturally, largely targeted primarily to farmers. This portion of the chapter describes some of the more widespread tax incentives in the Farm Act.

Contributions of Real Property for Conservation Purposes

Congress reformed the rules for charitable contributions of real property for conservation purposes in the *Pension Protection Act of 2006*. Individual donors of real property for conservation purposes could take a deduction of up to 50 percent of their contribution base (rather than the existing 20 percent limitation). The deduction was enhanced even more for farmers and ranchers who could take a deduction of up to 100 percent of their contribution base. However, this special treatment was temporary and expired at the end of 2007. The Farm Act restores it for charitable donations of conservation property through 2009.

> **COMMENT**
>
> This provision in the Farm Act is one of the few that affects individuals who are not engaged in the business of farming or ranching.

Disabled Farmers

In 2006, the IRS announced that it intended to treat all payments made under the Conservation Reserve Program as subject to self-employment tax, including payments made to disabled and retired farmers. The Farm Act reverses the IRS' intended treatment. Payments under the Conservation Reserve Program received by disabled and retired farmers who receive Social Security benefits will be excluded from self-employment income for federal tax purposes and for purposes of Social Security benefits.

Farm Losses

One of the revenue raisers in the Farm Act is designed to prevent taxpayers from abusing the rules allowing losses from farming to offset losses from nonfarming activity. Taxpayers receiving certain government subsidies, such as ones from the Commodity Credit Corporation, are limited as to the amount of net Schedule F losses from farming they may take. The limit for any given tax year is the greater of $300,000 (or $150,000 for a married taxpayer filing separately) or the taxpayer's net farm income for the prior five tax years.

> **EXAMPLE**
>
> Todd Yeager has $1 million of net income from a farming business in each tax year 2010 to 2014. Todd incurs a $5 million farming loss in 2015. Under the Farm Act, the farming loss in 2015 is limited to the greater of $300,000 or $5 million (which represents Todd's total net farm income for the prior five tax years). The farming loss would be allowed in full in 2015.

More Incentives

Along with these tax incentives, the Farm Act also:

- Increases the cap on agricultural bonds;
- Authorizes the issuance of forestry conservation bonds;
- Enhances the treatment of certain farm-related like-kind exchanges;
- Provides enhanced depreciation for certain race horses; and
- Gives timber producers some tax relief.

STUDY QUESTIONS

---

7. The HEART Act increases the minimum penalty for failure to file a federal tax return within 60 days of the due date (with extensions) to the lesser of $___ or ___ percent of the net amount of tax due.

   a. 100; 50
   b. 135; 100
   c. 200; 100
   d. 300; 150

8. The Farm Act extends until 2010 the _____ deduction of the contribution base for charitable donations of conservation property by farmers and ranchers.

   a. 20 percent
   b. 50 percent
   c. 75 percent
   d. 100 percent

AMT PATCH

History of the AMT

Nearly 40 years ago, Congress created the alternative minimum tax (AMT) so that a handful of very wealthy taxpayers would not avoid taxation. The idea worked well at the beginning, but over time inflation has eroded the value of the dollar. That handful of very wealthy taxpayers has grown to be many millions. Even more taxpayers—especially taxpayers with household incomes of between $75,000 and $100,000—would be liable for the AMT for the 2008 tax year but for the so-called AMT patch. The patch insulates these individuals from AMT liability by giving them higher exemption amounts and allowing these taxpayers to use most nonrefundable personal credits to offset AMT liability.

2008 Patch

The *Emergency Economic Stabilization Act of 2008* patch raises the AMT exemption amounts for 2008 and allows taxpayers to take nonrefundable personal credits to reduce AMT liability. The 2008 exemption amounts under the new law are:

- $66,250 for married couples filing jointly and surviving spouses;
- $44,350 for single individuals and heads of household; and
- $33,125 for married couples filing separately.

PLANNING POINTER

For the first time, the patch abates AMT liability stemming from the exercise of incentive stock options (ISOs) before 2008. The treatment is effective for any unpaid tax liability as of the date of enactment of the new law. Additionally, all individuals, including those who paid their ISO AMT liabilities, may accelerate the refund of the minimum tax credit that has not been used.

EMERGENCY ECONOMIC STABILIZATION ACT OF 2008

As part of a $700 billion financial markets rescue package enacted in October, Congress enacted The *Emergency Economic Stabilization Act of 2008*, which features:

- An AMT patch for 2008(discussed above); and
- A package of extenders, energy tax breaks, and disaster relief.

Extenders

More often than not, when Congress passes a tax cut, it intends the tax break to be temporary. Lawmakers make tax breaks temporary so their cost is kept low (at least on paper). The *Emergency Economic Stabilization Act of 2008* extends a host of temporary tax incentives through 2009, including:

- State and local sales tax deduction (which had expired January 1, 2008);
- Higher education tuition deduction (which had expired December 31, 2007);
- Teachers' classroom expense deduction (which had expired December 31, 2007);
- Charitable contributions of IRA proceeds (which had expired December 31, 2007); and
- Research tax credit (which had expired December 31, 2007).

COMMENT

The *Emergency Economic Stabilization Act of 2008* also enhances the child tax credit. Under current law, the credit is refundable to the extent of 15 percent of the taxpayer's earned income in excess of a $10,000 floor ($12,050 as adjusted for inflation for 2008). The bill reduces the floor to $8,500.

> ### COMMENT
>
> The *Emergency Economic Stabilization Act of 2008* also corrects what many practitioners see as a disconnect between the preparer penalty standard under Code Sec. 6694(a) and the taxpayer penalty standard. In the *Small Business and Work Opportunity Tax Act of 2007*, Congress voted to change the long-time Code Sec. 6694(a) preparer penalty standard from *realistic possibility of success* to a reasonable belief that the position would *more likely than not be sustained* on its merits. The *Emergency Economic Stabilization Act of 2008* replaces the more likely than not language in Code Sec. 6694(a) with *substantial authority*, effectively equalizing the preparer and taxpayers standards at substantial authority for undisclosed, nonabusive positions.

Disaster Relief

The *Emergency Economic Stabilization Act of 2008* targets tax relief to taxpayers in 10 states in the Midwest recovering from floods, tornadoes, and storms in 2008 (the Midwestern Disaster Area). These taxpayers may be may be eligible for targeted tax breaks, such as suspension of casualty loss limitations, increased expensing, enhanced depreciation, and loans from qualified plans. The new law also targets more limited relief for taxpayers recovering from Hurricane Ike in Louisiana and Texas (the Hurricane Ike Disaster Area). Finally, the new law includes temporary tax relief for taxpayers affected by all federally declared disasters nationwide.

> ### COMMENT
>
> The *Emergency Economic Stabilization Act of 2008* also extends some Hurricane Katrina incentives first enacted in 2005 to help taxpayers in New Orleans and the Gulf Coast.

Energy Incentives

The *Emergency Economic Stabilization Act of 2008* extends and enhances a number of energy tax incentives. Producers of renewable energy benefit from extended incentives targeted to them. Renewable sources include solar, biomass, and wind facilities. The *Emergency Economic Stabilization Act of 2008* also enhances solar energy tax incentives and creates a new tax credit for taxpayers that purchase a plug-in-electrical vehicle.

Troubled Asset Relief Program

The *Emergency Economic Stabilization Act of 2008* creates the Troubled Assets Relief Program (TARP). The program allows the Treasury Department to acquire bad mortgage debts and other troubled assets from banks and other institutions by direct purchase or through auction. Once the Treasury Department acquires these assets, it can implement changes in executive compensation, such as setting compensation amounts in a direct purchase situation and, under the auction program, limit the deductibility of compensation under Code Sec. 162(m). Golden parachute payments likewise will be prohibited or curtailed for top executives of companies that participate in TARP.

Basis Reporting

Under the *Emergency Economic Stabilization Act of 2008*, brokers must report the adjusted basis of publicly traded securities, including stocks, bonds, and other financial instruments designated by Treasury. However, basis reporting does not kick in immediately. It applies to stock acquired in 2011, mutual funds acquired in 2012, and other securities acquired in 2013.

> **COMMENT**
>
> Basis reporting is estimated to raise $6.7 billion over 10 years, helping to partially offset the cost of the tax incentives in the *Economic Stabilization Act of 2008*.

> **COMMENT**
>
> The *Emergency Economic Stabilization Act of 2008* also:
> - Changes the tax treatment of nonqualified deferred compensation plans maintained by foreign corporations;
> - Limits the Code Sec 199 deduction for oil and gas production;
> - Tightens the rules for oil and gas companies to pay taxes on overseas income; and
> - Extends the FUTA surtax and the oil spill tax.

2001 TAX CUTS

EGTRRA was one of the largest tax acts in recent history. Congress lowered the marginal income tax rates, provided relief from the so-called marriage penalty, and temporarily repealed the federal estate tax. However, all of these provisions are temporary and will expire at the end of 2010. The cost to make them permanent is estimated at more than $3 trillion during the next 10 years. Although the Bush Administration would like Congress to make the 2001 cuts tax permanent, lawmakers are likely to wait until after the November presidential election to take any action.

STUDY QUESTIONS

9. The *Emergency Economic Stabilization Act of 2008*:

   a. Extends many temporary tax incentives and includes an alternative minimum tax (AMT) patch for the 2008 tax year

   b. Provides tax relief for military personnel and their families

   c. Grants higher bonus depreciation caps for luxury automobiles

   d. All of the above are included in its provisions

10. The AMT patch passed late in 2008 also applies for the 2009 tax year. ***True or False?***

CONCLUSION

As the federal government continues to seek how to best assist economic recovery, Congress continues to use the Internal Revenue Code in an attempt to boost consumer and business spending and stimulate the economy. Like past tax acts, many provisions in the 2008 tax acts are temporary and will be allowed to expire or will be renewed in future years. The on-again/off-again nature of these tax breaks creates many planning challenges for practitioners and their clients. In addition, the sunsetting of many provisions in EGTRRA after 2010 presents more planning challenges.

Mortgage Workouts and Foreclosures: Tax Alternatives and Consequences

The U.S. housing market is in its worst shape in a generation. Housing values are down and, as a result, the refinancing of existing variable-rate or adjustable rate mortgages (ARMs) has been curtailed. The fallout is a massive increase in the number of foreclosures and, to an increasing extent, a mortgage workout environment in which mortgage lenders know that they are never getting 100 cents on the dollar and, therefore, are open to "workouts" in which either/or principal or interest on existing mortgages is reduced. There are tax consequences to the homeowner in these situations, blunted somewhat but not entirely by recent Congressional legislation. This chapter looks at the most common mortgage workout and foreclosure scenarios and explains their tax consequences to the homeowner, as well as alternative strategies to minimize taxpayers' tax liability.

LEARNING OBJECTIVES

Upon completion of this chapter, you will be able to:

- Understand the bifurcated tax impact of a foreclosure;
- Determine income that results from a partial or full forgiveness of mortgage debt;
- Cite key exceptions to income recognition for mortgage debt forgiveness;
- Compare the different tax consequences among a mortgage workout, foreclosure, a deed in lieu of foreclosure, a short sale, and a sale by a bankruptcy court.
- Determine when a mortgaged property is considered a principal residence in order to qualify for valuable tax exclusions made possible under two recent tax law changes;
- Describe what basis reduction is required if one of the exclusions to debt cancellation income is used; and
- Determine how gain or loss on the sale of the mortgaged residence is computed, including the computation under a recent law change for residences converted from second-home to principal residence status.

INTRODUCTION

Tax consequences of either a mortgage workout or foreclosure (or fore-closure-like transfers such as a short sale or a deed in lieu of foreclosure) involve two distinct potentially *taxable events:*

- Income upon the forgiveness of indebtedness is realized by the home-owner under Code Sec. 108. Whether this income is recognized at the time depends upon whether one or more of several exceptions carved out of Code Sec. 108 apply. Those exceptions include cir-cumstances involving a principal residence, insolvency, bankruptcy, or farm debt; and
- Gain or loss on the sale or deemed sale of the residence (or a reduction in the homeowner's basis in the property, which will increase the likeli-hood of gain recognition on any future sale of the residence). This tax consequence, too, has an exception to taxation. Under Code Sec. 121, up to $250,000 ($500,000 for joint filers) of gain is exempt from tax if the residence is the taxpayer's principal residence.

Many homeowners in the current subprime mortgage environment will find that they have forgiveness of indebtedness income that is exempt under a recently enacted principal residence exclusion. They also typically will realize a loss on the foreclosure sale of their residence that cannot offset any other income. If they have held their property for many years, however, the homeowners may realize a gain on a foreclosure sale, which triggers capital gain tax payable unless a partial or full exclusion as a principal residence is available.

Recent sellers of vacation or other second home property in the same circumstance will find themselves not so lucky: their property is ineligible for any principal residence exclusion to shield forgiveness-of-indebtedness taxable income to the extent the property's sale price does not satisfy the mortgage amount. At the same time, that taxable income cannot be offset by any loss realized on the foreclosure sale of the property.

PRINCIPAL RESIDENCE

Having the mortgaged property classified as the taxpayer's principal resi-dence is a key component to maximizing tax relief. Characterization of the property as a principal residence:

- Allows all (or some of) debt forgiveness to be excluded from taxable in-come under the Code Sec. 108(h)(2) principal residence exclusion; and
- Allows most if not all of the gain from the sale of the home—whether as part of a foreclosure action or years later in the case of a mortgage workout—to escape tax through the Code Sec. 121 home sale gain exclusion.

Under Code Sec. 121, up to $250,000 of gain from the sale of the taxpayer's principal residence ($500,000 for married filing jointly taxpayers) may be excluded from gross income if, during the five-year period ending on the date of the sale or exchange, such property has been owned and used by the taxpayer as the taxpayer's principal residence for periods aggregating two years or more. Pro-rata use of the exclusion also may apply when the property has not been the taxpayer's principal residence for at least two years, provided a sanctioned unanticipated circumstance triggers the earlier move.

> **COMMENT**
>
> If the home is not a principal residence, certain other limited tax relief may remain available upon forgiveness of mortgage indebtedness, including the insolvency exclusion for forgiveness of indebtedness income. See the discussion of this exclusion later in this chapter.

If a principal residence has a home office within it for tax purposes, the principal residence exclusions continue to apply, but any depreciation deductions previously taken as part of the home office deduction generally must be recaptured as ordinary income. Depreciation taken on a second home that is then converted into a principal residence also must be recaptured under a similar regime.

Determination of Principal Residence

Generally, the home in which a person lives is considered to be the taxpayer's principal residence. However, the determination of whether a residence is in fact his or her principal residence for tax purposes depends upon all the facts and circumstances of each case. An individual can have only one principal residence at a time. If a taxpayer owns two homes at the same time, the principal residence is generally the one that is occupied more of the time. However, once a taxpayer has acquired principal residence status, it can remain a principal residence for tax purposes depending on the circumstances even if the taxpayer has already moved to a new principal residence. For example, a homeowner may move to another state for employment while vacating his or her residence that is either on the market for sale or in foreclosure proceedings.

Ultimately, the determination of a taxpayer's principal residence is based on all the facts and circumstances. Relevant factors in addition to the length of occupancy in determining the taxpayer's principal residence include:

- The taxpayer's place of employment;
- The principal place where the taxpayer's family lives;
- The address used by the taxpayer on tax returns, driver's license, automobile registration, and voter registration;

- The mailing address used by the taxpayer for bills and correspondence;
- The location of the taxpayer's banks; and
- The location of religious organizations and recreational clubs with which the taxpayer is affiliated.

Ownership and Use Tests

To claim the full home sale exclusion of gain on the sale of the residence the homeowner must meet the ownership and use tests. During the five-year period ending on the date of the sale (or deemed sale in the case of certain foreclosure alternatives), the homeowner must have:

- Owned the home for at least two years (satisfying the *ownership test*); and
- Lived in the home as his or her principal residence for at least two years (meeting criteria of the *use test*).

> **CAUTION**
>
> A partial exclusion from gain on the sale of a principal residence is available when criteria of the ownership and use test or 2-year test are not met but taxpayer sells due to change of employment, health problems, or unforeseen circumstances. See the discussion later in this chapter.

No period of ownership or use is needed, however, to use the principal residence gain exclusion of debt forgiveness income under Code Sec. 108. All that is necessary is that the property has been the taxpayer's principal residence before vacating the premises, which has not thereafter been put to another use. Nevertheless, the ability to show that the home was a principal residence for an extended period before vacating can only serve to help the homeowner provide principal residence status at the time of vacating the property.

STUDY QUESTIONS

1. All of the following can help to maximize tax relief in case of a foreclosure sale of a homeowner's principal residence *except:*
   a. Home sale gain exclusion under Code Sec. 121
   b. Automatic waiver of the full ownership and use test requirements for the period preceding the sale
   c. Exclusion of debt forgiveness from taxable income under Code Sec. 108(h)(2)
   d. All of the above provide tax relief in foreclosure sales

> **2.** Which of the following is *not* a consideration in addition to length of occupancy in determining a homeowner's principal residence?
>
> **a.** Place of employment of the homeowner
> **b.** Location of recreational clubs with which the individual is affiliated
> **c.** Address used on driver's license and voter registration
> **d.** All of the above may be relevant factors in determining the homeowner's principal residence

DEBT FORGIVENESS INCOME

The operative Internal Revenue Code sections in determining income recognition in situations as debt forgiveness are

- Section 61, Gross Income Defined; and
- Section 108, Income from Discharge of Indebtedness.

Code Section 61(a) provides that: "Except as otherwise provided in this subtitle, gross income means all income from whatever source derived, including (but not limited to) the following items....61(a)(12) Income from discharge of indebtedness."

Code Section 108(a)(1) provides that: "Gross income does not include any amount which (but for this subsection) would be includible in gross income by reason of the discharge (in whole or in part) of indebtedness of the taxpayer if—

- 108(a)(1)(A) the discharge occurs in a title 11 [bankruptcy] case,
- 108(a)(1)(B) the discharge occurs when the taxpayer is insolvent,
- 108(a)(1)(C) the indebtedness discharged is qualified farm indebtedness,
- 108(a)(1)(D) in the case of a taxpayer other than a C corporation, the indebtedness discharged is qualified real property business indebtedness, or
- 108(a)(1)(E) the indebtedness discharged is qualified principal residence indebtedness which is discharged before January 1, 2013."

COMMENT

The principal residences exclusion under 108(a)(1)(E), above, was first enacted by the *Mortgage Forgiveness Debt Relief Act of 2007* to cover the periods January 1, 2007, through December 31, 2009. The *Emergency Economic Stabilization Act of 2008*, signed into law on October 3, 2008, extended this temporary provision to run until December 31, 2012.

Most homeowners seeking a mortgage workout or going into foreclosure fall into the category of subsection 108(a)(1)(B) (being insolvent) or 108(a)(1)(E) (owing qualified principal residence indebtedness). The exception is the vacation home owner who, typically, has a different principal residence and has other assets (including equity in a principal residence) that prevents use of the insolvency exclusion.

STUDY QUESTION

3. Specific exclusions from inclusion of amounts in gross income by reason of discharges of indebtedness are described in
   a. Code Sec. 61(a)
   b. Code Sec. 108(a)(1)
   c. Code Sec. 1082(a)(2)
   d. None of the above lists specific circumstances for excluding income from discharge of indebtedness

The Tax Benefit Rule

Separate from Code Sec. 108 exclusions is a common law principle under which the portion of indebtedness that would have been deductible if paid does not need to be recognized if forgiven. In the mortgage forgiveness situation, forgiving past interest due generally comes under this rule.

> **EXAMPLE**
>
> At the time Jefferson and Lavinia Smiths' lender in a mortgage workout forgave $100,000 of the Smiths' current $325,000 mortgage debt, they also owed mortgage interest of $4,500 that had been in arrears. The lender also forgave that $4,500 in order to give the Smiths a clean start. Since that back interest would have been an itemized deduction for the Smiths if paid, forgiveness of that interest does not trigger recognition of $4,500 in taxable income.

Fraud or Fee Gauging

In some cases, a portion of the amount of the "forgiven" indebtedness actually may arguably be considered a return of monies to the borrower as settlement of liability on the mortgage holder's part for fraudulent practices in obtaining the original mortgage. Regardless of what may be technically the correct argument, however, the lender may not be willing to admit to possible liability by reducing the amount of debt income reported on Form 1099-C, *Cancellation of Debt*.

Fraudulent fees that were added to principal may not be income when "forgiven" because they were not owed under law.

STUDY QUESTIONS

---

4. The tax benefit rule holds that the portion of indebtedness that a borrower could have deducted had it been paid does not need to recognize it as income if the lender forgives the debt. *True or False?*

5. Because they were not legally owed, fraudulent fees added to principal by mortgage holders may not be income when they become "forgiven." *True or False?*

New Principal Residence Exclusion

Discharged indebtedness is normally included in gross income unless a specific exception applies (as explained above). The *Mortgage Forgiveness Debt Relief Act of 2007,* passed at year-end 2007, created the latest exception to income recognition by adding Code Sec. 108(a)(1)(E). Under that provision, the amount any discharged indebtedness secured by a qualified principal residence will not be included in gross income but will instead reduce the basis of the taxpayer's principal residence. This provision so far is only temporary, spanning any mortgage debt forgiven from January 1, 2007, through December 31, 2012.

> **EXAMPLE**
>
> Eve Wickam purchased her main home in 2006 and has a $310,000 mortgage debt. Eve is unable to make her mortgage payments and her lender ultimately forecloses in early 2008 when her mortgage debt has been paid down to $300,000. The lender sells the home for $240,000 in satisfaction of the debt later that year. Eve has $60,000 in income from the discharge of indebtedness. Under the *Mortgage Forgiveness Debt Relief Act of 2007,* Eve may exclude the $60,000 from income under the principal residence exclusion.

In return for using the exclusion, the taxpayer must reduce the basis of his or her principal residence (but not below zero) by the amount of qualified principal residence debt that is excluded from the homeowner's income. Typically, however, this basis reduction does not hurt the homeowner at all, because any gain realized on the sale of the residence is typically sheltered by the Code Sec. 121 home sale exclusion of $250,000 ($500,000 for joint filers).

The exclusion does not apply to a debtor in a Title 11 bankruptcy case. Rather, the exclusion of income from discharged indebtedness due to bankruptcy applies. However, the exclusion of debt discharged on a principal residence applies to insolvent taxpayers not involved in Title 11 bankruptcy cases, unless the taxpayer elects to have the exclusion due to insolvency apply.

Under the *Mortgage Forgiveness Debt Relief Act of 2007,* no home equity borrowing is allowed to be considered under the mortgage forgiveness exemption unless it can be considered as acquisition indebtedness. *Acquisition indebtedness* is a debt that cannot exceed $2 million and that is used for the acquisition, construction, or substantial improvement of the principal residence of the individual and is secured by the residence.

Refinancing and second mortgage (home equity loan) amounts are included in this overall allowance but only to the extent the amount of the refinancing or home equity loan does not exceed the amount of the existing balance of the original acquisition indebtedness unless it is used to construct or improve the principal residence (including fees paid and included in loan principal to the extent loan proceeds are used for the house).

CAUTION

The new law considers any nonqualified mortgage loan to be "on top" as far as computing what amount has been forgiven and, therefore, considered fully in whatever excess of indebtedness over fair market value exists. As a result, any mortgage debt forgiveness is not excluded under the qualified residence exclusion to the extent that it does not exceed any *cashout amount* (described next) or any portion of the mortgage that exceeds $2 million.

COMMENT

Homeowners who took out super jumbo mortgages may need to recognize income to the extent that the amount of debt forgiveness exceeds the qualified mortgage amount greater than $2 million.

EXAMPLE

The Morgans have a $2.2 million mortgage taken on a home that was worth $2.3 million on their closing date, but that now has a fair market value of only $1.95 million. The mortgagee forecloses and forgives the $150,000 mortgage amount in excess of fair market value (at foreclosure, the Morgans had already paid down the mortgage to $2.1 million). The Morgans may exclude only $50,000 of the forgiveness amount is excluded under the principal residence exception carved out by the new law. Because the existing mortgage of $2.1 million is $100,000 over the $2 million limit, that $100,000 cannot not excluded by the qualified residence exclusion. (However, the insolvency or other exception under Code Sec. 108 also may help the Morgans exclude that balance.)

Additionally, the *Mortgage Forgiveness Debt Relief Act of 2007* also helps homeowners whose mortgage debt may have been reduced through a *restructuring* (also known as a *mortgage workout*). In some cases, a lender may permit a homeowner to make partial payments for several months and then catch up in the future with additional payments. Other times, a lender may be willing to adjust the loan to carry a lower interest rate, either temporarily or permanently.

COMMENT

Homeowners who are approved for a mortgage workout may be responsible for some out-of-pocket expenses, such as recording fees.

COMMENT

Debt used to refinance qualifying debt is eligible for the exclusion, but it is considered refinanced debt only up to the amount of the original acquisition indebtedness, just before the refinancing. In other words, no cashout due to refinancing qualifies for the exclusion (unless, of course, the refinanced excess itself goes to the qualifying use of a capital construction project that increases the value of the home).

CAUTION

Debt forgiven on second homes, credit cards, or car loans can never qualify for the new tax-relief provision.

The Housing Act created a new program (HOPE for Homeowners) to help distressed homeowners refinance into government-insured mortgages. The new mortgages will be offered by FHA-approved lenders that will refinance the loans of individuals who are at risk of losing their homes to foreclosure. The program is open only to owner-occupants who are unable to afford their current mortgage payments. They must have a mortgage debt-to-income ratio greater than 31 percent as of March 31, 2008.

Insolvency Exclusion

Code Sec. 108(d)(3), Insolvent, provides:

For purposes of this section, the term "insolvent" means the excess of liabilities over the fair market value of assets. With respect to any discharge, whether or not the taxpayer is insolvent, and the amount by which the taxpayer is insolvent, shall be determined on the basis of the taxpayer's assets and liabilities immediately before the discharge.

Being *legally* insolvent is not the same as being *functionally* insolvent. Retirement savings that cannot be accessed without penalty still count as assets having value for Code Sec. 108 legal insolvency. In addition, some assets are shielded from creditors under state law, but they do not work themselves into the definition of insolvency for federal tax purposes. These assets include insurance policies, personal residences, retirement plans, and annuities.

The insolvency exclusion as allowed under Code Sec. 108(a)(3) (and as defined under Code Sec. 108(d)(3)) is limited to the amount by which the taxpayer is insolvent immediately before the discharge.

STUDY QUESTIONS

6. How is a homeowner's basis in a principal residence affected under the *Mortgage Forgiveness Debt Relief Act of 2007* by excluding discharged indebtedness from his or her gross income?

   a. The basis is reduced by the amount of qualified principal residence debt excluded

   b. The basis is reduced by the amount of gain excluded

   c. The basis is neither increased nor reduced by the exclusion from income

   d. None of the above is the effect on the basis of the borrower's residence

7. The Code Sec. 108(a)(3) insolvency exclusion is:

   a. The amount by which the taxpayer's liabilities exceed the fair market value of his or her assets just prior to their declaration of insolvency

   b. The amount of the taxpayer's functional insolvency

   c. Limited to the taxpayer's acquisition indebtedness

   d. Limited to the balance of a borrower's mortgage loan principal

Bankruptcy Exclusion

Discharge of indebtedness income is excluded from gross income if the taxpayer is bankrupt. A taxpayer is bankrupt for this purpose when the debt discharge occurs in a *Title 11 case,* a case under Title 11 of the United States Code, also referred to as the Bankruptcy Code.

This exclusion applies only if the debtor is under the court's jurisdiction in a bankruptcy case and the debt discharge is either granted by the court or is made pursuant to a court-approved plan of liquidation or reorganization.

The bankruptcy exclusion takes precedence over the insolvency exclusion. If a taxpayer is in bankruptcy and is also insolvent, the exclusion is not limited to the amount of insolvency. Both the insolvency and the bankruptcy exclusions take precedence over the farm indebtedness exclusion.

Basis Reduction Triggered by Exclusions

Principal residence exclusion. Taxpayers who exclude indebtedness income under the principal residence exclusion of Code Sec. 108 are required to reduce the basis of their principal residence by the amount excluded from gross income. Unlike basis reductions required under Code Sec. 1017 for other Code Sec. 108 exclusions, the reduction for the principal residence exclusion is immediate rather than postponed until the next tax year (Code Sec. 108(h)(1)).

When a sale of the residence takes place, either at a foreclosure or in a later year in the case of a mortgage workout, the portion of any gain allocable to the Code Sec. 108 basis reduction caused by the principal residence exclusion is covered under the general Section 121 gain exclusion of $250,000 ($500,000 for joint filers) on the sale of a principal residence. Any gain in excess of the $250,000/$500,000 exclusion is taxed at capital gains rates, with no portion subject to recapture as ordinary income. This result applies even though the indebtedness income that otherwise would have been taxed but for the Section 108 exclusion would have been taxed as ordinary income.

Insolvency or bankruptcy exclusion. In contrast to basis reduction in the case of the principal residence exclusion of forgiven mortgage debt, if the insolvency or bankruptcy indebtedness exclusion under Section 108 is used, the basis reduction occurs at the start of the next tax year (Code Sec. 1017(a)) and any gain on a subsequent sale attributable to the exclusion amount is recaptured as ordinary income (Code Sec. 1017(d)). Also in those situations, the Section 121 home sale $250,000/$500,000 exclusion is not available to exclude that recaptured income (Code Sec. 121(d)(6)), unlike any basis reduced accounted for because of the principal residence exclusion. In a sale of a residence that takes place in the same tax year as the debt excluded under the insolvency or bankruptcy exclusion, however, the basis of the residence is not reduced by the excluded amount. Rather, the basis of other assets, if any, owned by the taxpayer at the start of the following year is reduced.

Election. A homeowner who qualifies for either the principal residence or the insolvency exclusion may elect whichever exclusion is most beneficial. In absence of an election, the principal residence exclusion applies. The principal residence exclusion is generally preferable. Even in a loss situation, electing the insolvency exclusion may require the reduction of other tax attributes, whereas use of the principal residence exclusion only requires reduction of the taxpayers' basis in their residence.

STUDY QUESTIONS

8. Which of the following has the highest precedence in exclusion of income?

   a. Bankruptcy exclusion
   b. Insolvency exclusion
   c. Farm indebtedness exclusion
   d. All types of discharges receive equal treatment and have equal precedence levels

9. A joint filing couple excludes indebtedness income using Code Sec. 108 under the principal residence exclusion and reduces the basis in their principal residence. When they later sell the property, any gain exceeding the maximum $500,000 exclusion for joint filers (assuming they meet the full ownership and use tests):

   a. Is taxed as ordinary income to the extent of the prior basis reduction
   b. Is taxed at capital gains rates to the extent of the prior basis reduction
   c. Is treated the same as had the couple claimed the insolvency or bankruptcy exclusion
   d. None of the above is the treatment of the excess gain

STATUS OF THE MORTGAGE(S)

The relief from mortgage debt on the residence is what may generate taxable forgiveness of indebtedness income for the homeowner. Even if any forgiven mortgage debt is excluded under one of the Code Sec. 108 exclusions, it may affect the amount of gain eventually realized on the sale of the underlying property since excluded debt forgiveness reduces the homeowner's tax basis in the property. If the forgiven debt as evidenced by the mortgage note is not excluded, it is taxed to the homeowner in the year of forgiveness as ordinary income (unless the homeowner can claim an insolvency, bankruptcy, or farm Section 108 exclusion instead).

EXAMPLE

The Smiths find themselves unable to keep up with their $4,000 per month mortgage payments on their principal residence. They had been paying $2,200 a month on a "teaser" adjustable rate mortgage that they had planned to refinance before the higher interest rate kicked in. Unfortunately, their home is now worth less than the remaining mortgage total and, consequently, the Smiths cannot refinance. Nevertheless, their current mortgage holder is willing to drop the mortgage amount by $100,000 (which would reduce the payments to $3,000 a month) rather than face holding a house that it cannot sell. If the Smiths had purchased their home for $400,000, which was their basis in the property, they must reduce their basis by $100,000, the amount of debt forgiveness income excluded under the principal residence exclusion. Assume further that five years from now, Mrs. Smith, who is now the sole owner because of divorce settlement, sells the home for $825,000. With a basis of $300,000, she will realize $525,000 in gain, of which $250,000 is excluded (assuming current law remains the same).

Nonrecourse Mortgages

Whether the mortgage is recourse or nonrecourse also determines the amount of debt forgiveness subject to potential income tax. Most homeowners have taken out a recourse mortgage on their property. A *recourse mortgage* is considered a personal note in which the homeowner remains personally liable on any amount that cannot be satisfied from the proceeds of a sale of the underlying property to which it is secured. Even if the mortgage lender in practice never attempts to collect from the homeowner personally for payment after a foreclosure, the mortgage may still be technically considered a recourse mortgage for tax purposes. State statutes, on the other hand, may prohibit collection of any excess mortgage debt over the home's value on foreclosure, even for debt otherwise designated as "recourse." In those situations, the property may be considered "as if nonrecourse" and no indebtedness income would result.

Under Code Sec. 108, a *nonrecourse mortgage* (defined as a debt solely secured by the property with the borrower under no personal obligation for the debt) does not generate forgiveness of indebtedness income.

Second Mortgages (Home Equity Loans)

The use of the mortgage money in the case of a refinancing of an original mortgage or a second mortgage (home equity loan) is also critical to the tax impact of debt forgiveness income and the amount of deductible interest.

Even though a home equity loan is made against equity in a principal residence, that fact alone does not give the homeowner the benefit of the principal residence exclusion of any forgiven debt under Code Sec. 108. *Qualified principal residence indebtedness* is defined only as debt incurred to buy or make capital improvements to that principal residence. Cashout refinancing unrelated to home expenses such as loans to pay college tuition, buy a car, pay medical bills, put a down payment on a vacation home, or any other purpose other than the purchase or capital improvement of the principal residence, does not count, either for the Section 108 principal residence exclusion or for increasing the taxpayer's basis in the home for purposes of determining gain under Section 121 on its sale.

Credit Card Debt

Credit card debt, unfortunately, can never be considered a second mortgage for debt forgiveness purposes. Even though purchases may have gone directly into capital improvements within the home, or even if incurred as a cash advance to cover an initial down payment on the purchase of the home, the forgiveness of credit card debt (as is the case for all unsecured debt) always gives rise to forgiveness of indebtedness income. Such income, however, may sometimes be excluded under the insolvency or bankruptcy exception.

STUDY QUESTIONS

10. For federal tax purposes, a nonrecourse mortgage generally:

   a. Generates forgiveness of indebtedness income upon the property's sale to the same extent as does a recourse mortgage
   b. Does not generate forgiveness of indebtedness income over and above the fair market value of the property
   c. Creates more forgiveness of debt income taxable as ordinary income because the borrower has taken on no personal obligation
   d. None of the above applies to taxation of nonrecourse mortgages

11. A home equity refinancing for more than the original remaining acquisition indebtedness that was used to pay a portion of a child's college tuition and pay off medical expenses is ineligible either for the Code Sec. 108 principal residence exclusion or for increasing basis for purposes of later minimizing any gain under Code Sec. 121. *True or False?*

FORECLOSURES AND RELATED SITUATIONS

The inability to make mortgage payments on time can lead to one of several situations that may give rise to forgiveness of indebtedness income.

These include straight foreclosures, mortgage workouts, deeds in lieu of foreclosures, short sales, and bankruptcy court-ordered sales.

Foreclosure

The foreclosure process varies depending on state law but all follow the same general procedure. A mortgage lender begins contacting the delinquent borrower shortly after payments fall into arrears. If the amount due continues to be in arrears after a reasonable time (generally, about 90 days), the lender hands the matter over to an attorney for formal foreclosure proceedings.

Foreclosure proceedings generally start with the service of a notice of default on the borrower. If payment and costs are not paid within a time specified within that notice pursuant to law (varying from state to state) for "curing" the default, the lender's attorney sets a court date to reduce the outstanding arrearage and the mortgage debt to a judgment. Once a judgment is obtained, the lender will request that the property be auctioned off to satisfy the judgment. The lender will almost always enter the first bid in the foreclosure sale equal to the amount of the outstanding debt. If there are no other bidders, the lender becomes the owner of the property. Most states allow the residence to be "redeemed" by the homeowner by paying the outstanding mortgage debt, real estate taxes paid by the lender, interest, and other costs. The time period varies from state to state. Once the redemption period is over, the lender will place the home on the market to recoup the mortgage debt, interest, and expenses paid.

Generally, the lender is unable to sell the house for what is owed and, if the note is a recourse note, must decide whether to pursue the former homeowner for the balance. Typically, however, a homeowner of a personal residence that goes into foreclosure has exhausted most other assets to prevent a forced sale of the home, which discourages the lender from undertaking the costly process of pursuing the borrower's other assets. This process may not be the case, however, in connection with vacation property.

When the lender purchases the mortgaged property at the foreclosure sale, it may be referred to as a *bid in at a foreclosure sale* and a lender usually makes such a purchase when there are no other bids. Another variation is a *strict foreclosure,* under which a court orders the property to be conveyed to the lender in full satisfaction of the mortgage debt. Usually, however, an independent third party purchases the foreclosed property under a court-ordered sale of the property.

The result of a foreclosure for homeowners is not only the loss of their home but also the tax consequence that arises from any forgiveness of the unpaid indebtedness. On the mortgage lender's side, foreclosure general results in recovery of only about 60 percent of the investment.

> **COMMENT**
>
> In the midst of the subprime mortgage crisis, the Better Business Bureau is warning homeowners about foreclosure rescue scams. As a result of such scams, borrowers need to exercise care in entering into workout agreements. Generally, dealing directly with the lender or mortgage servicer is advised.

Foreclosure Alternatives

With decreasing home values, refinancing to a better mortgage rate with another lender is generally not possible, leaving many recent homeowners unable to switch from their current mortgages under which a reset interest clause now has raised their scheduled monthly mortgage payments to levels they are unable to handle.

It is often in the best interests of both the homeowner and the lender to seek a solution to nonpayment of monthly amounts other than through foreclosure. Major alternatives are described here.

Mortgage workouts. A mortgage modification or workout generally consists of a change in the contractual interest rate (or scheduled resets in the case of ARMs) and/or term of an existing mortgage in order to lower monthly payments. The lender or mortgage servicer agrees to a workout or modification when the alternative is a foreclosure sale in which the mortgage debt likely would not be fully paid.

When a lender determines that foreclosure is not in its best interest (because the typical foreclosure nets the lender only about 60 cents on the dollar), the lender may offer a mortgage workout, under which the terms of the mortgage are changed to result in a lower monthly payment that the homeowner is likely to be able to handle.

Deed in lieu of foreclosure. Rather than the lender exercising its right to foreclose on the property, the borrower may be able to reach an agreement with the lender simply to transfer title back to the lender. In return for this deed in lieu of foreclosure, the lender usually agrees to accept the deed so transferred as full settlement and cancels the remainder of the borrower's mortgage debt.

The deed in lieu of foreclosure route usually is taken when there is not much chance that the borrower will be able to pay the deficiency judgment on the mortgage note using other assets. In that case, the lender accepts the deed as full settlement. Before considering this option, many lenders require the homeowner to try for at least 90 days to sell the home for its fair market value. The deed in lieu of-foreclosure option may not be available if other liens, such as other creditor judgments, second mortgages, and IRS or state tax liens, have been placed on the property's title.

Short sales. A *short sale* is generally a sale by the owner in which the net selling price will not cover to balance of the mortgage—that is, the sale comes up short in paying off the mortgage balance. In cases of short sales, the lender must agree to the sale in order to release the lender's lien on the property for purposes of conveying free-and-clear title to the purchaser. Some homeowners, in addition, wish to avoid the community stigma of having a foreclosure sale sign on their front lawn and would prefer a sale conducted quietly. A sale by the owner also works, of course, in "nonshort" situations: when the fair market value of the residence exceeds debt obligation plus costs (broker commissions and closing costs). If the borrower has significant equity in the home, the sale by owner may be an alternative to a foreclosure sale in which participants are accepting rock-bottom prices. Especially if the homeowner has a purchaser in mind, the lender is often willing to postpone the start of foreclosure proceedings.

Bankruptcy. Bankruptcy law changed in 2005 and, as a result, the solution to indebtedness income may be worse than recognizing the debt itself in the amount of collateral damage done. The Bankruptcy Code allows the borrower more time to get current on past-due payments. Even if catch-up payments cannot ultimately be made, bankruptcy can:

- Temporarily stop foreclosure proceedings;
- Provide a workout of unsecured debt (thereby enabling the borrower to make the mortgage payments); and
- Prevent a deficiency judgment from requiring future payments on the excess of the mortgage balance over the home's value.

State law will determine whether a personal residence of an individual in bankruptcy is protected from the claims of creditors, including secured mortgagees. Potential protection of the residence from sale under the bankruptcy laws is a compelling reason for an individual to consider the bankruptcy alternative.

TIMING OF DEBT INCOME RECOGNITION

A debt is canceled or forgiven when, considering all the facts and circumstances, an identifiable event occurs that make it evident that the debt will never be paid. Thus, the debtor recognizes discharge of indebtedness income when:

- The debt is canceled, reduced, or forgiven; or
- The encumbered property is transferred and the debt is otherwise difficult if not impossible to collect.

In many foreclosure situations, the abandonment of the security interest in the debt by the lender (that is, at foreclosure) is the evidence required to prove that the debt will not be paid for purposes of the lender taking a bad debt deduction. This is particularly true for nonrecourse debt but is also convincing when the borrower has no significant other assets.

For a "walk away" (that is, when the homeowner just vacates the premises one day), debt forgiveness does not take place for tax purposes when the borrower starts to walk away from or abandon the property. Rather, debt forgiveness for tax purposes occurs when the lender gives up on collection of the recourse mortgage, either by formal notice or sufficient inaction. This usually occurs in the case of a mortgage workout through a formal, written agreement; in the case of a short sale or a deed in lieu of foreclosure, when title to the house passes; and in the case of a straight foreclosure, at the time of sale unless the lender leaves open its legal right to pursue the borrower's personal obligation on the mortgage note over and above the mortgage amount satisfied by the foreclosure sale.

Second Mortgage Situations

Especially in home equity (second mortgage) loan situations, where the home equity lender is second in line for any proceeds from a foreclosure sale, the home equity lender may simply accept the fact that the payments have stopped and will not take any further action. However, such lenders frequently will leave the recorded lien on the property so that if real estate values eventually rise and the home eventually is sold, the lenders may get their money back. In these cases, there is no forgiveness of the debt simply because collection stops.

FORM 1099-C, *CANCELLATION OF DEBT,* DUE DILIGENCE

A lender or mortgage servicer must report a discharged indebtedness of $600 or more during a calendar year. Form 1099-C, *Cancellation of Debt,* is used. Form 1099-C must be furnished to the debtor by January 31 of the year following the discharge of indebtedness.

Taxpayers need to be aware that failure to receive a Form 1099-C is not proof that the homeowner does not have income from cancellation of an indebtedness.

The receipt of Form 1099-A, *Acquisition or Abandonment of Secured Property,* does not establish a discharge of debt. Similarly, the simple receipt of a Form 1099-C does not establish a discharge of debt. However, a borrower who receives a Form 1099-C must be prepared to rebut the assumption by the IRS that the amount and the tax year are correct.

The IRS generally prefers the borrower and lender to resolve disputes concerning information reported on the Form 1099-C. These disputes typically involve:

- Debate over amount; or
- Debate over tax year.

> **COMMENT**
>
> Form 1099-C does not include information regarding entitlement to any of the exclusions under Code Sec. 108. It is up to the homeowner to claim the exclusions in reporting such potential income on his or her personal tax return.

STUDY QUESTIONS

12. A court-ordered conveyance of property to a lender in full satisfaction of the homeowner's mortgage debt is a:

 a. Strict foreclosure
 b. Nonnegotiable foreclosure
 c. Bid in foreclosure sale
 d. Curing the default sale

13. In a deed in lieu of foreclosure:

 a. The homeowner temporarily transfers the deed back to the lender and catches up on back mortgage payments
 b. The lender agrees to accept the sale price obtained and release its lien to convey free-and-clear title to the purchaser
 c. The lender accepts a deed as full settlement, cancels the remaining debt, and takes title to the property
 d. The transfer of deed becomes part of the homeowner's bankruptcy estate

SALE OF THE MORTGAGED RESIDENCE

Independent of any forgiveness of indebtedness arising out of a foreclosure sale (or a short sale or the transfer of a deed in lieu of foreclosure) is the sale itself for tax purposes. Although the debt forgiveness and sale typically take place simultaneously in most foreclosure sales, they are considered independently for tax purposes.

Basis in Residence

The adjusted basis that a homeowner has in his or her residence has no direct relationship to the amount of income, if any, to be realized and recognized under Code Sec. 108 on the forgiveness of debt. It does, however, have everything to do with the amount of potential gain or loss realized by the homeowner on the sale of his or her residence. Gain or loss is determined by subtracting net sales price from the taxpayer's adjusted basis in the principal residence.

A homeowner's adjusted basis in the residence is a component that directly affects the amount of gain realized on the sale of the residence (Net sales price – Adjusted basis = Gain realized).

Adjusted basis is immediately relevant only if a foreclosure or other sale takes place, rather than a mortgage workout. Mortgage workouts, however, usually reduce the tax basis in the residence, which in turn creates a greater amount of potential gain when the residence is eventually sold in a future tax year.

Pre-May 7, 1997, ownership. If a homeowner bought his or her present home before May 7, 1997, and had owned a home prior to that purchase, the likelihood is that his or her basis in the current home may be lower than the price paid for the property. Prior to May 7, 1997, a homeowner who sold a principal residence could defer tax on all gain attributable to the sale if the selling price amount was "rolled over" and used to purchase the homeowner's next principal residence. Gain was deferred to the extent that the purchase price of the new home was equal to or greater than the selling price of the new home. That rolled over amount lowered the adjusted basis of the new home by the amount of the rolled-over untaxed gain. Therefore, the basis of any principal residence property acquired before May 7, 1997, may be lower than the purchase price of the residence under this rule if a prior home had been owned.

Capital improvements. Capital improvements to the property (in contrast to repairs) also increase the homeowner's tax basis in the property by the cost of those improvements (material and labor).

Depreciation. On the other hand, prior depreciation on the residence (taken either when it was previously a rental property or to the extent used partially as a home office) will reduce adjusted basis by the amount of depreciation taken.

The market value of the residence is important when a foreclosure sale, a short sale, or a deed in lieu of foreclosure solution is pursued. Market value can determine the amount of indebtedness forgiveness realized as well as gain realized on the sale or the "deemed sale" of the residence.

Selling Price

Aside from determining basis, the selling price of the residence is essential in determining any gain or loss realized on the sale of the residence. A sale can either be in the form of a short sale or a foreclosure sale to an unrelated third party; or it may be a "deemed sale" under which the mortgage lender takes title and possession of the property. In the latter cases, determining fair market value at the time of transfer is used to determine "selling price" under the computation of gain or loss for tax purposes.

Sale to unrelated third party. Determining the selling price of a sale of the residence, whether as a short sale or in foreclosure, is simple. The same computation is used as in a regular, unforced sale of any residence: the price that the third party pays for the residence, less any closing expenses related to closing title. That amount is not reduced by any offset claimed by the mortgage holder or any other lien holder (for example, by contractors who worked on the house).

EXAMPLE

In a foreclosure sale, Rick Hansen has sales proceeds from his property of $500,000. Rick nets $40,000 after paying closing fees of $1,000 and $459,000 to the first and second mortgage holders for the property. Assuming that his basis in the property is $175,000, his gain is $324,000 ($499,000 net sales price less $175,000 basis). Further assuming that Rick can claim the $250,000 home sale gain exclusion, he realizes $74,000 as taxable long-term capital gain when his home is sold in foreclosure.

Transfer to recourse mortgage lender. In situations under which "sale price" for purposes of determining taxable gain is dependent on a determination of market value, miscalculations can occur. From a pragmatic viewpoint, it is important for the parties to determine market value before the IRS becomes involved through receiving a Form 1099 information return.

Determining market value usually becomes an issue if the property is not sold to a third party but rather when title reverts to the lender. This reversion may be at a foreclosure sale, in which the lender bids in at the amount of the mortgage because either no bidder or only under-bidders come forward. Or market value may become an issue if the lender agrees to take title to the property in lieu of foreclosure. Valuation rather than an actual sale of the residence in the open market to a third party determines the "selling price" in the case of deed in lieu of foreclosure situations.

COMMENT

Homeowners should be watchful for inaccurate valuations, in which the lender says the property is worth less as the lender takes a deed in lieu of foreclosure. The IRS Taxpayer Advocate and other consumer watchdogs have warned that lenders often have little incentive to value the property precisely. The homeowner, however, may have an interest in having a higher value for the property. Obtaining a higher value for the property means less ordinary income debt forgiveness while increasing gain from the sale that is taxed at maximum 15 percent capital gain rate. This may be especially relevant to vacation property for which neither the Code Sec. 108 principal residence exclusion nor the home sale exclusion of gain is available.

Home Sale Exclusion of Gain

Eligibility. A homeowner may exclude from gross income up to $250,000 of gain from the sale or exchange of his or her principal residence. Married taxpayers filing jointly as well as qualifying surviving spouses may exclude up to $500,000. The exclusion can be used once every two years.

To be entitled to a full home sale gain exclusion, a taxpayer must own and use property as principal residence for periods totaling 2 out of 5 years before sale. The 5-year period can be suspended for up to 10 years for absences due to service in the military, the foreign service, on account of employment in the intelligence community, or as a member of the Peace Corps.

A partial exclusion is available when the ownership and use test or 2-year test is not met but taxpayer sells due to change of employment, health problems, or unforeseen circumstances. Special rules ease application of the rules in cases of deceased or former spouses or involuntary conversions. Information returns may not be required. If the property was acquired in a like-kind exchange, the ownership/use period is 5 years.

New rules for property converted from other residence to principal residence. Under a loophole-closing provision in the *Housing Assistance Tax Act of 2008,* conversions of a residence from a second home to a principal residence can no longer effectively allow the homeowner to use the principal residence home sale exclusion under Code Sec. 121 to shelter all or a substantial portion of the gain attributable to periods during which the residence had not been used as the taxpayer's principal residence. The impact of this new twist in the law, however, will only slowly impact current homeowners because a period of nonqualified use for this purpose with respect to a piece of property is defined as any period (other than any period before January 1, 2009) during which the property is not used as the principal residence of the taxpayer, the taxpayer's spouse or the taxpayer's former spouse. As a result, the pro-rata gain attributable to pre-2009 periods may continue to be sheltered under the Code Sec. 121's $250,000/$500,000 maximum exclusion.

Gain is allocated between periods of qualified and nonqualified use on the basis of the respective amounts of time the property is employed for qualified and nonqualified uses. Specifically, the Internal Revenue Code provides that gain is allocated to periods of nonqualified use based on the ratio which the aggregate periods of nonqualified use during the period the property was owned by the taxpayer bears to the total period of time the property was owned by the taxpayer.

Computation of Gain

The basic computation to determine taxable gain or loss on the sale of a residence is as follows:

Selling price
- Adjusted basis and selling expenses
- Reduction in tax basis due to excluded debt forgiveness income
= Gain or loss realized (if a positive number)
- Home sale gain exclusion, if gain realized on a principal residence
= Gain (recognized) or Loss (unrecognized and not deductible)

No allowable netting of debt discharge income against gain on sale.
Although the excess of mortgage debt over home value is forgiveness of indebtedness income, the IRS considers the loss realized on the home in selling it for less than was paid for it to be nondeductible as a personal loss under Code Sec. 162(c). The general accepted rule—and one followed by the IRS—is that a loss from the sale portion of the foreclosure transaction cannot offset the income from the cancellation of indebtedness portion.

No investment loss allowed. Despite the trend particularly in recent years of calling a home an "investment," and despite significant appreciation in certain homes that proved that claim true in the abstract, the Internal Revenue Code continues to consider a home that is lived in by the tax-payer as exclusively personal use property. As such, any loss on the sale of the residence is a personal loss and cannot be used as a deduction against other types of investment gains, such as in the stock market or in the sale of raw land.

STUDY QUESTIONS

14. Why does a vacation homeowner benefit by having his or her home valued as high as possible when ownership of his or her residence is transferred to the lender as part of debt forgiveness?

   a. Higher value increases the former homeowner's gain taxed at maximum 15 percent capital gains rates but lowers any potential ordinary income from debt forgiveness that is generally taxed at a much might rate

   b. The former homeowner's credit rating generally is less affected when the value is greater

   c. The higher value of the property whose debt is forgiven can be used to offset more investment gains

   d. The homeowner is losing the home anyway and therefore does not benefit either way

---

15. Under Code Sec. 162(c), why may a loss from selling a home for less than was paid for it not be deducted?

   a. The IRS considers the loss is a nondeductible personal loss that may not offset income from the cancellation of indebtedness

   b. The loss may only be netted against other long-term capital gains

   c. The loss occurs in a separate reporting period from the timing of the purchase, which could adversely affect tax revenues

   d. The loss may be deducted

CONCLUSION

In a straight foreclosure, the lender—under its legal right to do so—conducts a foreclosure sale in which the proceeds of the sale, less expenses, are used to pay off the homeowner's mortgage. If the proceeds from the sale do not repay the entire mortgage, the lender can either pursue additional payment from the homeowner on the mortgage note as a personal obligation or it can "forgive" any outstanding amount.

If all or part of the mortgage debt after the foreclosure sale is forgiven, that forgiven debt is income to the former homeowner and is taxed to him or her unless one of several statutory exclusions applies. The *Mortgage Forgiveness Debt Relief Act of 2007* effectively protected through 2009 an estimated 1 million recent "subprime" homeowners through enactment of the qualified principal residence exclusion. The *Emergency Economic Stabilization Act of 2008* extended that protection another three years, through 2012, effectively making this part of "permanent" planning for the near future. Thousands more are protected by the insolvency exclusion. Many long-time homeowners with now-onerous home-equity loans, vacation homeowners, and those with "jumbo" mortgages, however, are not protected. And for those who may qualify for one of the statutory exclusions, danger of tax liability lurks if respect for their rules and limitations are not scrupulously observed.

A foreclosure sale also triggers gain or loss to the homeowner separate and apart from the mortgage debt forgiveness. Here, again, as in the case of debt forgiveness, an exclusion may apply if the property is a qualified principal residence. Most recent homeowners in the subprime crisis are there because their homes have depreciated since the borrowers purchased their property; such homeowners will realize a nondeductible loss on any foreclosure. For those who are now going through mortgage workouts, as well as individuals who have owned their homes for a number of years, however, the prospect of paying capital gains on the sale of their mortgaged property in the future remains a hazard that should not be ignored, despite the present home sale exclusion.

The transfer of a deed in lieu of foreclosure or a short sale may also trigger similar tax issues and exclusions. Even if the homeowner is fortunate enough to be able to come to a mortgage workout arrangement with his or her current lender and remain in the home, forgiveness-of-indebtedness-income issues can arise.

Most homeowners generally are in a frantic state when foreclosure looms. Having an advisor with a cool head who knows the rules, their myriad permutations, and alternative paths is essential under these circumstances. Hopefully, this chapter provides advisors with the knowledge needed to more ably assist in this crisis.

Tax Relief for a Business in Distress

This chapter explores transactions that give rise to losses companies may claim because of an economic downturn or a specific event. Many of these transactions involve two taxpayers: a buyer and seller, a borrower and lender, or an issuer and investor. The chapter also offers a refresher course in important deductions that may be taken as part of business operations, such as bonus depreciation, first-year expensing, tax treatment of tangible/intangible assets, and start-up expenses, which Congress has put into place as incentives to continue doing business during the inevitable cyclical ups and downs of the marketplace.

LEARNING OBJECTIVES

Upon completion of this chapter, you will be able to:

- Decide when losses can be recognized;
- Apply the distinctions among features of depreciation, expensing, and amortization;
- Explain bad debt deductions;
- Describe the impact of foreclosures, repossessions, and debt-related mortgage transactions;
- Determine the tax consequences of discharge of indebtedness;
- Understand net operating losses and their impact on assets; and
- Determine in what ways Congress's latest attempt at helping struggling businesses, the *Emergency Economic Stabilization Act of 2008*, has altered the rules.

INTRODUCTION

Taxpayers generally take for granted that tax deductions are always advantageous, improving cash flow; that any business operating losses are temporary; and that bills will be paid, investments will pan out, and loans and mortgages will be repaid. But as American businesses have discovered in the last few years, the economy may turn expectations upside down. A business may struggle. No matter how well run, a business may be "distressed," i.e., lose money. What does a company do when it has losses? What if a borrower cannot pay a mortgage, or a customer cannot pay a bill? Suppose an investment goes bad. How much is the tax loss and how should it be treated? Are losses bad—or good?

HOW ACCOUNTING BASICS APPLY TO BUSINESS LOSSES

Before the chapter examines how features of tax accounting drive treatment of business losses, this section explores how basic operational accounting choices that businesses make also affect their optimal handling of losses.

Tax Year

The first order of business in addressing a business loss is determining whether the proper and most advantageous time period is being used to measure it. A business must have a measurement period for determining and reporting its income and losses—its *tax year.* Instead of lifetime accounting or transaction accounting, the income tax has always been based on annual accounting. The taxpayer must aggregate all transactions in determining net gain, loss, income, and deductions for the annual accounting period. Imposing tax at relatively short intervals reduces the problem of deferral; the government collects revenue periodically and predictably. This allows for easier budgeting and minimizes the need for interest charges to counteract deferral. Measuring income at relatively short intervals also eases income tax administration.

The tax year may be the same as the calendar year, or it may be a fiscal year, i.e., a different 12-month period chosen by the business for keeping its books and records. Most businesses can use any 12-month period if the books and records requirement is met. A business with a seasonal market that culminates in the sale of products during the summer, for example, may choose a natural fiscal year that begins October 1 and ends the following September 30. However, a partnership or S corporation is limited in its tax year to a *required year,* which is usually the calendar year. There is a business purpose exception applicable to these entity types.

To change its tax year, a company must apply under Rev. Proc. 2002-39 and show a business purpose for the change. The annual period cannot substantially distort income. The business may apply for an automatic change of tax year if it has not changed its tax year for 48 months. Automatic approval is available under Rev. Proc. 2002-37 and must be requested on Form 1128, *Application to Adopt, Change, or Retain a Tax Year.* The business can also qualify for automatic approval under the 25-percent gross receipts test, if the business's gross receipts in the last 2 months of the 12-month period are at least 25 percent of the total gross receipts of the requested period for the past 3 years.

EXAMPLE

XYZ Beach Co. took in $1.2 million of its annual receipts of $2.5 million in gross receipts in July and August of this year. In the previous year it took in $1 million of its $2 million in annual receipts during July and August, and $0.9 million of $2.2 million in gross receipts the year earlier. XYZ Beach Co. will be automatically approved for a September to August fiscal year because it has realized at least 25 percent of its annual gross receipts during July and August—the last two months of the tax year that it is requesting.

Tax Reporting

The business's income and loss is determined for the tax year and reported on the appropriate annual tax return—Form 1040, Form 1120, Form 1120S, or Form 1065 for that tax year. The end of one tax year cuts off the measurement of events that affect the year's income or loss; subsequent income and losses are reported on a separate return for the next tax year.

The applicable tax return forms are as follow:

- A business such as a *sole proprietorship* or *single-member limited liability company (LLC)* that operates under a distinct name may nevertheless be the alter ego of an individual and report its taxes on the individual's Form 1040. If an individual runs the business without creating a separate entity or if the LLC is taxed as a sole proprietorship, the business's operations are reported on Form 1040, Schedule C. The resulting income or loss is then included in the individual's taxable income reported on Form 1040;

- A *corporation* reports its operations on Form 1120, *U.S. Corporation Income Tax Return.* Because the corporation is a separate entity, its income and losses are reported separately at the entity level and do not carry over to income or loss of the individual(s) that owns the corporation;

- An exception to use of Form 1120 applies to Subchapter S corporations, which do "pass through" their income and losses to the owners (the stockholders) and are taxed as a passthrough entity similar to a partnership (and file Form 1120-S); and

- A *partnership* reports its operations on Form 1065, *U.S. Return of Partnership Income.* Its income and losses flow through to its owners, the partners. A Subchapter S corporation is a flowthrough entity that in many respects is taxed like a partnership. If the partnership or S corporation has a loss for the year, the individual owner can claim the loss on the Form 1040 and reduce his or her taxable income.

Accounting Method

Another issue that goes directly toward measurement of losses is determining what method of accounting is required and, if options are available, which method—cash or accrual, or a special variation such as a hybrid method— is most advantageous to a particular business. Depending on the method used, the business's reported income (or loss) will vary:

- The *cash method* captures and reports payments and receipts as they are actually made; and
- The *accrual method* reports income when the taxpayer has the right to receive the income and losses at the time when they are incurred, for example, when property is bought or sold or services are performed.

Most individuals use the cash method to report their personal income and expenses; most businesses use the accrual method to report their income and expenses and determine their profit or loss. Once the item is accrued, the actual payment of the item does not change the time for reporting the income or expense.

Under an accrual method of accounting, a business owner generally deducts business expenses when both of the following apply:

- The all-events test has been met; and
- Economic performance has occurred.

The all-events test is met when:

- All events have occurred that fix the fact of liability; and
- The liability can be determined with reasonable accuracy.

Economic performance generally occurs as the property or services are provided.

Accounting for prepayments. Expenses generally cannot be deducted in advance, even if they are paid in advance. This rule applies to both the cash and accrual methods. Examples include prepaid interest, prepaid insurance premiums, and any other expense paid far enough in advance to, in effect, create an asset with a useful life extending substantially beyond the end of the current tax year. If a long-term contract or other agreement is broken and termination fees are paid, however, those fees are deductible in the year paid.

Accounting for late payments. Because a tax loss is a component of taxable income, a bad economy in which payments are made late may either lower or raise taxable income: the cash basis allows a business not to recognize income until a customer actually pays, whereas it also means delaying expense deductions until the business pays its own bills.

STUDY QUESTIONS

---

1. Under the gross receipts test, a business may automatically qualify for approval for a change in tax year if the gross receipts in the last 2 months of the 12-month period are:

a. At least 25 percent of the total gross receipts of the requested period for the past 3 years

b. At least 25 percent of the total gross receipts for the preceding year

c. At least 25 percent of the total gross receipts for 2 of the previous 5 tax years

d. None of the above describes the qualifications

2. A calendar year business pays its office cleaning service in December 2008 for cleaning through the end of 2009, thereby getting a reduced price and a guarantee that a certain cleaning crew will be on duty. The prepayment:

a. Can be deducted from the business's 2008 federal tax liability

b. Cannot be deducted from 2008 federal taxes

c. Must be amortized for each quarter in the coverage period

d. Cannot be deducted for either 2008 or 2009, because a cash basis taxpayer can only pay an expense in the year it should be deducted in order to be entitled to the deduction

---

TAX ACCOUNTING

Accelerating and Deferring Income Recognition and Deductions

Regardless of the tax year and the accounting method the company chooses, the taxpayer will have some discretion when to recognize income or deductions, gains or losses. This recognition strategy involves the techniques of deferral and acceleration, and affects income tax liability for two or more tax years, without affecting the business's overall tax liability. For example, the use of accelerated depreciation will reduce income in an earlier year but increase income in the subsequent year. However, the overall depreciation that can be deducted does not change. What does change, however, is the time at which the deduction is taken and, therefore, when tax must be paid. The longer the same amount of tax can be deferred, the greater the benefit under a time-value-of-money analysis.

The use of deferral and acceleration depends on whether the taxpayer determines that it is advantageous to modify the amount of income or loss shown on the return for a particular year. If the taxpayer is likely to have losses for the year, accelerating a deduction may not be helpful. On the other hand, the deduction may create or increase a net operating loss. This can be carried back to an earlier tax year by a business taxpayer and can be used to obtain a refund if the taxpayer owed taxes in that earlier year. Taxpayers also should consider acceleration and deferral techniques to even out income between any two years, because the average tax rate based on tax brackets will then be as low as possible. Ideally, too, the time value of money should be a factor, making the deferral of tax liability beneficial provided it does not result in a jump in the following year's tax rate not commensurate to the amount of interest saved on the deferred tax.

> **EXAMPLE**
>
> ABC Co. has a choice: either accelerate incurring certain expenses in the current year and add to the company's overall net losses for the year, or postpone incurring those expenses until the next year, which looks like it will be a profitable year due to ABC Co.'s position in the marketplace. If ABC Co.'s prior year reports showed a significant profit on which the company paid income taxes, it makes sense for ABC to incur the additional expense this year (as long as it also makes economic business sense). By incurring the expense this year, ABC can claim a net operating loss (NOL) when it files its taxes for this year and carry the NOL back to last year, amend that tax return, and apply for a quick refund of income taxes already paid for that year.

Depreciation

Depreciation is generally required for tangible property that will be used over a period of years. *Depreciation* is the process of allocating and deducting the cost of property throughout the property's entire period of use (its recovery period). The cost of the property cannot generally be deducted all in one year because this would "distort income." Other items, such as startup expenses, can be written off (amortized) over a period of years. The Internal Revenue Code generally allows the IRS to set certain recovery periods for various property types. The Code also regulates depreciation by setting out rules for the use of *straight-line depreciation* (depreciation taken for the cost of property using an even rate each year throughout the item's recovery period) or *accelerated depreciation* (depreciation that allows for higher deduction amounts in the early years of use and then lower deduction amounts in the "out years"). In either straight-line or accelerated depreciation, however, total depreciation deductions over the asset's recovery period remains the same; just the timing of those deductions over the same set period varies.

Deferral and acceleration using depreciation. The effect of depreciation is to defer an expense deduction and thus, in one sense, accelerate income. That is, income taxed in Year 1 may be used to buy Asset A, which has a recovery period of five years. Under the depreciation rules, the total expense of purchasing Asset A may not reduce the income in Year 1 and the expense must be spread out over five years.

Many Code provisions allow taxpayers options regarding how much they can defer a deduction or accelerate income, giving businesses flexibility to adjust these items in response to fluctuations in taxable income. For example, depreciation may be taken on an accelerated basis (e.g., 200-percent double-declining balance) or on the straight-line method of claiming equal deductions for business property each year.

2008 bonus depreciation. Bonus depreciation is an additional first-year depreciation deduction temporarily offered that exceeds the amount allowed under any of the general methods approved in the Internal Revenue Code. Bonus depreciation is computed before regular depreciation is computed under the modified accelerated cost recovery system (MACRS) for the year the property is placed in service, but after any Code Sec. 179 expensing (explained later). The *Economic Stimulus Act of 2008* (P.L. 110-185) permits businesses to take 50-percent bonus depreciation, available only for property acquired after December 31, 2007, and before January 1, 2009, and placed in service before January 1, 2009 (with a limited extension for "long-production-period" assets acquired before 2010). Bonus depreciation also had been offered briefly in the past, first to help businesses reinvest after the terrorist attacks of 9-11-01 and, again, after Hurricane Katrina hit the Gulf Coast.

Taxpayers will take bonus depreciation unless they elect not to apply it to a particular class of property. They then apply one of the conventional depreciation methods to the remaining basis of the property.

PLANNING POINTER

Bonus depreciation accelerates a large portion of available depreciation into the year of purchase; it does not *create* more depreciation. A business that does not have sufficient current income to absorb available bonus depreciation still may find it advantageous to elect bonus depreciation in cases in which the business's two previous years were profitable. In such a case, the bonus depreciation creates a net operating loss (NOL) (described later) that may be carried back to the prior two years and entitle the business to an immediate refund.

COMMENT

Unlike first-year expensing, bonus depreciation is not phased out as the company's investment in qualifying property increases. Thus, bonus depreciation is particularly valuable to larger companies operating at a profit.

Most new tangible property with a regular MACRS recovery period of 20 years or less, water utility property, computer software (off-the-shelf), or qualified leasehold property is eligible for bonus depreciation if it is acquired after December 31, 2007, and placed in service before January 1, 2009. The placed-in-service date is extended through December 31, 2009, for qualifying commercial and noncommercial aircraft and certain other types of property with a long production period. Property acquired pursuant to a binding contract entered into before January 1, 2008 does not qualify for bonus depreciation. The production, manufacture, or construction of property for the taxpayer's own use must begin in 2008.

The placed-in-service date is extended through 2009 for property with a recovery period of 10 years or longer, transportation property, and certain aircraft. The property in this case must have an estimated production period exceeding one year, be subject to the uniform capitalization rules, and have an estimated cost exceeding $1 million.

For bonus depreciation to apply, the property must be purchased for use in a trade or business, to be held for investment or for the production of income. The property must be new. However, property converted to business use by the original purchaser will qualify for bonus depreciation.

STUDY QUESTIONS

3. What effect can techniques to defer or accelerate income and/or deductions have on the taxpayer's multiyear tax liability?

   a. Even out taxable income and therefore lower the overall effective tax rate for any two tax years
   b. Produce no increase or decrease in tax liability because overall income and deductions remain the same when added up over any two-year period
   c. Increase the tax liability when multiple years are considered
   d. Rule out the eligibility of a business to claim bonus depreciation

4. The placed-in-service date for 2008's bonus depreciation is extended through 2009 for any property that has a recovery period of 10 years or longer or is transportation property, has a production period exceeding one year, is subject to the uniform capitalization rules and has an estimated cost of

   a. $100,000 or more
   b. $250,000 or more
   c. $500,000 or more
   d. More than $1 million

First-Year Expensing

Under Code Sec. 179, a qualifying business that purchases depreciable assets can immediately opt to write off a substantial portion of the cost of property, regardless of what the depreciation rules require. For tax years beginning after 2007, the maximum Code Sec. 179 expense deduction was $125,000 with the deduction phased out by the amount that the cost of the property placed in service during the year exceeds $500,000 (with the dollar amounts adjusted for inflation). However, the *Economic Stimulus Act of 2008* (P.L. 110-185) raised the dollar limit to $250,000, but only for 2008. After 2008, the limit drops to $125,000 for 2009 and 2010, indexed for inflation, and $25,000 for subsequent years, with no inflation adjustment. The investment limit is increased to $800,000 for 2008.

> **COMMENT**
>
> Unlike 2008 bonus depreciation, enhanced expensing under the *Economic Stimulus Act of 2008* applies "in case of any taxable year beginning in 2008," which includes tax years that run over into 2009.

Like bonus depreciation, the deduction for first-year expensing is triggered in the year that the property is placed in service. The property must be purchased for use in the taxpayer's trade or business. Property acquired in an exchange can be expensed, but not to the extent of the basis attributable to the basis of the old property.

> **PLANNING POINTER**
>
> As in the case of bonus depreciation, a business should consider making an expensing election even if the company does not have the income to cover it in the current year. The expensing can create an NOL that may be carried back to a profitable year and result in an immediate refund. Taxpayers also should consider electing first-year expensing even if there will be no immediate tax benefits, for example, because of a lack of income in the current or the two carryback years. The election preserves the option to carry forward the deduction. If it is not preserved in this way, the deduction cannot be taken in the future and will be lost. The taxpayer will be limited to recovering the cost of the property using depreciation only.

The amount of the deduction for expensing phases out when the business's investment in property eligible for the writeoff hits stated levels. Under the *Economic Stimulus Act of 2008,* the deduction phases out by the amount that the cost of the property placed in service during the year exceeds $800,000.

The expense deduction for 2008, therefore, can be taken until the purchases of eligible property total $1.05 million ($250,000 maximum expensing for 2008, phased out dollar-for-dollar starting at $800,000).

> **COMMENT**
>
> Under the lower expensing limit, the writeoff was a considerable benefit for small businesses. With the higher limit and increased phaseout threshold, expensing can benefit larger businesses in 2008.

The maximum Code Sec. 179 writeoff is limited to the taxable income from the taxpayer's trade or business. Taxable income from any other trade or business conducted by the taxpayer can be used, however, and not necessarily the one for which the asset is placed into service. Potential deductions that exceed taxable income generally can be carried forward and added to the subsequent year's deduction limit.

The basis of the property must be reduced by the amount of the expense deduction.

Taxpayers taking an expensing deduction do not have to make an alternative minimum tax (AMT) adjustment.

A taxpayer makes an election to take first-year expensing on Form 4562, *Depreciation and Amortization (Including Information on Listed Property)*, showing the total expense deduction and the portion allocable to each item. Fiscal year filers will use Form 4562-FY, *Depreciation and Amortization (Including Information on Listed Property)*. For years beginning before 2011, the taxpayer can revoke the election without the IRS's consent. After 2010, IRS consent is needed to revoke an election.

Interaction of Depreciation and Expensing

To maximize deductions, it is recommended that taxpayers apply first-year expensing to the asset(s) with the longest writeoff period, and apply other expensing or depreciation to assets with shorter writeoff periods. Taxpayers should apply bonus depreciation after taking Code Sec. 179 expensing but before taking regular depreciation. By adopting this strategy, overall deductions (Section 179, bonus depreciation, and regular depreciation) are taken as soon as possible in the largest amounts possible, starting with the current year.

In making its elections, a business should also determine whether it is located in a state that follows the expensing rules of the *Economic Stimulus Act of 2008* or that has chosen not to allow increased expensing by decoupling from the federal law.

AMT/R&D Credit in Lieu of Bonus Depreciation

When use of credits is preferable. Although the *Economic Stimulus Act of 2008* included 50-percent bonus depreciation to encourage businesses to increase investment in depreciable property, unlike previous stimulus packages the legislation did not offer taxpayers an extended loss carryback. Companies that have experienced loss positions for several years cannot take full advantage of bonus depreciation because these businesses do not have any taxable income against which to take the deductions. The *Housing Assistance Tax Act of 2008* in part remedies that disadvantage for corporations that have unused prior AMT credits or research and development (R&D) tax credits. These businesses can elect not to take bonus depreciation but rather apply an amount of the forgone bonus depreciation to freeing up their AMT and R&D credits. An electing corporation must use the MACRS straight-line method to depreciate any eligible qualified property placed in service in the tax year of the election and in any later tax year (Code Sec. 168(k)(4)(A)(ii)), as added by P.L. 110-289).

EXAMPLE

ABC is a calendar year corporation. It places one item of eligible qualified property costing $100,000 in service on June 1, 2008, and elects to claim a credit for a portion of its unused AMT and research credits instead of taking bonus depreciation under the *Economic Stimulus Act of 2008*. The property is seven-year MACRS property and the half-year convention and double-declining balance method apply. Depreciation determined for purposes of item (1) is equal to $57,145, the sum of the $50,000 bonus depreciation that could have been claimed ($100,000 × 50 percent) and the $7,145 regular first-year MACRS deduction ($50,000 basis after reduction by bonus allowance × 14.29 percent first-year table percentage for seven-year property subject to the double-declining balance method). Depreciation determined for purposes of item (2) is $14,290 ($100,000 × 14.29 percent first-year table percentage). The bonus depreciation amount is $8,571 (($57,145 – $14,290) × 20 percent), assuming this amount is less than 6 percent of ABC's unused pre-2006 AMT and research credits.

> ABC must use the MACRS straight-line depreciation method and half-year convention to compute its regular tax depreciation deductions (and AMT deductions) over the asset's seven-year recovery period because it made the accelerated credit election. The allowable 2008 depreciation deduction is $7,145 ($100,000 × 7.145 percent first year straight-line table percentage for seven-year property subject to the half-year convention).
>
> By making the accelerated credit election, ABC's first-year depreciation deduction is reduced from $57,145 to $7,145. However, the corporation may claim a refundable accelerated research or AMT credit in the amount of $8,571.
>
> The remaining amount of $50,000 ($57,145 − $7,145) will be deducted over the remaining recovery period of the asset using the straight-line depreciation method.

The amount of unused credits that may be claimed is limited to 20 percent of the difference between (1) the aggregate bonus depreciation and regular depreciation that would be allowed on eligible qualified property placed in service during the tax year if bonus depreciation were claimed and (2) the aggregate straight-line depreciation that would be allowed on the eligible qualified property placed in service during the tax year if no bonus depreciation were claimed (Code Sec. 168(k)(4)(C)(i), as added by P.L. 110-289). The increased credits are refundable. The amount claimed is limited to the lesser of $30 million or 6 percent of the total credits accumulated from tax years beginning before January 1, 2006.

For purposes of this computation, in general, eligible qualified property is property that is eligible for bonus depreciation under Code Sec. 168(k) except that it must be acquired after March 31, 2008 (rather than after December 31, 2007) and placed in service before January 1, 2009 (before January 1, 2010 in the case of property with a long production period and certain noncommercial aircraft).

Impact. Forgoing 50-percent bonus depreciation on property acquired after March 31, 2008, does not mean that depreciation over the life of the asset will be any less. Bonus depreciation simply accelerates depreciation and forgoing it, therefore, only delays the depreciation of that asset. However, if a corporation makes this election, the MACRS straight-line depreciation method must be used.

COMMENT

The placed-in-service dates for bonus depreciation and this accelerated credit election are not identical. Although each ends on December 31, 2008, bonus depreciation starts on January 1, 2008, whereas the accelerated credit election starts April 1, 2008.

STUDY QUESTIONS

---

5. Under the *Economic Stimulus Act of 2008* for tax years beginning in 2008, the maximum amount of property placed in service eligible for the expensing writeoff before the phaseout of the dollar amount of the deduction begins is:

   a. $125,000
   b. $500,000
   c. $800,000
   d. $1.05 million

6. The Code Sec. 179 limits for the year _____ depreciation deduction carryovers.

   a. Are reduced by
   b. Are increased by
   c. Are treated independent of
   d. Are increased by AMT or R&D credits but reduced by

BAD DEBTS: CODE SECTION 166

A taxpayer can deduct totally worthless nonbusiness bad debts and totally or partially worthless business bad debts, in the year they become worthless:

- *Worthless business bad debts* are deductible as ordinary losses (which offset other income or generate NOL); and
- *Worthless nonbusiness bad debts* are deductible as short-term capital losses (taken on Schedule D of Form 1040 and able to be carried forward under the general capital loss carryforward rules).

Secured debts are not considered totally worthless until the creditor either disposes of the collateral or shows that the collateral is worthless. A taxpayer cannot write off a debt after it has been sold. A business bad debt includes worthless debts of a corporate taxpayer that are not evidenced by a security. It also includes debt held by a noncorporate taxpayer and created or acquired in a trade or business, or debt the loss or worthlessness from which was incurred in the trade or business.

The amount deductible is the taxpayer's basis in the debt, not the debt's fair market value or the face value.

Capital Contribution Versus Debt

Taxable income that is offset by a deduction does not give rise to a bad debt deduction. There must be a bona fide debt and a valid debtor-creditor relationship involving an enforceable obligation to pay a fixed or determinable sum of money. The taxpayer must intend to seek repayment of the debt.

A transfer between shareholders and their corporations, between family members, or between affiliated corporations may create a bona fide debt, but the transfer will be scrutinized for treatment as a gift or a contribution to capital.

Contributions to capital are not bona fide debts. The scrutiny is most strict for advances made to corporations by controlling shareholders. The same goes for advances by parties who are not shareholders but who have a close relationship to the corporation. The lender's ownership of stock may itself effect a return of capital. Allowing the lender to write off what is essentially an equity interest as a bad debt produces a deduction that corresponds with no real loss. For a bad debt deduction, the taxpayer must genuinely intend to create a debt with a reasonable expectation of repayment, consistent with the economic reality of the transaction.

Subsequent Recovery

Recovery of a totally worthless debt is taxable unless there is no tax benefit. An amount recovered on a partially worthless debt reduces the basis on the balance of the debt that has not been written off.

Partial Worthlessness

A partially worthless business debt can be deducted if:
- The taxpayer can demonstrate that a portion of the debt cannot be recovered;
- The taxpayer has charged off the debt during the tax year;
- The partial worthlessness applies to a specific debt; and
- The debt is unsecured.

The taxpayer must reduce his or her basis in the debt and the amount deductible in later years should the debt become totally worthless. The taxpayer is not required to write off a partially worthless business bad debt prior to the time it becomes totally worthless.

Losses and Bad Debts

A creditor's loss on the compromise of a debt owed by a solvent debtor is a loss, not a bad debt, because the settlement extinguishes the debt and leaves no balance that may be regarded as a bad debt. In contrast, a loss on the compromise of a debt owed by an insolvent debtor is a bad debt. A loan of property other than money that is not returned yields a loss, not a bad debt. A taxpayer can deduct a loss on a bad debt with a related person, even though the taxpayer cannot deduct a loss in a sale or exchange with a related person.

When a taxpayer guarantees another person's debts, however, the loss of a guarantor who made a payment and cannot recover it from the debtor is a bad debt, not a loss. The loss is like a nonbusiness bad debt. However, courts disagree; the Tax Court has treated loss of the payment as an ordinary loss deduction, not a bad debt.

If a creditor acquires property that satisfies a debt without foreclosure, the creditor's basis is the fair market value of the property when transferred, even if the conveyance does not extinguish the debtor's liability. The portion of the debt not satisfied is a bad debt. A transaction coming within the literal language of both the loss provisions and the bad debt provisions must be treated as a bad debt. The taxpayer has a short-term capital loss under the bad debt rules. If the property does not have an ascertainable fair market value, the creditor's basis is the full amount of the debt.

If a corporation forgives the debt of a stockholder to the corporation, the IRS regards the canceled debt as a constructive distribution that generally is treated as a dividend.

Foreclosure, Surrender, or Tax Sale

An individual owner's loss of property is deductible if incurred in a trade or business or transaction for profit. A lender is entitled to a loss deduction on the compromise or settlement of a solvent debtor for an amount less than the debt.

Forfeiture. Forfeiture of a down payment or deposit to purchase or lease property is deductible for a transaction entered into for profit. For example, the forfeit of payments on a building upon the failure to make the last payment is a loss. If the property is a capital asset, a forfeiture of money to purchase the property is a capital loss. A sale or exchange has occurred when the forfeiture is accompanied by a release of the purchaser's obligation to make further payments under the contract. Forfeitures and deeds in lieu of foreclosures, transfers of property in payment of an obligation, condemnations, dispositions of installment obligations, and significant modifications or retirements of debt instruments are generally sales or exchanges.

Satisfaction of a debt. Acquiring property in partial or full satisfaction of a debt is a taxable exchange of debt for property. The debtor can realize gain or loss on the disposition of the property. The creditor's basis in the property is its fair market value. If the value is not ascertainable, the creditor's basis is the amount of the debt satisfied by receipt of the property. The creditor can have a bad debt loss if the property's value is less than the creditor's basis for the debt or record a gain if the value exceeds the basis of the debt. Accrued interest is included in the basis of the debt if it was previously included in income. Payment made for a right to redeem property from a tax sale is included in the property's basis, even if the redemption expires.

Foreclosures and repossessions. A lender may foreclose or repossess property on which the taxpayer owes a debt secured by the property. This is treated as a sale, resulting in gain or loss, even if the taxpayer voluntarily returns the property. Any canceled debt is ordinary income to the borrower (subject to certain exclusions carved out by the Internal Revenue Code). If the debtor is personally liable for the debt, the amount realized on the foreclosure is the smaller of the debt or the property's fair market value, plus any proceeds received on a foreclosure sale. Any leftover debt that is forgiven is ordinary income.

A property owner may have a loss or gain on the loss of mortgaged property through foreclosure, surrender, or abandonment to the mortgagee (lender). A tax sale is treated like a foreclosure. Gain or loss is the difference between the full amount of the debt and the adjusted basis of the property. If the mortgagor remains liable for the deficiency, the amount realized is the bid price. The compromise of mortgage debt is treated as discharge of indebtedness income to the mortgagor (borrower). A solvent mortgagor realizes income on the cancellation of any mortgage debt.

> ### COMMENT
>
> The *Mortgage Forgiveness Debt Relief Act of 2007* provided significant relief to homeowners if the mortgaged property is the taxpayer's principal residence. Debt forgiveness, in whole or in part, of a mortgage loan secured by a principal residence will not be considered forgiveness-of-indebtedness income. This temporary relief provision initially applied for 2007 through 2009; the *Emergency Economic Stabilization Act of 2008* extended it through 2012. The exception to debt forgiveness income for business real property was unaffected by this new law and continues to be available to qualifying businesses.
>
> Taxpayers who run their business out of their home can qualify for this business-related exception only if the business is conducted in a structure separate from the main principal residence. Otherwise, any debt forgiveness must fall within the principal residence exception to be excluded.

No sale or exchange. Collections of claims or debt, compromises of debt, and grants of options to purchase are generally not sales or exchanges. An abandonment is not a sale or exchange unless the property abandoned is real estate subject to nonrecourse debt. A cancellation of a contract or lease is generally not considered to be a sale or exchange, but contract and lease rights may be sold or exchanged. A contract for a deed can be considered a sale or exchange of real property.

However, merely surrendering purchased property may not be treated as a sale or exchange. The courts have split on identical facts, in which the purchaser forfeited payments, there was no release, and the purchaser had occupied the building. In one case, the seller unilaterally declared that the purchaser had forfeited his rights to the building. If there is no sale or exchange, the loss is ordinary for tax purposes. A corporation that breached a contract to purchase stock of another corporation and lost a $500,000 deposit could take an ordinary loss. A deposit lost on a lease is also considered an ordinary loss. Payments forfeited to the seller are ordinary income when no sale or exchange has occurred.

Exceptions and exclusions. Debt canceled in a Title 11 bankruptcy case (which involves a plan of reorganization to maintain continued business operations) is not included in income, and the taxpayer must accordingly reduce its tax attributes. If the debtor was insolvent (i.e., had total liabilities that exceeded the fair market value of all assets) before the debt cancellation, the canceled debt similarly is not included in income, and tax attributes must be reduced. This exclusion applies after the bankruptcy exclusion.

A business using the cash method of accounting does not realize income from canceled debt if payment of the debt would have been a deductible expense. A taxpayer employing the accrual method has already deducted the expense and must include the canceled debt in income.

If discharged debt is qualified farm indebtedness or qualified real property indebtedness, the debtor can exclude from income the amount discharged, even if he or she is solvent.

COMMENT

As mentioned earlier but worth repeating: The exclusion of income from mortgage forgiveness that has been created by the *Mortgage Forgiveness Debt Relief Act of 2007* applies *only* to principal residences that are used by the owners at the time of the debt forgiveness. The exclusion does not apply to rental properties. Note, further, however, that indebtedness on real property used in a trade or business is subject to its own exclusion.

Tax attributes. If the taxpayer is allowed to exclude canceled debt from income, in return it must reduce tax attributes by the same amount, applying the following order:

1. NOLs (current and carryover);
2. General business credits carryovers;
3. Minimum tax credit carryovers,
4. Net capital losses or capital loss carryovers;
5. Basis of assets;
6. Passive activity loss and credit carryovers; and
7. Foreign tax credit carryovers.

For business real property debt, basis must be reduced in the following order:

1. Real property used in business and securing the canceled debt;
2. Personal property used in business and securing the debt;
3. Other property (except inventory and receivables);
4. Inventory and receivables; and
5. Personal use property.

For farm debt, basis should only be reduced in the following order:

1. Depreciable property;
2. Land; and then
3. Other qualified property.

The basis of assets is a tax attribute that may be reduced when discharge of indebtedness income is excluded because of bankruptcy or insolvency. Taxpayers can elect to reduce the basis of depreciable property before reducing other attributes. Any gain on the sale of the property is treated as depreciation and must be recaptured as ordinary income. The basis reduction is made on the first day of the year following the tax year in which the debt was discharged.

Lender's perspective. If a lender takes property in satisfaction of a debt, the transaction is considered to be a sale or exchange, and the borrower may recognize gain or loss. The loss will be deductible if the property is business or investment property, but not if it is personal use property such as a residence. It does not matter whether the lender took ownership of the property through foreclosure, repossession, a voluntary conveyance, or abandonment of the property. If the lender cancels debt greater than the property's fair market value, the excess may be taxed as ordinary income to the borrower.

STUDY QUESTIONS

> **7.** Which of the following is *not* considered part of a creditor's basis in property received in satisfaction of a debt?
>
> **a.** The difference between the basis of the debt and the current value of the property
> **b.** Accrued interest previously included in the creditor's income
> **c.** Fair market value of the property
> **d.** All of the above are included in the creditor's basis of property received

---

8. If a debtor business becomes insolvent and its debt cancelled, the debt:

   a. Is treated as ordinary taxable income to the debtor

   b. Is not included in income and the borrower's tax attributes must be reduced

   c. Is treated as long-term capital gain taxed to the debtor at maximum capital gains rates

   d. None of the above affects the debt

TREATMENT OF LOSSES

Losses may be deducted if not compensated by insurance, reimbursement, or other payment method. Only the entity or individual who sustained the loss can deduct it, unless the Internal Revenue Code provides for the transfer of the loss. An individual can deduct a loss only if incurred in a trade or business or transaction entered into for profit, or if the loss results from theft or casualty, such as a fire or storm. The standards for determining whether a loss was incurred in a trade or business are substantially the same as the standards for determining whether expenses are deductible as a trade or business expense.

Some losses are subject to special rules:

- Worthless securities and other securities transactions;
- Foreclosure, surrender, or a tax sale of real property; and
- Registered obligations.

A trade or business loss is deductible in computing adjusted gross income, whereas a loss from a transaction entered into for profit may be a miscellaneous deduction, unless the loss results from a sale or exchange or is attributable to rental or royalty-producing property. The deduction may be disallowed or the amount may change if the taxpayer converts property from business to personal or investment use, or vice versa.

Limits for Deducting Losses

The amount of loss that a taxpayer may deduct can vary depending on a number of factors, described here.

Not-for-profit limits. If an activity is carried on without the intention of making a profit, the taxpayer cannot use a loss from the activity to offset other income. For example, losses that relate to hobbies, sports, and tax shelters are not considered to be derived from "for profit" business activities and therefore cannot be deducted.

At-risk limits. Generally, a deductible loss from a trade or business or other income-producing activity is limited to the amount that the business owner has "at risk" in the activity for the tax year. Such an amount includes the cash and adjusted basis of property contributed by the taxpayer to the activity as well as borrowed funds (for which the taxpayer has personal liability or has pledged assets) used in the activity. Losses that exceed the amount "at risk" for a particular tax year may be carried forward for use in the following tax year, so long as the taxpayer has a sufficient amount at risk to take the loss.

Passive activities. A *passive activity* generally is related to an investment interest in a business in which the taxpayer does not materially participate, or a rental activity. In general, deductions for losses from passive activities may only offset income from passive activities. Any excess loss or credits not currently claimable may be carried over to later years. Suspended passive losses (that is, losses that must be carried over in this manner), however, are fully deductible in the year the taxpayer may sell or otherwise dispose of the interest. This end-of-business deduction is permitted regardless of whether income is sufficient to cover it, thereby creating a loss that may be deducted against nonpassive income in that case.

Net Operating Losses

A trade or business has a *net operating loss (NOL)* when its allowable deductions exceed its gross income for the tax year. The treatment of the NOL depends on whether the business is operated through a corporation, partnership, or a noncorporate entity. The noncorporate-entity category includes a *disregarded entity* such as single owner limited liability company that elects not to be a corporation. A noncorporate entity also includes an individual who operates a trade or business as an unincorporated sole proprietorship that is taxed only at the individual level.

Individuals. Individual taxpayers may have an NOL as the result of other than trade or businesses losses, although such circumstances are less common. In addition to business losses, an individual may include in his or her NOL computation deductions due to:

- Employee business expenses;
- Casualty and theft losses;
- Moving expenses for a job relocation; and
- Expenses of rental property held for production of income.

The starting point in determining whether an individual has an NOL is the line on Form 1040 designated for the amount of adjusted gross income (AGI) minus itemized deductions or the standard deduction. If that result is a negative number, an NOL may exist and further computations for exclusions and adjustments are required.

Individuals also are subject to limitations on certain deductions that can go into a NOL computation. Excluded from the NOL computation are any deductions for personal exemptions, net capital losses, the "section 1202 exclusion" amount from the sale of qualified small business stock, and the section 199 domestic production activities deductions. NOLs themselves are also excluded.

Corporations. A corporation is entitled to deduct its NOL at the entity level from its corporate revenue. An ordinary taxable corporation (commonly called a C corporation after subchapter C of the Internal Revenue Code) is normally a distinct taxpayer from its shareholder(s).

A C corporation may not deduct a shareholder's NOL, and shareholders may not deduct the corporation's NOLs. Further, because a corporation is a separate taxpayer, NOLs do not automatically flow between successor entities.

A corporation generally computes its NOL in the same way as does an individual taxpayer, with the same 2-year carryback and 20-year carryforward sequencing rules. A corporation, however, takes different deductions and modifications depending on the nature of its business-entity status. A corporation also files different forms to claim an NOL deduction:

- Individuals use Form 1045, *Application for Tentative Refund;* Schedule B, or Form 1040X, *Amended U.S. Individual Income Tax Return,* for carrybacks; and
- Corporations use either Form 1120X, *Amended U.S. Corporation Income Tax Return,* or Form 1139, *Corporation Application for Tentative Refund.*

If a business is not a corporation, its losses pass through to its owners. A partnership itself cannot use NOL deductions, but the losses are available to flow through to the partners and be used against other income of the partners. The partners can take the loss up to the amount of their basis in their partnership interest at the end of the year. If the losses exceed a partner's basis, the excess losses are carried forward and allowed as a deduction in subsequent years, to the extent there is sufficient basis.

If the business is operated by an individual as a sole proprietorship, the business's NOL again can be used against the individual's other income. Any excess NOL could be carried over to another year to offset the business's income.

NOL carryback and carryforward. Generally, an NOL can be carried back 2 years and carried forward 20 years—the carryover period. The first year of the carryover period is the year after the NOL arises; thus, it becomes important to determine the correct year in which gross income is recognized and deductions are taken.

A 10-year carryback is available for certain classes of liability losses: product liability, workplace liabilities, and environmental remediation. For NOLs from years ending in 2001 and 2002, as part of the 9/11 recovery program, the carryback period was 5 years. Under the *Emergency Economic Stabilization Act of 2008*, a 5-year NOL carryback period is also allowed for qualified disaster losses attributable to a federally declared disaster occurring after December 31, 2007, and before January 1, 2010.

In any case, the carryback and carryover periods cannot be extended; any portion of the NOL remaining after the 20-year carryforward period is lost. It may be possible, however, to use an expiring NOL by accelerating the recognition of income.

Amended return. A corporation must file an amended return, resulting from an NOL carryback, within 3 years of the due date for filing the loss year return or within 2 years from the time the tax was paid. The due date for filing the loss year return includes any extensions to file the return. An NOL carryover is deducted with the ordinary tax return for the year to which it is carried.

Computation of NOL. A business with a current year NOL must first carry back an NOL to the earliest year available. Any excess NOL can be used in the succeeding year. A single NOL may be carried to multiple years, if the entire NOL was not used in the first year. The taxpayer can elect to waive the carryback period and begin to carry the losses forward. This election is irrevocable. The extended 5-year and 10-year carryback periods can also be waived. If the NOL occurs in the corporation's first year, there is no carryback period.

A business can choose in any tax year not to carry back its NOL for that year. If that election is made, it is irrevocable and the business can use the NOL only in the 20-year carryforward period. The election also applies to any NOL when the taxpayer is subject to the AMT.

The computation of the NOL for any tax year is determined under the law that applies to that year, disregarding the law for the year to which the NOL is carried. The deduction allowed is calculated under the law that applies to the year of the deduction. Any calculations involving any other year in the carryback or carryover period are made under the law for that year.

Tax liability for the carryover year is calculated using the full NOL before any reductions. Thus, NOLs are fully usable in the year the debt is discharged. If not fully used, the NOL is reduced by the amount of the cancelled debt. Cancellation income that is excluded from taxable income must be applied to reduce tax attributes. Normally, the first attribute is the NOL, but the taxpayer can elect to reduce the basis of property instead.

> **COMMENT**
>
> If NOLs are likely to expire unused, it makes sense to reduce them. On the other hand, NOLs have more immediate tax saving value than reducing the basis of an asset. Basis reduction reduces taxes more gradually upon depreciation or sale of the property. An NOL can reduce taxable income dollar-for-dollar in the next year.

An NOL is treated as used in a year to which it can be carried, even if the taxpayer did not file a timely amended return to take the NOL deduction. The NOL is deemed absorbed and reduces the NOL available in later years. The amount used is based on the correct measure of taxable income. Errors that cannot be corrected because of the statute of limitations are ignored.

A short tax year has the effect of reducing the carryback and carryover periods. An NOL generated by a short year required to change tax years is generally not subject to carryback.

Modifications affect the deductible amounts for computing NOLs and restrictions on some corporations' use of NOLs:

- The NOL deduction itself is not allowed when computing the year's NOL. A contrary rule would negate the limits on the carryover of the NOL and could allow NOLs to be counted twice;
- If a C corporation becomes an S corporation, NOLs from the C corporation years cannot carry over to the S corporation years. This prevents C corporations from trying to pass their NOLs to shareholders for individual use;
- Life insurance companies technically cannot take an NOL but are entitled to an analogous *operations loss deduction;* and
- Exempt organizations can take an NOL when computing their unrelated business taxable income.

A corporation that qualifies as a real estate investment trust (REIT) in some years and not in others cannot carry back an NOL from a REIT year to a non-REIT year, although the year counts toward the maximum carryback period.

NOL trafficking. Congress and the IRS oppose trafficking in NOLs. This occurs when a corporation has more NOLs than it can use and sells or transfers the NOLs to a making-money corporation in a corporate reorganization or other change of ownership. The idea is that NOLs are intended to benefit the corporation that suffered the losses, and that transactions motivated by NOL trafficking distort the economic benefits of acquiring or consolidating a business.

NOLs (and other corporate attributes) belong to the corporation that created them. However, another corporation acquires the NOL in the liquidation of a subsidiary corporation or in certain asset acquisitions. If a corporation acquires assets in a nontaxable reorganization, it succeeds to the NOLs of the acquired corporation. However, Code Sec. 382 imposes limits on loss trafficking, i.e., it limits the amount of the acquired corporation's NOL that may be used each year by the acquiring corporation. Application of the limits is triggered by an ownership change. The loss allowed to the acquiring corporation is the value of the old NOL corporation's stock multiplied by the *long-term tax-exempt rate* determined by the IRS.

In some situations, the Code Sec. 382 limit is increased by recognized built-in gain on assets of the acquired corporation whose value exceeded their basis when acquired. This increase applies to asset sales within five years after the NOL is acquired.

The 2008 Farm Act (the *Heartland, Habitat, Harvest, and Horticulture Act of 2008,* P.L. 110-234), enacted in June 2008, limits the amount of farming losses that a taxpayer receiving certain subsidies may use to offset nonfarming business income. The limit for any tax year is the greater of $300,000 or the net farm income received during the last five years. Losses that are limited may be carried forward to subsequent years. The provision applies to farmers that are not C corporations and that receive payments under Title I of the Farm Act or loans from the Commodity Credit Corporation. This measure applies to tax years beginning on or after January 1, 2010. The definition of *farming* is expanded to include commodity processing, without regard as to whether the processing is incidental to an agricultural or horticultural activity. The limitation is applied at the partner or shareholder level for partnerships and S corporations.

STUDY QUESTIONS

---

9. Which of the following types of losses may **not** be included in computing an individual's net operating loss (NOL)?

   a. Moving expenses

   b. Losses from an employee's work

   c. Losses on rental property

   d. All of the above may be included in an individual's NOL

10. Any loss amount remaining after the current _____ period for carrying an NOL forward is _____.

   a. 2-year; currently deductible as a lump sum

   b. 5-year; applied as a passive activity loss against passive activity income

   c. 20-year; lost due to expiration

   d. None of the above applies to NOLs carried forward for more than their carryforward period

---

IMPACT OF THE EMERGENCY ECONOMIC STABILIZATION ACT OF 2008 ON BUSINESSES HAVING FINANCIAL DIFFICULTIES

The *Emergency Economic Stabilization Act of 2008* (Public Law 110-343, Oct. 3, 2008) is intended to help most businesses most significantly in an indirect way. It is designed to create an economic environment in which credit is more readily available to smooth out a business's cash-flow and capital investment needs. Also indirectly creating an environment conducive to business success, this new law pumps $150 billion into the economy in the way of new and extended tax breaks and incentives.

In addition to the general relief, however, the *Emergency Economic Stabilization Act of 2008* also targets certain struggling businesses with direct tax assistance. These targeted groups include the financial services industry and businesses hit hard by devastating hurricanes and other natural disasters in 2008.

Financial Services Industry

Many of the nontax provisions in the *Emergency Economic Stabilization Act of 2008* legislation deal with the government purchase—directly or through auction—of the assets of banks and other financial institutions holding mortgage securities and similar assets that have become difficult to value. Nontax provisions also address the use of mark-to-market accounting. Under the tax provisions, companies participating significantly in the sale of assets to the government will find a new $500,000 limit on the compensation of key executives whose companies sell more than $300 million in assets through government-sponsored auctions. Companies selling assets directly to the government may also be subject to specially negotiated limits on executive compensation and claw-backs of remuneration paid based on erroneous financial statements.

Also of assistance to the financial services industry is the favorable guidance that the IRS released in September and October 2008 that enables several large banking reorganizations to move forward without fear of triggering certain tax rules.

Disaster Area Victims

The new law provides temporary, but significant, tax relief to victims of the severe storms, tornadoes, and flooding that swept through the Midwest in 2008 and—to a lesser extent —victims of Hurricane Ike in Texas. Additionally, Congress authorized national relief for other locations declared disaster areas by the president in tax years beginning after December 31, 2007, with some exceptions.

Midwestern Disaster Area. The tax incentives in the Midwestern Disaster Area mirror many of the ones enacted in 2005 after Hurricanes Katrina, Rita, and Wilma devastated the Gulf Coast. These breaks include:

- Increased expensing for demolition, environmental remediation, and cleanup costs;
- Enhanced depreciation for qualified disaster property, education, and housing tax benefits; and
- A higher standard mileage rate for charitable use of vehicles.

The Midwestern Disaster Area encompasses presidentially declared disaster areas named in Arkansas, Illinois, Indiana, Iowa, Kansas, Michigan, Minnesota, Missouri, Nebraska, and Wisconsin between May 20, 2008, and before August 1, 2008.

Hurricane Ike Disaster Area. The incentives targeted to the Hurricane Ike Disaster Area are much more limited than those for the Midwestern Disaster Area. Congress authorized temporary tax-exempt bond financing and low-income housing tax relief for certain areas damaged by Hurricane Ike.

The Hurricane Ike Disaster Area encompasses parts of Louisiana and Texas, which were declared disaster areas by the president on September 13, 2008.

National disaster relief. Victims of natural disasters that are not covered by the Midwestern Disaster Area or Hurricane Ike Disaster Area tax relief provisions are nevertheless entitled to modified tax benefits through 2009. Taxpayers affected by natural disasters after December 31, 2007, and before January 10, 2010, are offered tax help in the form of enhanced NOL carrybacks, increased expensing for qualified disaster expenses, special depreciation for qualified disaster property, and other targeted tax breaks.

NOLs attributable to federally declared disasters. A special five-year carryback period election for net operating losses (NOLs) has been created for qualified disaster losses under the *Emergency Economic Stabilization Act of 2008.* The amount of the NOL that qualifies for this five-year carryback is limited to the corporation's overall NOL for the tax year in which the NOL occurs. Remaining NOLs (if any) are subject to the general two-year carryback period and are also subject to specific ordering rules. This tax break covers qualified disaster losses attributable to a federally declared disaster occurring after December 31, 2007, and before January 1, 2010.

Expensing of qualified disaster costs. Taxpayers may elect to deduct their qualified disaster expenses when those expenses are paid or incurred, rather than charging them to a capital account. The election is available for amounts paid or incurred after December 31, 2007, in connection with a disaster declared after that date. *Qualified disaster expenses* include only expenditures related to federally declared disasters occurring before January 1, 2010.

Bonus depreciation for qualified disaster assistance property. An additional 50-percent depreciation allowance can be claimed for real and personal business property that is purchased to rehabilitate or replace similar property that is destroyed or condemned as a result of a presidentially declared disaster. The provision applies to property placed in service after December 31, 2007, with respect to disasters declared after that date and occurring before January 1, 2010.

CONCLUSION

Net income remains a preferable economic position to net losses; the tax law cannot change that result for any business. Nevertheless, business success is not necessarily measured by artificially created periods within which net income or losses may be calculated. This reality is recognized at least in part by the tax law through the availability of depreciation schedules, accrual accounting, capital loss carryforwards, and net operating loss carrybacks and carryforwards.

The ways in which the Internal Revenue Code recognizes the arbitrariness of accounting methods and periods, however, is itself imperfect. The Internal Revenue Code creates definite timelines within which certain tax benefits—including loss deductions—must be taken. Businesses that are most adept at working with these rules clearly have an edge, in good economic times and bad.

CPE NOTE: When you have completed your study and review of chapters 1-3, which comprise Module 1, you may wish to take the Quizzer for this Module.

For your convenience, you can also take this Quizzer online at **www. cchtestingcenter.com**.

MODULE 2: SMALL BUSINESS PLANNING — CHAPTER 4

Limited Liability Companies: Traps and Opportunities

This chapter examines the current opportunities associated with operating a business as a limited liability company (LLC). The chapter devotes special attention to the tax and nontax advantages and disadvantages of selecting the LLC entity structure.

LEARNING OBJECTIVES

Upon completion of this chapter, you will be able to:

- Understand the tax and nontax advantages of operating a business as an LLC;
- Compare the key tax and nontax differences and similarities among LLCs and other business forms; and
- Recognize the current drawbacks and pitfalls associated with LLCs, including self-employment tax issues, conversion issues, and disregarded entity issues.

INTRODUCTION

The limited liability company enjoys significant popularity among the business community, especially closely held companies and family-owned businesses. An estimated 1.2 million LLCs operate throughout the United States today. Regarded as a *hybrid entity*, the LLC appeals to many businesses because it combines the positive corporate characteristic of limited liability, which is afforded to all LLC members, with the passthrough tax treatment of partnerships. In addition to numerous tax benefits, LLCs offer owners substantial management and operational flexibility.

The formation and operation of LLCs, as well as the various aspects of its business relations, are governed by state law. However, despite the popularity of LLCs and the fact that they originated in the United States more than 30 years ago, there is still no provision in the Internal Revenue Code specifically governing the federal tax treatment of LLCs. An LLC is not a federal tax entity but can elect how to be treated for federal tax purposes under the check-the-box regulations. The federal tax treatment of LLCs is governed by a patchwork of IRS guidance and regulations.

Notwithstanding the major tax and nontax benefits associated with operating a business as an LLC, this business structure is not without its drawbacks. This chapter provides an overview of the tax and nontax advantages and disadvantages of LLCs. The chapter also addresses the current traps and opportunities associated with operating as an LLC in today's business environment that have surfaced during the past several years through litigation and IRS rulings.

DEFINITION AND CHARACTERISTICS OF LIMITED LIABILITY COMPANIES

A *domestic LLC* is a legal business entity created under state law. All 50 states and the District of Columbia have enacted statutes governing the formation and operation of LLCs. Like a corporation, members of LLCs are not personally liable for the debts and obligations of the company. At the same time, LLCs possess the passthrough characteristics of partnerships or sole proprietorships for federal income tax purposes. All income, profits, losses, credits, and deductions pass through to LLC members according to the LLC's operating agreement and are reported on members' individual income tax returns.

Most, if not all, state regulations provide that an LLC's profits and losses be allocated among members as specified in the LLC's operating agreement. However, if the operating agreement is silent on how allocations are to be made, the general default rule is that profits and losses are to be allocated on the basis of each members' capital contributions, which may be the agreed upon value of the contributions (to the extent they have been received by the LLC and not returned) or their book value. Under the default provisions, allocations of profits, losses, deductions, credits, and other items of income are made according to the same standard, whether it be pro rata or per capita. LLC members should establish in the operating agreement whether allocations of deductions, credits, and items of income will be treated differently than the allocation of profits and losses. For example, income tax deductions for depreciation expenses can be allocated among members in proportion to their capital contributions. Thus, an additional advantage of the LLC is that this business entity may make disproportionate distributions.

Moreover, most state laws allow LLCs to be formed to hold nonbusiness assets, such as investments. For federal income tax purposes, the income and expenses associated with such investment assets are also passed through to the LLC's members and reported on their individual income tax returns. However, some states prohibit certain types of businesses from operating as LLCs. Banks, insurance companies, trust companies, and nonprofit organizations are examples of businesses that cannot be operated as LLCs in some states. Special rules also apply to foreign LLCs.

LLC FORMATION

LLCs are generally formed by filing *articles of organization,* or a comparable state document such as a *certificate of formation,* with the appropriate state agency. Such a document is certified by the state. All states and the District of Columbia permit the formation of LLCs. In general, the articles of organization will include the name of the LLC, the name and address of its registered agent, and the LLC's principal place of business. Many states may also require that the articles of organization list the names and addresses of the LLC's managers, or a statement that the LLC is manager-managed rather than member-managed, in order to put potential creditors and others contracting with the company on notice about the business's management structure. Other information that states may require in the articles of organization are:

- The LLC's duration or a statement that the LLC's life is to be perpetual;
- Names of the members and/or managers at the time of the LLC's formation;
- Capital contribution information; and
- Members' rights and duties.

Most states permit LLCs to have a perpetual life. Additionally, many "modern" LLC statutes also allow less than unanimous consent of the members to continue the business if certain events occurred that would otherwise result in termination or dissolution of the LLC. These statutes also may allow members to transfer their ownership interests as well.

LLC OPERATING AGREEMENT

An *LLC operating agreement* is the document that sets forth how the business of the LLC will be governed. Although some states may not require a formal operating agreement, it is a fundamental document that is imperative for any LLC to have because it sets forth the specific rights and duties of the LLC members as well as the operation and management of the company. In most cases, LLC members will draft an operating agreement to include, among other items:

- How profits and losses are to be shared;
- The types of membership interests;
- Rules regarding the admittance and withdrawal of members;
- Capital account rules;
- Distribution rights;
- Voting rights;
- Other management rights; and
- Transfer rights and/or restrictions of membership interests.

STUDY QUESTIONS

1. Which of the following is *not* a significant benefit of operating as an LLC?
   a. Passthrough tax treatment and limited personal liability
   b. The ability of the LLC to hold nonbusiness assets
   c. The ability of the LLC to make disproportionate distributions
   d. All of the above are benefits of the LLC entity type

2. All of the following are typically elements of LLC operating agreements *except*:
   a. Capital account rules
   b. Transfer rights for membership interests
   c. Voting rights
   d. All of the above are items usually included in LLC operating agreements

MANAGEMENT

Designation by Operating Agreement or Under State Statute

Typically, LLCs are either member-managed or manager-managed. The LLC's operating agreement may provide for management, in whole or in part, by one member or a select group of members. The LLC's operating agreement also usually specifies how managers are to be elected by the members. State statutes governing LLCs generally allow every member to participate in management of the business. In a member-managed LLC, each member is an agent of the LLC for business purposes and has a vote in the business decisions of the LLC. If an LLC's members choose to be manager-managed, the manager(s) acts as an agent for the LLC and the nonmanaging members have no ability to make decisions or contract on behalf of the LLC, unless specifically provided otherwise in the LLC operating agreement. A managing member, alone or with others, is vested with the exclusive authority to make management and business decisions on behalf of the LLC. A managing member of an LLC possesses the responsibilities (and is subject to the restrictions) accorded to him or her by the members and set forth in an LLC agreement.

In the event that no member or members have been designated to manage the LLC's business affairs, most state statutes typically provide that management is vested in each member. A nonmanaging member, despite lacking authority over the LLC's business and management decisions, nevertheless continues to enjoy limited personal liability from the debts and obligations of the LLC. When there is no provision for managers set forth in the LLC agreement, then the management of the LLC is generally vested, depending on state statute, in all members.

Most state statutes governing LLC formation and operation do not restrict ownership in an LLC. Members of an LLC can include individuals, nonresident aliens, corporations, other LLCs, partnerships, pension plans, members of affiliated groups, and foreign entities. Additionally, there is no limit on the number of individuals or entities that can be members of an LLC, and all states now allow single-member LLCs (SMLLCs).

Noneconomic Members

Whether an LLC has more than one "member" may sometimes be difficult to determine. For example, some states permit an LLC to have a *noneconomic member* who does not own an economic interest in the entity. Although a noneconomic member is generally treated as a member under applicable state law, for federal tax purposes a noneconomic member is generally not treated as a member unless the nominally noneconomic member also owns an economic interest in the LLC.

ELECTING THE TYPE OF ENTITY

Check-the-Box Regulations

Certain types of entities are required to be taxed as corporations. Other entities, including LLCs, can elect how to be treated for federal tax purposes. An LLC is not a federal tax entity and there is still no provision in the Internal Revenue Code that specifically governs the treatment of LLCs for federal income tax purposes. Instead, under the IRS's *check-the-box regulations,* LLCs can elect how to be treated for federal tax purposes. The check-the-box regulations (Reg. §§301.7701-1, -2, and -3) took effect January 1, 1997, giving LLCs and other *eligible entities* (i.e., those not required by law to be treated as a corporation) the ability to choose their classification for federal tax purposes.

Under the check-the-box regulations:

- A single-member LLC (*SMLLC*) can elect to be taxed as a(n)
  — Disregarded entity (as a sole proprietorship),
  — Corporation (a regular C corporation, personal holding company, personal services corporation, or professional corporation), or
  — S corporation (accomplished by electing to be taxed as a corporation, then filing an S corporation election); and
- An LLC with more two or more members (*multimember LLC*) can elect to be taxed as a(n)
  — Partnership,
  — Corporation, or
  — S corporation (also accomplished by electing to be taxed as a corporation, then filing an S corporation election).

Once the entity makes a check-the-box election for its year of inception, generally the election is binding for at least five years. (The election procedures are detailed in the following section.)

Default Status

The IRS will automatically assign a classification to an LLC that fails, intentionally or unintentionally, to make an affirmative election under the check-the-box regs for federal income tax purposes. The IRS's default classifications are intended to reflect how the owner, or owners, of an LLC supposedly would have chosen to treat the LLC for federal tax purposes had they made an affirmative election.

Unless a domestic eligible entity elects otherwise, under the "default" rules:

- An entity with two or more owners that is not required by law to be treated as a corporation is classified as a partnership, and thus subject to general partnership tax rules; and
- An entity that is wholly owned by one individual is disregarded as an entity separate from its owner and taxed as a sole proprietorship.

Partnership Tax Rules

An LLC that elects to be—or by default is—treated as a partnership under the check-the-box regs for federal income tax purposes is subject to the partnership tax provisions of Subchapter K of the Tax Code. Additionally, other Internal Revenue Code provisions that are applicable to partnerships also apply to LLCs. An LLC taxed as a partnership files Form 1065, *U.S. Return of Partnership Income,* and issues Schedule K-1s to the LLCs members, who are treated as partners for federal income tax purposes. As such, the LLC's income, gains, losses, deductions, credits, and other tax items pass through the LLC to the members, who report those items on their personal income tax returns (Forms 1040). In effect, the LLC and its members escape double taxation because income of the LLC is taxed only at the member level. Such flowthrough tax treatment also enables "special allocations" to be made to the LLC members.

COMMENT

Such federal tax default elections, or affirmative elections for that matter, have no bearing on an LLC's treatment for state law purposes, except that state tax law generally follows the federal tax election. Additionally, although LLCs are not subject to an entity-level federal income tax, they may be liable for paying other types of taxes, such as federal employment tax. LLCs having employees, for example, must pay federal employment taxes, which include federal income tax withholding, Social Security and Medicare taxes, and federal unemployment tax.

Disregarded Entity

An SMLLC that is disregarded as separate from its owner (disregarded SMLLC) under the default provisions does not file a separate tax return; instead, the SMLLC's profits, losses, deductions, credits, and other tax items are treated as those of the owner's. For example, in the case of an individual, the items are reported on Schedule C of the owner's individual income tax return, Form 1040. If, for any reason, a disregarded SMLLC admits another member, it is no longer treated as a disregarded entity but is instead classified as a partnership for federal tax purposes.

Election Procedures

An LLC may elect its classification or change it (subject to restrictions), by filing Form 8832, *Entity Classification Election*. A classification election filed on Form 8832 is effective on the date specified by the entity on the form or on the filing date if no date is specified. However, the effective date may not be more than 75 days prior to the date on which the election is filed and not more than 12 months after the filing date. If a taxpayer specifies an effective date that is more than 75 days prior to the filing, the election will become effective 75 days prior to the filing date. If the taxpayer selects an effective date that is more than 12 months after the filing date, the election will take effect 12 months after the filing date.

Once it has elected a classification under the check-the-box regulations, the LLC cannot, on its own, change the classification during the five-year period following the effective date of the election. To change its election, the LLC must obtain a letter ruling from the IRS waiving the five-year limitation. Generally, the IRS agrees to waive the five-year period. The five-year limitation applies only to a change in the entity's classification for tax purposes; it does not apply if the entity's business is transferred to another organization.

ADVANTAGES OF LLCS

Nontax Advantages

The LLC business structure offers several significant nontax advantages outside of the lucrative tax benefits possible. Additionally, the nontax and other business purposes for operating as an LLC may be closely connected to the associated tax benefits that LLCs enjoy. LLCs provide the major nontax benefits described here.

Limited personal liability. Both managing and nonmanaging members of LLCs enjoy limited personal liability for the debts and other obligations of the LLC. The ability to isolate the liabilities of the business, yet continue to act in a managerial capacity—making operational, management, and other business decisions on behalf of the company—with limited exposure gives the LLC a significant advantage over other business forms. This feature is especially significant for SMLLCs, because the owner may elect to operate the LLC as a disregarded entity (for example, as a sole proprietorship) but concomitantly continue to have limited personal liability for the LLC's debts and other liabilities. Moreover, an LLC does not need to designate a member of the business to be personally liable for the debts and obligations of the business. Every member of an LLC is protected from personal liability for the entity's liabilities.

> **COMMENT**
>
> Any debt of the LLC forgiven by a lender, therefore, is not Code Sec. 108 income from forgiveness of indebtedness income to the owners over and above the security for the debt.

Management and operational flexibility. An LLC offers its owners great flexibility in managing the business. There are no restrictions on the maximum number of LLC members (although LLCs electing S corporation status for federal tax purposes must adhere to those limitations). Additionally, most states do not restrict the types of members an LLC may include. Generally, LLC members may include individuals, corporations, other LLCs, and partnerships, as well as foreign entities. Moreover, all members may participate in the LLC's management and business operations, and may do so without losing their limited personal liability.

Transferability of membership interests. The LLC entity also enables members to retain managerial control of the business when "outside" individuals acquire an interest in the LLC from another member or members. Although an interest in an LLC can be assigned in whole or in part, a member may only assign his or her financial interest in the business.

Thus, an assignee of a member's interest only:

- Has the right to receive distributions (or liquidation proceeds) from the LLC to which the assigning member would have been entitled to receive; and
- May share in the LLC's profits, and losses, with no right to participate in the management of the LLC, become a member, vote on LLC matters, or, in most cases, inspect the LLC's business and financial records, unless the nontransferring members consent or the LLC operating agreement provides otherwise.

Because many family and closely held businesses tend to operate as LLCs, these restrictions on the transferability of members' interests are significant. The limitations restrict the authority to make business and management decisions to the LLC's owners.

Asset protection. As just described, an LLC member can only assign or transfer his or her economic interest in the company, restricting the assignee only to distributions from the entity with no managerial or operational control, unless the other members consent to the assignee becoming a member of the LLC. Thus, the LLC operates as an effective asset protection vehicle.

In general, a judgment creditor of a member, who is not also a creditor of the LLC, has only the right to petition a court for a *charging order*, which constitutes a lien on the debtor-member's interest in LLC distributions. If a member's interest is charged, the creditor merely has the right to receive distributions from the LLC to the extent to which the debtor-member would have been entitled and only to the extent of the amount of the outstanding principal and interest of the debt. However, an LLC is not *required* to make distributions to its members; thus, a charging order may be of little use to a creditor if the LLC does not make regular distributions. In some instances, an LLC may only make distributions to members as guaranteed payments or salaries for their services. In other cases, an LLC, such as one formed solely to hold investment assets (for example, real estate), may make few, or no, distributions until a much later, future date.

Tax Advantages

Generally, one of the most important factors when selecting a business form is the tax consequences associated with operating and managing a business through the chosen entity. There are several significant tax advantages that LLCs present in and of themselves, as well as compared to other business entities.

Election of federal tax treatment. A distinct advantage of choosing the LLC business form is the ability to elect how to have the entity treated for federal income tax purposes. As mentioned earlier, LLCs are eligible entities that may elect their classification for federal income tax purposes. Under the IRS's check-the-box regulations, an LLC chooses how to be taxed for federal income tax purposes.

In the event no affirmative election is made, an SMLLC will be treated as a disregarded entity for federal income tax purposes under the check-the-box regs. A multimember LLC that fails to make an affirmative election under the regulations will be automatically treated as a partnership by the IRS for federal income tax purposes.

Passthrough taxation. The IRS's check-the-box regulations provide LLCs the option of being treated as a separate entity and paying two levels of tax, or allow SMLLCs to be disregarded as a separate entity and have any tax liabilities imposed directly on the owner. Moreover, LLCs taxed as partnerships are subject to only one level of federal income tax because all items of income pass through to the individual members. However, the owners, being taxed as partners, must take into account income and loss on individual returns regardless of whether earnings are actually distributed by the LLC.

Capital contributions. For an LLC classified as a partnership, its members do not incur tax when the company is formed because the contribution of property to a partnership is generally not a taxable event under Code Sec. 721. An LLC electing to be taxed as a corporation is afforded tax-free capitalizations under Code Sec. 351. Thus, for federal tax purposes, no gain is realized or recognized on the capitalization of an LLC. Members take a basis in their respective LLC interests equal to the cash or value of the property they contribute to the business.

However, if an LLC member contributes *services* in exchange for a capital interest, he or she recognizes taxable ordinary income unless the interest he or she receives is not sufficiently vested. Additionally, a contribution of *property that is subject to debt* can trigger the recognition of gain by the contributing member if his or her basis in the LLC is less than the member's decreased share of liabilities with respect to the property. On the other hand, the grant of a profits interest in an LLC to a member who contributes services to the business generally does not trigger taxable income. Upon the disposition of a profits interest, the member realizes capital gain.

Debt financing. Distributions of loan proceeds to LLC members are non-events for tax purposes. In the case of an SMLLC, loan proceeds are not included in the owner's income. In the case of an LLC taxed as a partnership, the LLC's debt is treated as if it had been incurred directly by LLC members, thereby increasing the basis of their membership interests. This allows for deductions from the LLC's debt to pass through to the members and for the loan proceeds to be distributed tax-free.

Assumption of debt. In the context of transferring an existing business to a new LLC, assumptions of debt by the LLC are common. An SMLLC's assumption of a debt of its owner is a nonevent for federal income tax purposes. The assumption of a partner's debt by an LLC classified as a partnership is also a nonevent for tax purposes to the extent the debt remains allocated to the partner; it is treated as a distribution to the extent the debt is allocated to other partners.

STUDY QUESTIONS

3. On which document does the SMLLC classified as a disregarded entity report the company's profits, losses, deductions, and credits when the owner is an individual?
   a. Form 1065
   b. Schedule K-1 of Form 1065
   c. Form 8832
   d. Schedule C of Form 1040

4. A charging order against a debtor-member of an LLC grants a creditor:
   a. Rights to the member's distributions but not managerial control in the entity
   b. Rights to require distributions from the company to repay the debtor-member's liability
   c. Rights to require sale of the debtor-member's interest in the entity to pay his or her liability
   d. All of the above

COMPARATIVE ADVANTAGES OF LLCS

LLCs Compared with S Corps

An *S corporation* is a corporation that has elected to be taxed under Subchapter S of the Internal Revenue Code. As with an LLC that is taxed as a partnership under the default provisions, an S corp's income, gains, losses, deductions, and credits flow through to and are reportable on the shareholders' personal tax returns. Moreover, both the LLC and the S corp allow owners to benefit from the limited liability of a corporation and the passthrough taxation of a partnership.

However, LLCs are not subject to a number of ownership restrictions and capital structure limitations that apply to S corps. S corps cannot issue more than one class of stock, whereas there is no limit on the classes of stock LLCs can issue. Additionally, S corporations cannot have more than 100 members, whereas there is no limit to the number of owners of an LLC. Only individuals, estates, certain trusts, and certain charities may be shareholders of an S corp. Generally, corporations, partnerships, nonresident aliens, foreign trusts, and individual retirement accounts cannot be S corporation shareholders. LLCs also permit the special allocation of income, gain, and loss to members; S corporations do not, and pro-rata allocations must be made due to the single-class-of-stock restriction imposed on S corporations.

In general, contributions of appreciated or debt-encumbered property to an LLC are nontaxable, but contributions of such property to an S corporation are taxable in most cases. Distributions of appreciated property by an S corporation are generally treated as a sale by the corporation and cause a pro-rata recognition of gain at the shareholder level. Further, an LLC member will generally not recognize gain or loss on the sale or disposition of distributed property (an exception applies for distributions deemed to include a member's share of unrealized receivables or substantially appreciated inventory items).

LLCs Compared with C Corporations

For the small business owner, an LLC that by default is taxed as a partnership is typically a much better choice of entity than the C corp. Like C corporations, LLCs offer their members the protection of limited liability. However, income of C corps is subject to double taxation—once at the entity level and again at the shareholder level. Multimember LLCs that are taxed as partnerships benefit from one level of tax because all profits flow through to individual members who report the income on their individual income tax return. Additionally, corporations must comply with considerably more legal and accounting rules than those imposed on LLCs.

LLCs Compared with Limited Partnerships

Members of an LLC taxed as a partnership for federal income tax purposes are generally subject to the same restrictions and enjoy the same rights as partners of a limited partnership. Unlike a limited partnership, members of an LLC can fully participate in the management of the business without risking the loss of their limited liability protection. Both business forms are subject to the federal partnership rules under Subchapter K of the Internal Revenue Code. However, each member of an LLC is generally allowed to participate in the management of the business, whereas limited partners are generally prohibited from participating in the active management of the limited partnership.

DISADVANTAGES OF LLCS

Self-Employment Tax Uncertainty

Uncertainty surrounds the self-employment tax status of LLC members. It remains unclear whether an LLC member will be considered a general partner or a limited partner for self-employment tax purposes.

Passive Activity Losses

The passive activity loss (PAL) limitations of Code Sec. 469 may restrict the amount of losses that LLC members may deduct. In general, an LLC classified as a partnership for federal tax purposes may be indirectly subject to Code Sec. 469 because LLC members have to report the LLC's activities as either active or passive. The PAL rules provide that deductions from passive activities may only offset income from passive activities, which include most rental activities and all trade and business activities in which a taxpayer does not *materially participate*. Moreover, any credits from passive activities only offset taxes attributable to income generated from the LLC's passive activities.

Partners must satisfy the material participation rules of Code Sec. 469 in order to use losses from passive activities to offset active or portfolio income. Generally, limited partners in a partnership are treated as holding an interest in a passive activity. Currently, uncertainty surrounds whether a member of an LLC taxed as a partnership can materially participate in an LLC trade or business activity for purposes of Code Sec. 469.

Because LLCs taxed as partnerships are subject to the partnership tax rules, the PAL limitations that apply to partnerships should also apply to such LLCs. Most limited partners in partnerships are prohibited by state LLC statutes from materially participating in the management of a limited partnership, for example. However, the IRS has not specifically addressed, through guidance or regulations, how the PAL limitations and material participation rules apply to LLC members, who are not defined as *limited* or *general partners*. Thus, there is debate about whether an LLC member—specifically, a nonmanaging member—should be considered a limited partner for purposes of the PAL rules. If this were the case, nonmanaging LLC members would be subject to the stringent material participation standards.

At-Risk Basis Limitations

The tax losses of individual LLC members may be claimed only to the extent that the member's investment is *at risk*. Under Code Sec. 465, the *at-risk rules* limit a partner's deductible losses to an amount that includes only debt for which partners are considered at risk. A member of an LLC is generally considered at risk for amounts of cash and the adjusted basis of any other property contributed to the LLC, as well as the share of the LLC's debt to the extent that he or she is personally liable for repayment. Because LLC members generally are ultimately not personally liable for the debts and liabilities of the LLC, the LLC's debt is considered nonrecourse and LLC members are therefore not at risk for such LLC debt, even if the members have been allocated the entity's liabilities under partnership allocation rules. As such, the LLC's debt does not typically create at-risk basis for LLC members (although it does increase the general tax basis of their LLC membership interests), often making it difficult for LLC members to satisfy the at-risk rules of Code Sec. 465.

The at-risk rules of Code Sec. 465 prohibit LLC members from deducting losses in excess of their actual investment in the company. Even debt that is considered recourse under state law is considered nonrecourse under federal law and thus does not increase an LLC member's at-risk basis. Under the rules, the following apply:

- An LLC member who agrees in his or her individual capacity to personally guarantee an LLC liability, or enters into a contractual agreement to pay a liability on behalf of the LLC, may be considered at risk for the amounts that he or she guarantees;
- Under Code Sec. 465 a guarantor of an LLC liability is not considered at risk if there is a right of reimbursement against any member for the obligation; and
- If each member personally guarantees an LLC liability for a certain amount, each member would generally be considered at risk for such amount.

STUDY QUESTIONS

5. All of the following are advantages of the LLC as an entity choice compared with the S corporation structure *except:*

a. An unlimited number of members is permitted in LLCs; S corporations may have a maximum of 100 members

b. Passthrough of taxation is allowed for LLCs; S corporations are subject to double taxation

c. Corporations, partnerships, nonresident aliens, foreign trusts, and IRAs may be LLC members but not S corporation shareholders

d. Generally, contributions of debt-encumbered or appreciated property to an LLC are nontaxable, but such contributions are usually taxable for S corporation shareholders

6. A major advantage of the LLC entity choice compared with a limited partnership is:

a. Each LLC member may participate in managing the business, but limited partners are usually unable to actively participate in managing a limited partnership without risking the loss of their limited liability

b. An LLC taxed as a partnership is not subject to Subchapter K partnership rules, whereas a limited partnership is subject to those rules

c. An LLC member is taxed on business income only at the individual level, but limited partners are subject to double taxation

d. None of the above is an advantage of the LLC compared with the limited partnership

CURRENT TAX ISSUES ASSOCIATED WITH THE LLC

Conversion

Significant tax consequences may result from the conversion of another business form into an LLC, regardless of whether the conversion is intentional or unintentional. In either case, important tax consequences are the result.

Converting from a partnership. Conversion of a partnership to an LLC generally qualifies for favorable tax treatment because multimember LLCs by default are considered partnerships for tax purposes. The IRS has ruled (Rev. Rul. 95-37) that the same income tax consequences that apply to the conversion of a general partnership to a limited partnership apply to the conversion of a domestic partnership into a domestic LLC classified as a partnership for federal tax purposes (Rev. Rul. 84-52). As such, the conversion of a partnership into an LLC classified as a partnership will not result in gain or loss to the partners.

Generally, the conversion of a partnership into an LLC occurs when partners of an existing partnership contribute assets to a newly formed LLC in exchange for proportionate membership interests. This type of conversion does not cause a termination of the partnership for tax purposes; therefore, no gain or loss is recognized by the partnership, its partners, the LLC, or LLC members. The conversion of a partnership into an LLC is not a sale, exchange, or liquidation of a partner's interest because each partner in the converting partnership continues to hold an interest in the resulting LLC. The basis of a partner's interest in the LLC will be the same as his or her basis in the partnership, as long as the partner's share of partnership liabilities does not change.

Additionally, there is no change in the holding period for purposes of determining whether gain from any sale of the interest in the resulting LLC qualifies as long-term or short-term capital gain (Rev. Rul. 95-37). The conversion of a partnership into an LLC also does not require the close of the partnership's tax year.

Converting from a C corporation. Generally, the conversion of an existing corporation into an LLC taxed as a partnership is treated as a liquidation of the corporation and as such, is a taxable event with tax consequences at both the entity and shareholder levels. The conversion is treated as if the corporation had completely liquidated and distributed its assets to the shareholders, who then contribute their share of the distributed assets to the newly formed LLC in exchange for membership interests. As such, shareholders in a C corporation may have to recognize gain at the shareholder level when they exchange their stock for an interest in the LLC (Code Sec. 331).

The corporation and its shareholders will be taxed on their respective gain or loss from the liquidating distributions. These tax consequences typically discourage corporations from converting into LLCs that elect under the check-the-box regs to be taxed other than as corporations—especially corporations that hold appreciated assets—because costly gain may be recognized by the corporation on disposition of such assets.

Converting from an S corporation. S corporations are generally subject to the same liquidation provisions as C corporations and, as such, an S corporation recognizes taxable gain on liquidation of the entity. When an S corporation is converted into an LLC, the S corporation's gain is passed through to its shareholders, under the Subchapter S rules, who recognize their pro-rata share of the gain and receive a corresponding basis increase in their stock. In general, this result will prevent additional gain from being recognized when the stock is exchanged for an interest in the LLC.

Converting from an SMLLC to a multimember LLC. Special tax consequences apply when an SMLLC that is disregarded as an entity separate from its owner (disregarded SMLLC) for federal tax purposes admits a second member. A disregarded SMLLC that adds a second member becomes an LLC classified as a partnership for federal tax purposes upon acquiring a second member (Reg. §301.7701-3(f)(2)), unless the LLC elects to be taxed as a corporation. Generally, the owner of the SMLLC is treated as having contributed the assets of the SMLLC to the newly formed multimember LLC in a tax-free transaction under Code Sec. 721. However, depending on the transaction, there may be different tax results.

If a second person *purchases a partial interest* in an SMLLC from the owner, the buyer is treated as having purchased a pro-rata interest in each of the LLC's assets. The original owner of the SMLLC recognizes gain or loss on the pro-rata sale of each LLC asset to the new member. Both members are then treated as contributing their interests in the LLC assets to the newly formed partnership (Rev. Rul. 99-5).

EXAMPLE

Tom Liston, who is not related to Bill Siebert, purchases 50 percent of Bill's ownership interest in an LLC for $10,000. Bill does not contribute any portion of the $10,000 to the LLC. Bill and Tom continue to operate the LLC as co-owners. After the sale, no entity classification election is made under the IRS's check-the-box regulations to treat the LLC as a corporation for federal tax purposes.

> For federal tax purposes, prior to the sale, the LLC is disregarded as an entity separate from its owner. The LLC is converted to a partnership when Tom purchases an interest in the disregarded entity from Bill. Tom's purchase of 50 percent of Bill's ownership interest in the LLC is treated as the purchase of a 50 percent interest in each of the LLC's assets, which are treated as held directly by Bill for federal tax purposes. Immediately thereafter, Bill and Tom are treated as contributing their respective interests in those assets to a partnership in exchange for ownership interests in the partnership.

When a second person *contributes capital* to an SMLLC, both the original owner and the second member are treated as making a capital contribution to the new partnership, and neither party will generally recognize gain or loss. The transaction is treated as a nontaxable contribution to a partnership in exchange for a partnership interest.

EXAMPLE

Partner Patrick McGonagle owns Oldham Farm, LLC. Bobby Byer makes a $10 million capital contribution for a half interest, with that $10 million put to work in the business. Patrick and Bobby are treated as forming a new partnership and (assuming Oldham Farm is debt-free) recognize neither gain or loss.

Converting from a multimember LLC into a disregarded SMLLC. An LLC classified as a partnership for federal tax purposes becomes a disregarded entity on the date that the LLC shrinks to having only one member (Reg. §301.7701-3(f)(2)), unless the LLC elects to be taxed as a corporation. When one of two members in an LLC sells his or her interest to the remaining member, the LLC's partnership status terminates and the LLC is thereafter treated as a disregarded entity for federal income tax purposes (Rev. Rul. 99-6). The selling member will recognize gain or loss on the sale of his or her "partnership" interest in the LLC. The buying member, who becomes the sole owner of the disregarded SMLLC, is treated as having assets from both the seller and his or her share of the assets received in a deemed liquidation of the "partnership." As a result, the partnership's termination can be taxable for the single owner of the disregarded SMLLC, as well as for the selling LLC member whose interests have been acquired. The buyer's holding period in the assets acquired directly from the "partnership" in the deemed liquidation includes the LLC's holding period.

> **EXAMPLE**
>
> Bartlett, LLC, has two members, Susan Seller and Paul Purchaser, and is classified as a partnership for federal income tax purposes. It has no cash or unrealized receivables. On September 18, Susan sells half her interest in Bartlett to Paul, who owns the other half interest in the LLC, for $100. Paul now owns the entire company, so the "partnership" is deemed to be liquidated. Susan and Paul are both deemed to receive a liquidating distribution of each of their interests in the LLC. Susan, whose basis in the company was $40, recognizes a gain of $60. Paul does not receive any cash or unrealized receivables and, as such, he does not recognize any gain. Paul's holding period in the half interest in Bartlett he already owned includes the company's holding period, but Paul's holding period in the half interest he purchased from Susan will begin on September 19.

If all members of an LLC sell their interests to a third party, who becomes the LLC's sole owner, the sellers are treated as selling their "partnership interests," whereas the buyer is treated as purchasing assets of the LLC (Rev. Rul. 99-6). The sellers recognize gain and loss on their "partnership interests." The LLC's partnership status is thus terminated for federal tax purposes and the LLC is then treated as a disregarded entity, unless the LLC elects to be taxed as a corporation.

> **EXAMPLE**
>
> On May 10, Susan and Paul sell Bartlett, LLC, to Barbara Buyer. The "partnership" is deemed liquidated. Susan and Paul both recognize gain on the sale of their membership interests. Barbara is treated as buying the assets of Bartlett, LLC, and her holding period will begin on May 11.

STUDY QUESTIONS

7. C corporations may prefer not to convert into LLCs because:

a. Liquidating distributions trigger tax on gain or loss if the LLCs elect tax treatment other than as corporations

b. The shareholder's basis in the LLC ownership interest is less than in the former's corporate shares

c. The resulting entity must create a single class of ownership interests, even if the former C corp had issued multiple classes

d. None of the above is a reason for C corporations not to convert into LLCs

> **8.** If a second individual contributes capital to a single-member LLC:
> **a.** The transaction is taxable for the existing member of the SMLLC, who recognizes gain
> **b.** The new member is considered to have acquired stock in a corporate entity
> **c.** The transaction generally is treated as a nontaxable contribution in which neither party recognizes gain or loss
> **d.** None of the above is the tax result of the conversion from an SMLLC

Self-Employment Tax Issues

Although the LLC business form provides owners many tax and nontax benefits, there are certain pitfalls to the structure that, in part, stem from a body of law that is still in the developmental stage as applied to LLCs. One such pitfall is the ambiguity that surrounds whether members of LLCs taxed as partnerships must pay self-employment tax on all their earnings derived from the company or only on amounts representing reasonable compensation for services provided to the LLC.

Self-employment income. Self-employment income is "net earnings from self-employment." Such earnings generally include income from any trade or business carried on by an individual, as well as the individual's distributive share (whether distributed of not) of income from any trade or business conducted by a partnership in which the individual is a partner under the tax law (Code Sec. 1402(a)). Self-employment taxes are levied on an individual's self-employment income when it exceeds $400 in a tax year. Certain types of income are typically not considered self-employment income, such as real estate rentals, dividends, interest, and capital gains.

Code Sec. 1402(a)(13) exclusion. Code Sec. 1402(a)(13) excludes from self-employment income the "distributive share of any item of income or loss of a limited partner...other than guaranteed payments...to that partner for services actually rendered to or on behalf of the partnership" [emphasis added]. A limited partner has limited liability for the debts and obligations of the partnership, but he or she has no right to participate in the day-to-day management of the business. A general partner, however, usually has liability for the debts of the partnership but participates in the management of the business.

Guaranteed payments are amounts that a partner receives for services he or she renders to the partnership, or for the partnership's use of capital contributed by the partner, and that are determined without regard to the income of the partnership. Thus, while limited partners generally may exclude from self-employment income their respective share of partnership distributions attributable to their limited partnership interest, they must include in self-employment income guaranteed payments received for services provided to the partnership.

Additionally, under Code Sec. 1402(a)(13), a partner's distributive share of income attributable to a *limited partnership interest* is excluded from self-employment tax even if the partner also has a general partnership interest or receives guaranteed payments from the partnership that are otherwise subject to self-employment tax. This distinction between limited partnership and general partnership interests essentially enables limited partners to bifurcate their partnership distributions between those subject to self-employment tax (guaranteed payments and income attributable to general partnership interests) and those distributions that are not (income attributable to limited partnership interests).

Although Code Sec. 1402(a) addresses the self-employment tax consequences of limited partners in a partnership, there are no Code provisions and no regulations that provide similar clarification on the self-employment tax of certain members of LLCs taxed as partnerships (multimember LLCs). Specifically, there is continued uncertainty as to the self-employment tax consequences for nonmanaging members of a multimember LLC.

The proposed regs. In 1997, the IRS issued proposed regulations (Prop. Reg. §1.1402(a)-2(h)) under Code Sec. 1402(a)(13) that effectively equated nonmanaging LLC members to limited partners in a partnership for self-employment tax purposes. Under the proposed regs, all members of a multimember LLC (taxed as a partnership for federal income tax purposes) would be treated as a limited partner, unless the member:

- Has personal liability for the debts and other obligations of the partnership;
- Has authority to contract on behalf of the partnership; or
- Participates in the partnership's business for more than 500 hours during the year (the *500-hour test*).

Thus, under the proposed regs, an LLC member would be required to pay self-employment tax on profits distributed to him or her by the LLC if he or she:

- Has personal liability for the LLC's debts and other liabilities;
- Possesses the authority to negotiate and enter into contracts on the LLC's behalf; or
- Participates in the LLC's business for more than 500 hours during the entity's tax year.

An exception in the proposed regs also provides that *service partners* in professional service partnerships would never be treated as limited partners for self-employment tax purposes. Under the regs, a *professional service partnership* is one in which services are provided in the areas of:

- Medicine;
- Law;
- Engineering;
- Accounting;
- Actuarially science; or
- Consulting.

The intent of the proposed regs was to exclude from an individual's self-employment net earnings those amounts that were essentially returns of capital contributions invested in the partnership.

Congressional moratorium. However, criticism of the proposed regs led Congress to pass legislation prohibiting the issuance or finalization of any regulations relating to the definition of a limited partner for self-employment tax purposes before July 1, 1998. Opponents argued that the proposed regulations could lead to the imposition of self-employment tax on income that could not accurately be characterized as self-employment income. To date, the proposed regs have not been finalized—or withdrawn.

Bifurcation of member interests. The language of the proposed regs effectively likens an LLC's managing members to general partners in a partnership and nonmanaging members to limited partners for self-employment tax purposes. Under the proposed regs, imposition of self-employment tax on LLC members depends on their level of participation in the business and also the type of services they provide. In most circumstances, an LLC member does not have personal liability for the debts and obligations of the LLC, as provided under state law. Thus, a member will be delineated as a limited partner under the proposed regs for purposes of self-employment tax unless he or she is a managing member of the LLC (because a managing member generally has the authority to contract on the LLC's behalf) or spends more than 500 hours working for the LLC. Thus, managing member's earnings and distributive income from the LLC would generally be subject to self-employment tax, while the distributive income of nonmanaging members would be excluded from self-employment tax.

The proposed regs, however, would allow for the bifurcation of an LLC member's distributive share of income in certain circumstances and if certain requirements are met, such as compliance with Code Sec. 704(b). Under the proposed regs, an LLC member who has both managing and nonmanaging membership interests would be able to bifurcate his or her distributive share of income between the two, thereby minimizing exposure to self-employment tax.

Self-employment tax of LLC managing-members. Without clear guidance, there remains ambiguity regarding how to apply Code Sec. 1402(a)(13) to managing LLC members that actively manage the business. One approach would classify LLC members as limited and general partners. Under this rationale, an LLC member may be considered a "general partner" to the extent he or she meets one of the exceptions under the regs (i.e., the member has liability for the LLC's debts, has the power to contract on behalf of the company, or participates in the LLC's business for more than 500 hours during the year). An LLC member would be considered a "limited partner" to the extent that, for example, he or she does not have liability for the LLC's debts or does not have authority to contract on behalf of the LLC.

Single-Member LLCs and the Issues of Disregarded Entities

A single-member LLC (SMLLC) can be either a corporation or a single-member disregarded entity for federal income tax purposes. To be treated as a corporation by the IRS, an SMLLC has to file Form 8832 and elect to be classified as such. An SMLLC that does not elect to be a corporation will be classified by the IRS under the check-the-box regulations as a disregarded entity, which is taxed as a sole proprietor for federal income tax purposes.

One drawback to operating as an LLC is a lack of consistent federal and state treatment of LLCs for income tax purposes. States generally follow the federal tax treatment of LLCs for income tax purposes; however, there is a lack of uniformity, consistency, and transparency in certain areas. Historically, the federal government has disregarded state classifications of businesses for some federal tax purposes. Courts have repeatedly observed that, although state laws of incorporation control various aspects of business relations, the laws do not necessarily control (but may only affect) federal tax provisions. In effect, single-member LLCs may be allowed certain advantages provided by state law, but they are also subject to federal tax liabilities that may supersede state rights granted to the LLC and its members.

For example, the interaction of the IRS's disregarded entity rules and federal employment tax with state tax provisions have created some problems for single-member LLCs. Specifically, problems may arise between state employment tax laws that set forth distinct requirements for the reporting, collection, and payment of employment taxes that conflict with the federal disregarded entity rules. Although a disregarded entity's tax status is transparent for federal tax purposes, due to the IRS's check-the-box regulations, it is not necessarily transparent for state law purposes. For instance, the owner of an SMLLC is not personally liable for the debts and obligations of the LLC. However, because the entity is disregarded as separate from its owner, the owner is generally treated as the employer of the disregarded SMLLC's employees. Therefore, the owner is personally liable for applicable employment taxes, regardless of the limited liability afforded to the owner under state law.

Employment Tax Changes

In August 2007 the IRS issued final regulations (T.D. 9356) to treat single-member LLCs that are disregarded entities as separate entities for employment tax (and excise tax) reporting purposes. The provisions of the final regulations pertaining to employment taxes are effective with respect to wages paid on or after January 1, 2009. As such, the disregarded SMLLC will be treated as a corporation for employment tax obligation purposes. After January 1, 2009, the SMLLC will be responsible for collecting, reporting, and paying over employment tax obligations using the name and employer identification number (EIN) assigned to the LLC. Although under the final regulations, a disregarded SMLLC will be treated as a corporation for employment tax purposes, the SMLLC will continue to be disregarded for other federal tax purposes. The purpose of the final regulations is to alleviate administrative burdens that have plagued disregarded entities due to different employment tax reporting requirement rules.

The final regulations provide that a disregarded SMLLC is to be treated as a separate entity for employment tax purposes. As such, the entity will bear ultimate responsibility for the LLC's employment tax obligations, and the owner may no longer have to worry about personal liability for such taxes. However, the IRS can still seek to collect unpaid employment taxes from an SMLLC owner under the Code Sec. 6672 trust fund penalty tax, which allows the IRS to personally assess and collect an LLC's unpaid employment taxes from the SMLLC's owner, if the owner is considered a *responsible person*. A disregarded SMLLC is to be treated as a corporation for purposes of employment taxes and related reporting requirements.

STUDY QUESTIONS

---

9. Under the 1997 IRS proposed regulations, a member of a multimember LLC taxed as a partnership for federal income tax purposes would be subject to self-employment tax if:

a. The member receives guaranteed payments for services rendered to the LLC

b. The member is not personally liable for any of the debts and liabilities of the LLC

c. The member is prohibited from entering into contracts on the LLC's behalf

d. None of the above would subject the LLC member to self-employment tax

---

---

10. Under the final regulations of T.D. 9356 for single-member LLCs, after January 1, 2009, a disregarded SMLLC entity is to be:

a. Treated for all federal tax liabilities as a sole proprietorship

b. Treated as a corporation for income tax purposes but a disregarded entity for employment tax purposes

c. Treated as an S corporation passthrough entity

d. None of the above reflects the final regulations

CONCLUSION

The tax and nontax benefits of operating a business as a limited liability company must be balanced with the various pitfalls associated with the LLC structure. Although the limited liability company is no longer a "new" business structure, LLCs continue to provide new tax challenges as the IRS works to develop more guidance and regulations clarifying the federal tax treatment of these state law entities. The federal tax treatment of LLCs is an evolving area and will continue to develop over time. Additionally, the federal tax treatment of LLCs will, as highlighted in this chapter, have likely ramifications for state tax and nontax LLC issues. Therefore, it is imperative to stay abreast of the IRS guidance and case law that develops and expands on the tax and nontax treatment of LLCs.

MODULE 2: SMALL BUSINESS PLANNING — CHAPTER 5

Retirement Savings for Small Businesses

This chapter explores the various retirement plan options available for employers, with particular emphasis on the options specific to smaller companies. Many small employers may be tempted to dismiss the idea of establishing a retirement plan for their workers as too difficult and expensive. This chapter will hopefully persuade course participants to consider the many tax advantages of retirement plans for small employers and the features of today's qualified plans that can reduce both the cost and complexity of implementing and maintaining them.

LEARNING OBJECTIVES

Upon completion of this chapter, you will be able to:

- Compare the advantages and disadvantages of qualified and nonqualified retirement plans;
- Analyze the tax benefits of a qualified retirement plan;
- List the basic steps in establishing a qualified retirement plan;
- Describe the requirements of maintaining a qualified retirement plan;
- Contrast features of the various types of 401(k) plans;
- Understand the basics of the new DB/K plan; and
- Describe the options offered by the various IRA-based plans.

INTRODUCTION

Every savvy, forward-looking U.S. worker hopes to set aside funds to plan for retirement. However, finding the extra cash to save may be quite difficult for the average worker, especially those employed in small businesses, where working capital (and therefore salaries) is not as plentiful. Additionally, small business owners are often not able or willing to provide assistance with employees' retirement savings.

To assist individual employees in their retirement saving efforts, as well as encourage employers to adopt retirement plans, the U.S. Internal Revenue Code provides a variety of tax-advantageous vehicles through which employees may save funds for retirement. In addition, employers can offer retirement plans for employees' that, if they meet certain qualifications under the Tax Code, create tax advantages for both parties.

However, with any qualified retirement savings plan for which the government affords tax breaks, there are complex requirements, under the tax code and the *Employee Retirement Income Security Act of 1997 (ERISA)*, for maintaining the plans. For example, plans must be updated to reflect changes in the law and information about the plan must be reported annually to employees as well as to the IRS. If a plan falls out of compliance or is inappropriately used for the advantage of the wrong parties, it must be corrected to avoid penalties or the loss of its qualification for special tax treatment.

After describing the steps in establishing and maintaining qualified retirement plans, this chapter describes the various types of plans which may or may not be appropriate, taking into account the employer's particular resources and objectives. Some qualified plans, called *defined benefits plans* are structured so that the employee is guaranteed to receive a specific amount of benefits upon retirement; and require employers to make contributions. Other qualified plans, *defined contribution plans,* are more flexible, and give employers the choice, rather than the requirement, of contributing to the employee's retirement assets. Employers can also offer a 401(k) cash-deferred arrangement, which permits employees to make elective deferrals of their wages for payment into retirement plans, but with the significant tax advantages of a qualified defined contribution plan. Another option, the individual retirement arrangement (IRA), is a separate account to which employees may contribute funds, on a pretax basis, and grow their savings into tax-deferred future benefits. Some IRA plans even permit contributions by the employer.

TYPES OF BENEFIT PLANS

Three general areas relate to employee benefit plans for retirement:
- Employee welfare benefit plans;
- Employer compensation and payroll practices; and
- Qualified retirement plans.

Employee Welfare Benefit Plans

In a discussion about tax-advantageous retirement plans, Code Sec. 419 employee welfare benefit plans are not directly relevant, because these plans do not provide immediate retirement benefits to employees. Rather, they provide other important benefits that can include severance pay, supplemental unemployment benefits, health insurance, life and disability insurance, paid vacation and other fringe benefits. Welfare benefit plans assist employees, indirectly, in accumulating funds for retirement, by helping employees to avoid draining retirement savings because of more immediate cash needs caused by unemployment, healthcare costs, etc.

Compensation and Payroll Practices

To assist employees in their retirement efforts, employers can simply increase employee salaries, and advise employees to contribute the extra cash to their savings accounts. Although increasing salaries in the hope employees will save the extra compensation may be the easiest way for employers to help with retirement, this technique does not make use of the tax advantages for qualified retirement plans offered by the Code, nor does it impress upon the employees its value as an "additional employee benefit."

Retirement Plans

Employee retirement plans generally encompass all plans that provide retirement benefits with tax-advantages of varying degrees. There are two general types of plans: nonqualified and qualified.

Nonqualified plans. A *nonqualified plan* is, generally, a retirement plan that fails to meet the requirements of Code Section 401(a) for qualified plans. But even a nonqualified plan can provide benefits, such as the deferral of income tax recognition on contributions, under certain circumstances, which provides employees the benefit of time-value of money savings.

Nonqualified plans that meet the requirements for deferred compensation plans under Code Sec. 409A, are most often used to provide deferred compensation arrangements to corporate executives and key employees.

Nonqualified plans are not heavily regulated, require little administration, allow unlimited contributions, and have tax advantages, however, that are slight compared to those of qualified plans. Under Code Sec. 409A, income tax is deferred on the compensation paid into the plan, but only if there is:

- A "substantial risk" that the employee may forfeit his or her rights to the funds; or
- The plan meets certain requirements regarding distributions, acceleration of benefits, elections, etc.

Substantial risk of forfeiture means that the employee's eventual entitlement to the funds is contingent upon the employee providing substantial future services or meeting specific performance goals.

Unlike qualified plans, nonqualified plans do not allow employers an immediate tax deduction for plan contributions. Employers are not entitled to deductions for contributions until the funds are distributed, which is typically many years after the employer's contribution was made. Employees are taxed when they receive distributions from the plan.

Qualified plans. Qualified retirement plans are the more tax-advantageous type of plan for businesses. These plans are more heavily regulated than nonqualified plans, and have many requirements. For example, plan assets must be held in a qualified trust or custodial account and employers must offer benefits under qualified plans on a nondiscriminatory basis (with respect to salary level) to all rank-and-file employees, not only to highly paid executives and other key employees, and plans are required to contain "antialienation" provisions that state that the plan benefits cannot be assigned or alienated.

However, several plan options can make the requirements less burdensome and less costly for small businesses.

The combination of tax advantages plus variety and flexibility of plan types makes qualified retirement plans preferable for a majority of small businesses. Thus, qualified plans in their various types are the focus of this chapter.

WHY HAVE A QUALIFIED RETIREMENT PLAN?

Qualified retirement plans can afford many tax and nontax benefits to employers as well as to employees. For example, a qualified retirement plan can help employers attract and retain better employees, thereby reducing turnover and new employee training costs. Also, employers can immediately deduct their contributions (within certain limits) to a qualified plan and may even be entitled to receive a tax credit for the costs of implementing the plan.

Employees pay no income tax on employer contributions (within certain limitations) until the funds are distributed and also benefit from the tax-free accumulation of earnings. Employees generally may make pretax contributions from their compensation to a qualified plan (thereby lowering participants' taxable income).

Finally, one of the greatest advantages of qualified plans is that retirement savings from defined contribution plans are *portable;* eligible funds can be rolled over to another defined contribution plan (or IRA), in accordance with certain requirements, thereby helping employees continue to build their nest eggs and cut down on the excess paperwork caused by maintaining several retirement accounts.

COMMENT

For individuals with lower incomes, Code Sec. 25B provides (subject to various restrictions) up to a $1,000 nonrefundable "saver's credit" to encourage contributions to certain types of retirement plans, such as 401(k)s and IRAs. The amount of the credit is based upon the total contributions to qualified retirement plans plus elective deferrals (limited to $2,000), gross income, and filing status. The saver's credit is completely phased out for:

- Joint return filers with adjusted gross incomes (AGIs) exceeding $50,000;
- Head of household filers with AGIs exceeding $37,500; and
- Single or married separate return filers with adjusted gross incomes exceeding $25,000.

STUDY QUESTIONS

1. Which of the following is a benefit of nonqualified retirement plans compared with qualified plans?

    a. Higher deductions for employee contributions
    b. Same-year deductions of employer contributions
    c. Rank-and-file employees are automatically eligible for comparable benefit percentages as highly compensated employees
    d. Less government regulation

2. All of the following are generally ways employees may benefit prior to retirement from contributing to qualified retirement plans *except:*

    a. Portability features enabling employees to move qualified defined contribution plan funds without penalty to another employer's defined contribution plan
    b. Reducing their pretax salary by the amount of contributions or deducting contributions from federal income tax
    c. Claiming a saver's credit
    d. All of the above are ways employees can benefit from their qualified plan prior to retirement

GENERAL FEATURES OF ALL QUALIFIED RETIREMENT PLANS

Advantages

Tax savings for all. Retirement plans that meet the requirements of Code Sec. 401 are of great tax advantage to both employees and employers.
Following are specific tax benefits:

- Employer contributions to qualified plans are fully and immediately deductible under Code Sec. 219 by the employer, subject to certain limits;
- Employees can make pretax contributions to a qualified retirement plan;
- Employees are not taxed on employer contributions or on plan earnings. Employees only pay income tax upon distribution of funds;
- Employer and employee contributions grow in a trust (or custodial account) that is exempt from tax under Code Sec. 501(a)(1); and
- At the time plan distributions commence, an employee can further defer federal income tax by rolling over his or her eligible funds in a defined contribution plan (funds must be vested) to an eligible retirement plan (includes defined contribution plans, IRAs, etc.) under Code Sec. 401(a)(31), subject to certain required minimum distribution (RMD) amounts upon reaching retirement age.

> **COMMENT**
>
> Under Code Sec. 45E, a tax credit is available for a portion of a qualified plan's startup costs incurred by small employers that employ 100 or fewer workers who each receive at least $5,000 of compensation annually. This credit is limited to 50 percent of the cost of starting a qualified plan, up to a maximum of $500 per year, for the first three years of the plan. At that level, the credit is obviously of most value to the small employer.

Asset protection. Pursuant to bankruptcy laws (11 U.S.C. § 541(c)(2)), assets held in a qualified retirement plan are generally protected from both creditors of employees and creditors of employers, because they are required to contain "antialienation" provisions, under Code Sec. 401(a)(13) and ERISA.

Plan use of nonvested employer contributions. If an employee terminates employment, he or she is only entitled to the vested portion of the account balance, with respect to employer contributions. The employee forfeits the nonvested portion of his benefits, and those funds may be applied to pay administrative expenses of the plan, reduce future employer contributions, or increase the accounts of the remaining plan participants.

Disadvantages

Contribution limits. There are several disadvantages of qualified retirement plans. For example, the Code limits the amount of benefits that employers can provide and benefits must be given to all employees, without discrimination based upon employees' salary and length of service, in accordance with the nondiscrimination rules set forth in Reg. Sec. 1.401(a)(4)-2.

Administrative limits and costs. Additionally, administrative requirements of the plans can be costly for employers. The main requirements for qualification under Code Sec. 401 include the following:

- The retirement plan's assets cannot be diverted away from the plan and used for other purposes under Code Sec. 401(a)(2);
- Under Code Sec. 401(a)(4), benefits provided to and contributions provided on behalf of employees must not discriminate in favor of "highly compensated employees" as defined in Code Section 414(q);
- Contributions and benefits must not be denied to employees based upon a maximum age under Code Sec. 410(a)(2); and
- Unless otherwise instructed by the employee, the plan is required to pay benefits under Code Sec. 401(a)(14) within 60 days after the close of the plan year in which the latest of the following occurs
  — The date that the employee turns 65 years of age,

— The 10-year anniversary of the employee's participation in the plan, or

— The year the employee leaves the company.

Top-Heavy Rules

The *top-heavy rules* of Code Sec. 416 prohibit defined benefits plans from permitting more than 60 percent of the present value of the cumulative accrued benefits for "key employees" and prohibit defined contribution plans from permitting more than 60 percent of the aggregate value of the accounts of the key employees to exceed 60 percent of the value of all employee accounts under the plan. *Key employees* include officers of the company making more than $150,000 per year, a 5 percent owner of the company, and a 1 percent owner of the company making more than $150,000 per year.

COMMENT

With respect to rollovers, employees can avoid the 20 percent withholding requirement by rolling over their eligible distributions from a qualified defined contribution plan into another qualified plan through a direct trustee-to-trustee transfer. The transferee plan is required to separately account for the taxable and nontaxable portions of the funds under Code Sec. 402(c). Alternatively, employees may elect to personally roll over distributions from their qualified defined contribution plans, subject to the 20 percent withholding, within 60 days after funds are distributed from the old retirement plan. If a rollover is not done correctly, subject to several exceptions, Code Sec. 72(t) imposes an additional 10 percent tax on premature distributions made to employees before they reach the age of 59½.

Again, however, small businesses may add several flavors to their qualified retirement plans suitable to their own tastes. As a result, it is possible to avoid several of these administrative requirements and, therefore, lower overall plan maintenance costs.

STUDY QUESTIONS

---

3. Code Sec. 416 prohibits employers from reserving more than 60 percent of plan benefits for highly compensated employees under the:

a. Top-heavy requirement

b. Termination requirement

c. Asset protection requirement

d. Nonvested employer contribution rules

---

4. Which of the following is part of the timing requirements for determining when a distribution from a qualified retirement plan is available under Code Sec. 401(a)(14)?

   a. The year of the employees' fifth employment anniversary

   b. The year of termination of employment

   c. Their starting date of employment

   d. None of the above is a requirement of Code Sec. 401(a)(14)

ESTABLISHING A QUALIFIED PLAN

There are two basic steps in setting up a qualified retirement plan:

1. The employer must adopt a written plan and inform employees of the plan specifics; then
2. The plan assets must be invested and held in a tax-exempt trust or custodial account.

Selecting and Informing Participants of the Plan

Before an employer may begin funding and reporting deductions for its employee retirement contributions, the organization must adopt a specific written retirement plan, which fulfills the requirements of Code Sec. 401(a). The written plan must be adopted by the last day of the tax year in which the employer initiates the plan. Further, under Reg. §1.401-1(a)(2) the employer is required to communicate terms of the plan to eligible employees.

Types of plans. Employers may choose from three types of written retirement plans:

- An IRS-approved master plan;
- An IRS-approved prototype plan; or
- A written document individually designed for the employer that follows certain acceptable Internal Revenue Code guidelines.

Under a master plan, a single trust or custodial account is established for the joint use of all adopting employers. Under a prototype plan, a separate trust or custodial account is established for each employer. Employers are free to tailor the organization of an individually designed plan as they see fit. Sponsoring organizations such as a bank or mutual fund usually have master or prototype plans available for use. As a result, most qualified plans follow these two types of written plans, rather than completely customizing the terms of their plan from scratch.

Later sections of the chapter explore specific plan types and compare their advantages and disadvantages.

IRS determination letters. Because the consequences of a plan's qualification are so far-reaching, the IRS will review plan documents and issue determination letters stating whether a written plan meets the qualification requirements. To obtain a determination letter, the employer must file Form 5300, Application for Determination for Employee Benefit Plan. However, a plan is not required to obtain a determination letter. A determination letter may be obtained for either advance or retroactive qualification of a new plan or for a plan amendment.

> **COMMENT**
>
> For certain small employers with 100 or fewer employees receiving at least $5,000 of compensation in the preceding calendar year, Code Sec. 7528(b)(2)(B) requires the IRS to waive the user fee normally required when requesting a determination letter for plan qualification. At least one employee must not be considered highly compensated and the request must be submitted before the later of five years after the plan has been adopted or any remedial amendment period beginning within the first five years of adoption.

> **COMMENT**
>
> The IRS also issues determination letters with respect to the tax-exempt status of any related trusts.

An applicant for a determination letter may appeal a notice of proposed adverse determination issued by IRS to the IRS Appeals Office. Individual employees, as opposed to employer-sponsors, do not share this right. Employee administrative remedies are limited to the right to submit written comments on the application, pursuant to Rev. Proc. 2008-6. However, under Code Sec. 7476, any *interested party,* as defined under the regs, may bring an action in Tax Court for a declaratory judgment, once the IRS has issued or failed to issue a determination letter and all administrative remedies have been exhausted.

Creating an Account for and Investing the Qualified Plan Assets

As part of establishing a Code Sec. 401 qualified retirement plan, an employer is required to place the plan assets into a tax-exempt trust (or custodial account) for safekeeping. In setting up the plan, there are several ways to arrange investments:

- The employer (or the trustee) can select a professional investment firm "to manage the funds. However, an employer must exercise reasonable and good-faith judgment in selecting and continuously monitoring an investment firm in order to avoid liability in the event that the investments do not achieve a market return;

- The trust may purchase an annuity contract from an insurance company;
- The trust can purchase and hold life insurance for plan participants, if incidental to the retirement benefits; and
- The trust may purchase face-amount certificates from an insurance company. These certificates are treated like annuity contracts.

STUDY QUESTIONS

5. A single trust or custodial account set up for joint use without substantive changes by employers that adopt it is a(n):
   a. Master plan
   b. Prototype plan
   c. Individual plan
   d. Default plan

6. An employer may obtain a determination letter from the IRS for all of the following *except:*
   a. The tax-exempt status of a plan's trust
   b. Retroactive qualification of a new plan
   c. An amendment to an existing plan
   d. The IRS may issue a determination letter in all of the above circumstances

QUALIFIED PLAN ADMINISTRATION

In addition to the requirements for establishing a qualified retirement plan, a significant amount of work remains for employers in operating the plan on an ongoing basis. These administrative responsibilities include:

- Ensuring that all eligible electing employees are enrolled in the plan;
- Making contributions in accordance with the plan;
- Keeping the plan up-to-date and in compliance with all retirement plan laws;
- Managing the plan assets;
- Providing information and required disclosure to plan participants; and
- Distributing benefits in accordance with the plan.

Responsibilities of Plan Administrators

The *plan administrator* is an individual or group of people responsible for managing the day-to-day affairs of a qualified plan under Code Sec. 414(g). Generally, the plan administrator is specifically designated in the plan. If no person or group is designated, the employer is the administrator. If the plan administrator cannot otherwise be determined, the plan administrator is the person(s) actually responsible for the control, disposition, or management of the plan's assets.

The basic responsibilities of the plan administrator include:

- Hiring attorneys, accountants, consultants, and actuaries;
- Determining eligibility for plan participation and accrual of benefits;
- Advising participants or beneficiaries of their rights;
- Directing distribution of benefits;
- Preparing reports for participants and responding to information requests; and
- Keeping records and participant information.

Updating Plans

Plan administrators must ensure that a qualified plan is operated in accordance with, and amended as needed for compliance with, current federal rules, including ERISA. Because the retirement plan rules frequently change, existing qualified retirement plans must be updated to reflect new requirements.

New legislation usually gives qualified plans a remedial period to make adjustments of a year or more after the effective date of any new law. Although usually administrators immediately begin to operate the plan in accordance with new laws beginning on their effective date, plans have until the end of the remedial period to modify the provisions in the qualified plan's written documents to reflect the change.

> **COMMENT**
>
> Should an employer adopt or amend a plan and subsequently receive a determination letter from IRS denying its qualified status or discover a change in law, administrators usually may retroactively amend the plan to meet the new requirements. The change would then be effective beginning at the date of creation or amendment.

Correcting Plan Failures

Even after receiving a favorable determination letter of its qualified status, a plan may subsequently fail to satisfy the qualification requirements due to lack of compliance with changes in the law, problems caused by incorrect plan amendments, or problems caused by incorrect operation of the plan. Should a plan fail to remain compliant with all the requirements imposed on qualified plans, it risks having the IRS revoke its qualification status.

When a retirement plan is disqualified, it loses all of the special tax benefits available for qualified plans and the trust maintaining the plan assets is no longer considered tax-exempt. This not only affects the tax situation of the employer but also all employee participants. Because of this drastic result, the IRS (jointly with the Department of Labor) bends over backward to help plans maintain qualification, by allowing retroactive corrections. Nevertheless, the IRS and DOL have limited tolerance, so it is important for plan administrators to fix plan failures as soon as possible.

The IRS has established several correction programs that allow plan administrators to correct certain plan failures before the agency disqualifies the entire plan. As put forth by Rev. Proc. 2006-27 and later modified by Rev. Proc. 2007-49, these procedures are known collectively as the *Employee Plans Compliance Resolution System* (EPCRS). There are three correction programs within the EPCRS program:

- The Self-Correction Program;
- The Voluntary Correction Program; and
- The Audit Closing Agreement Program.

Self-Correction Program. Under the Self-Correction Program, plan administrators may correct "insignificant operational failures" without paying a fee or receiving a sanction. Because no IRS involvement is required, this is the cheapest and easiest method of the three for plans to correct failures.

Voluntary Correction Program. Under the Voluntary Correction program, plans may pay a fee and obtain the IRS's approval for corrections of all types of plan failures. These situations include failures related to the plan's operations, the plan's written documents, or the employer's eligibility. Requests for relief under a Voluntary Correction Program, however, must be made prior to an audit.

Audit Closing Agreement Program. The most formal and costly correction avenue of last resort is the Audit Closing Agreement Program. This option applies to plan failures discovered during an IRS examination. Plans must correct the failures, pay a fee under sanction, and enter into a closing agreement with the IRS. The IRS may also require the plan to alter its administrative procedures or obtain a favorable determination letter prior to execution of the closing agreement.

> **COMMENT**
>
> Qualified retirement plans may not correct plan failures under the EPCRS regime involving the misuse or diversion of assets from the plan.

Prohibited Transactions

Excise tax. In addition to maintaining the ongoing activities of the plan, the retirement plan administrator must ensure that no prohibited transactions occur between the plan and certain disqualified persons. The IRS assesses a 15 percent excise tax against disqualified persons on amounts involved in a retirement plan's prohibited transactions under Code Sec. 4975. Furthermore, if the transaction is not corrected within the tax year, Code Sec. 4975 imposes an additional 100 percent excise tax on the amount involved. Finally, the trust maintaining the retirement plan could lose its tax-exempt status under Code Sec. 503(a)(1)(A) if it has engaged in a prohibited transaction.

Prohibited transactions include the following:

- The plan's income or assets are transferred to disqualified persons for their own individual use or benefit;
- A fiduciary of the plan uses the plan's income or assets for his or her own interest;
- A fiduciary of the plan receives consideration from a party in a transaction involving plan income or assets; or
- The plan and a disqualified person engage in business dealings such as a sale, exchange, or lease of property; lend money or extend credit; or furnish goods, services, or facilities, other than transactions that are exempt under the regs for Code Sec. 4975.

Disqualified persons include the following:

- A fiduciary of the plan;
- Persons providing services to the plan;
- The employer;
- Any direct or indirect 50 percent owner of the employer (both individuals and corporations); and
- Family members of the previously mentioned individuals.

Correcting a prohibited transaction. If a disqualified person corrects a prohibited transaction as soon as possible, he or she may avoid the 100 percent excise tax on the prohibited transaction. According to IRS Publication 560, this means, "undoing it as much as you can without putting the plan in a worse financial position than if you had acted under the highest fiduciary standards."

If the disqualified person does not correct the prohibited transaction during the tax year of its occurrence, there is a grace period for correction, before the draconian Code Sec. 4975 excise tax is imposed. The disqualified person is allowed 90 days to correct the transaction after the day the IRS mails a notice of deficiency for the excise tax. Additionally, the correction period can be extended by the IRS for reasonable time needed to correct the transaction. IRS Publication 560 states that the IRS will abate, credit, or refund the excise tax if the prohibited transaction is corrected during the appropriate time period. Clearly, the IRS prefers to have problems corrected rather than to collect revenue from the excise tax. Expressed another way, the purpose of the excise tax is to force compliance rather than create revenue for the federal government.

Reporting and Disclosure

In addition to its efforts to maintain the ongoing operations of the plan, a plan administrator must file a variety of reports with respect to the plan's operations and compliance with all laws and governmental rules. The principal reports include an annual information return and a notice of changes in plan status. The plan administrator must also make appropriate disclosures to the plan participants.

Participant notification: summary plan description. Upon the formation of a qualified retirement plan, ERISA requires the plan administrator to give eligible employees a summary plan description that includes specific detailed information about the plan. The administrator must also give summary annual reports to participants under ERISA. The report must include a statement setting forth the type, amount, and value of the benefits to which the participants are entitled.

Information returns. Under Code Sec. 6058, qualified plan administrators must also file Form 5500, *Annual Return/Report of Employee Benefit Plan*, annually with the IRS. Schedule A must be attached to the Form 5500 if any benefits under the plan are provided by an insurance company, insurance service, or other similar organization. Schedule B must be filed by the administrator of a defined benefit plan that is subject to the minimum funding standards of the Internal Revenue Code.

Form 5500-EZ, *Annual Return of One-Participant (Owners and Their Spouses) Retirement Plan*, is a short-form information return that is filed by pension plans, profit-sharing plans, and 401(k) plans that cover:

- Only one individual or an individual and his or her spouse who wholly own the trade or business for which the plan is established; or
- Only partners and their spouses in a business partnership for which the plan is established.

Form 5500-EZ must be filed annually. However, plans having $100,000 or less in total assets at the close of the plan's accounting year do not have to file.

According to the instructions for both Form 5500 and 5500-EZ, each form and all of its accompanying schedules are due by the last day of the seventh calendar month after the end of the plan year beginning during the tax year at issue.

> **COMMENT**
>
> If two or more plans of a single business have combined assets of more than $100,000, Form 5500-EZ must be filed for each plan, even if one of the plans individually has $100,000 or less in total assets.

Notice of changes. In the annual summary plan provided to beneficiaries, the qualified plan administrator must include a summary of material changes in the plan under ERISA. The administrator must also alert the IRS to any material changes.

Administrators must file Form 6406, *Short Form Application for Determination for Minor Amendment of Employee Benefit Plan*, to obtain IRS approval of a minor change to a plan that has previously received a determination letter. Administrators must also file Form 5310-A, *Notice of Plan Merger or Consolidation, Spinoff, or Transfer of Plan Assets or Liabilities; Notice of Qualified Separate Lines of Business*, to notify the IRS of certain plan mergers, spinoffs, or transfers of plan assets.

PLAN TERMINATION

An employer may terminate a qualified retirement plan for several reasons. These include voluntary termination as a result of not having enough assets to pay required benefits to participants or involuntary termination by the Pension Benefit Guaranty Corporation (PBGC) for similar reasons. However, employees should not be adversely affected by a plan's termination. Code Sec. 411(d)(3) requires qualified plans to provide that if a plan is terminated, the employees will still be entitled to all benefits accrued as of the date of termination.

When a plan terminates, the plan administrator has several administrative duties to perform in preparation of the plan's termination. Under Title IV of ERISA, the administrator must provide written notice to the PBGC and to plan participants regarding the employer's intention to terminate the plan and the amount of employees' accrued benefits as of the proposed termination date. A notice of change in status regarding the termination must also accompany the plan's Form 5550 or 5550-EZ filed with the IRS, in accordance with Code Sec. 6057(b).

The plan is also required to distribute benefits to participants as soon as administratively feasible after the termination of the plan. Although the required time limit for distributions depends on the facts and circumstances of the situation, the IRS generally considers the outside date for distributions to be no later than one year after the date of termination, according to Rev. Rul. 89-87.

After the plan officially terminates, the administrator has the option of filing Form 5310, *Application for Determination for Terminating Plan*. The PBGC will determine whether distributions will retain their tax benefits to the participants and whether the plan meets minimum funding requirements. If the plan's assets are subsequently found to be insufficient to cover its liabilities to participants, the employer may be held liable to the PBGC for the outstanding liabilities. Because obtaining an IRS determination allows employers to preempt this possibility, employers routinely request it.

STUDY QUESTIONS

7. The cheapest and easiest method of correcting plan failures under EPCRS is:

   a. Self-Correction Program

   b. Retirement Plan Revision Program

   c. Audit Closing Agreement Program

   d. Voluntary Correction Program

8. All of the following are allowances the IRS offers for correcting a pro-hibited transaction by a qualified plan *except:*

   a. A 90-day correction period following IRS issuance of a notice of deficiency

   b. An extension by the IRS of its original correction period

   c. A refund of half of the penalty excise tax upon correction of the transaction

   d. All of the above are methods the IRS allows for correcting pro-hibited transactions

GENERAL TYPES OF QUALIFIED PLANS

Qualified retirement plans generally can be divided into two categories:
- Defined benefit plans; and
- Defined contribution plans

The differences between the two categories are described here.

Defined Benefit Plans

A *defined benefit plan*, technically defined under Code Sec. 414(j) as "any plan which is not a defined contribution plan," provides a guaranteed amount of annual or monthly payment to each plan participant beginning at retirement. The amount of payment is determined according to a set formula. Under Code Sec. 401(a)(25), the formula must be based on actuarial assumptions and described in the written plan documents. The amount of the benefit is based generally on the employee's years of service with the employer and either:
- The employee's final average earnings; or
- A specified dollar amount.

COMMENT

Under Code Sec. 415(b), annual employer contributions under a defined benefit plan are limited to the lesser of 100 percent of the employee's average compensation over the three consecutive calendar years during which the employee had the greatest aggregate compensation from the employer or $230,000 (as inflation-adjusted for 2008). (See IR-2007-171.)

Employer's investment risk. The employer sponsoring the plan is required under Code Sec. 430 to provide minimum funding for the benefits promised under the defined benefit plan. Funding is accomplished with annual (or more frequent) tax-deductible employer contributions to the tax-exempt trust that holds the plan's assets. As a result, even though some defined benefit plans allow or require employees to contribute to their accounts, the risk of investment loss lies solely on the plan employer/sponsor. If the assets of a defined benefit plan decline in value, the employer must contribute additional amounts necessary to provide the promised benefits. If the assets increase in value more than expected, the plan can use the excess value to balance out funding requirements in case of lean future years.

Minimum participation. Defined benefit plans are also subject to minimum employee participation requirements under Code Sec. 401(a)(26)(A). The plan must have minimum participation of the lesser of:

- 50 percent of the company's employees; or
- The greater of 40 percent of all employees or two employees (or if there is only one employee, then such employee).

Good for small business? As compared to the defined contribution plan (described next), a defined benefit plan may not be the preferable option for a small business. Because contributions to these plans are based upon what funding is needed to provide future benefits, actuarial assumptions and computations are necessary, and must be consistently updated to ensure the employer is making the proper contributions. This oversight generates considerable costs, which a small employer may avoid by using a defined contribution plan instead.

Consensus, based on the number of small businesses opting for defined contribution plans as opposed to defined benefit plans, clearly favors defined contribution plans. Generally, defined benefit plans leave most of the contributions up to the employer, which may need to pay less salary in order to fund those benefits. However, employers are hard pressed to do so when competing businesses offering defined contribution plans are able to pay more competitive salaries. The argument against defined benefit plans is bolstered when employers can explain to employees that if upon retirement they want guaranteed income, they can purchase an annuity using funds from their defined contribution plan accounts.

Defined Contribution Plans

A *defined contribution plan* is a qualified retirement plan defined under Code Sec. 414(i) in which the employer has the option of making discretionary contributions to the account of an employee participant. Unlike defined benefit plans, participants are not guaranteed to receive any specific amount of benefits upon retirement. Instead, the amount of benefits is the account balance at the employees' time of retirement, which reflects the amount of contributions, expenses, earnings, and forfeitures as allocated to participants under the plan. As a result of this setup, the risks—and benefits—of investment performance fall on the participants. The two most common types of defined contribution plans are money purchase pension plans and profit-sharing plans. Discussed later in the chapter are other plan varieties that are also popular: 401(k) plans and IRA-based plans. Finally, the chapter describes Keogh plans available for self-employed businesspeople.

Contribution limitations. Because defined contribution plans qualify under Code Sec. 401, both employers and employees are entitled to the previously mentioned tax advantages. However, deductions are limited. Under Code Sec. 404(a)(3), employer deductions for contributions to a defined contribution plan are limited to 25 percent of the employee's compensation paid during the year, with a maximum of $225,000 of employee income taken into account (as of 2008, adjusted upward each year for inflation). Under Code Sec. 415(c), employee deductions for contributions to a defined contribution plan are generally limited to the lesser of 100 percent of the employee's compensation or $46,000 (for 2008).

Money purchase pension plans. A money purchase plan, as described in Reg. §1.401-1(b)(1)(i), is a defined contribution pension plan requiring fixed and determinable employer contributions to the employee participants' individual accounts, whose amount is not based on profits. Failure to make the mandatory contributions subjects the employer to the Code Sec. 430 excise tax imposed on underfunded plans. Despite the fixed and determinable employer contribution requirement, however, money purchase plans are considered defined contribution plans because employers have some flexibility in choosing the basis upon which the payments are calculated. Usually, the amount of required employer contributions is based on the participant's compensation. However, the contribution amount could be based on other factors, such as length of service. Additionally, the formula for determining contributions can be weighted, allowing certain employees to receive larger contributions than other employees. This is permitted to the extent the allocation does not violate the nondiscrimination rules, as discussed below.

> **COMMENT**
>
> The percentage of employer versus employee contributions to a money purchase pension plan must be determinable. Otherwise, the contribution is not fixed and the plan therefore does not qualify as a money purchase plan.

Profit-sharing plans. Profit-sharing plans, as described in Reg. §1.401-1(a)(2), are defined contribution plans requiring employer contributions based on the amount of the company's profits. Although these plans must provide a definite formula for the allocation of company profits among the participants' accounts, they are considered more flexible than money purchase pension plans and defined benefit plans. This is because, under Code Sec. 401(a)(27), there is no requirement for the *amount* of profits from the business to be shared among plan participants. Furthermore, although the employer contributions are required to be *based* on the amount of profits from the business, contributions can actually be made from the businesses' gross income and are not required to be paid from the employer's current or accumulated profits. Under Reg. §1.401-1(b)(1)(ii), employers and employees can choose among a multitude of options as to when and how benefits are to be paid. Benefits can be paid after a fixed number of years, the attainment of a stated age, or on the prior occurrence of some event such as a layoff, illness, disability, retirement, death, or severance of employment. Benefits may also take the form of annuities, periodic payments, or lump sums. However, in all cases the minimum distribution requirements under Code Sec. 401(a)(9) and the distribution provisions of Code Sec. 401(a)(14), must be fulfilled.

STUDY QUESTIONS

9. If the assets of a defined benefit plan have greater-than-anticipated earnings:

  a. The earnings are divided as pro-rata shares among all plan participants currently receiving distributions

  b. The earnings are held within the plan for future years when earnings may be subpar

  c. The earnings may be invested in the company's stock or used to supplement dividends

  d. The earnings may be withdrawn by the plan's sponsor

---

10. The qualified retirement plan type that requires recurring employer contributions depending on company revenue but has no formula for determining the amount of business profits to be allocated to plan participants is the:

a. Defined benefit plan
b. Money purchase pension plan
c. Shared revenue plan
d. Profit-sharing plan

401(K) PLANS

The popular traditional Code Sec. 401(k) plan, also known as a *cash-or-deferred arrangement,* allows employees to elect a pretax income deferral and contribute that amount to an employer-sponsored plan; rather than receiving payment of those wages when earned. Most employers enhance the annual employee contribution by matching or partially matching employee contributions. Many, if not the majority of, 401(k) plans, call for a mandatory annual employer contribution regardless of employees' level of contributions. Although 401(k) plans may be intended to supplement defined benefit plans, most employers have opted to provide 401(k) plans as the exclusive vehicle in which retirement benefits for employees are provided. In addition, under Code Secs. 401(k)(2)(D) and 410(a)(1)(A), employers cannot deny participation in a 401(k) plan to employees employed less than one year with the company or less than 21 years of age.

> **COMMENT**
>
> Code Sec. 401(k)(1) allows profit-sharing and money purchase plans to also implement cash-or-deferred arrangements while retaining their qualified status. Without a 401(k) arrangement, the employer would have to withhold tax on the employee's deferred compensation and the employee would have to include as income the amount of deferred compensation contributions to the plan. This, in fact, is the situation when employees maintain their own individual retirement arrangements (IRAs) because such individual accounts cannot qualify under Code Sec. 401(a), as they are not . employer sponsored plans.

Although income recognition is deferred for employer-sponsored 401(k) plan employee contributions until the money is withdrawn from the plan, distributions from a 401(k) are taxed under Code Sec. 402(a) as ordinary income (as if they were compensation for current services). Employers can also offer Roth 401(k) plans (described in depth later), under which the tax treatment is reversed; employee contributions are made from after-tax salary, but distributions are tax-free.

Although a 401(k) plan may be a feature of a larger qualified defined contribution plan, in addition to the requirements for defined contribution plans, the 401(k) plan must also satisfy certain other requirements with respect to distributions, eligibility, coverage, nonforfeiture of elective contributions, etc.

Deferral and Contribution Limitations

Despite the higher overall limit for defined contribution plans, employees may not defer more than $15,500 into a 401(k) plan for 2008, under Code Sec. 402(g)(1)(B). Excess contributions are included in the employee's gross income, under Code Sec. 402(g)(1)(A). However, employees aged 50 years or older are allowed to make additional catch-up contributions to the plan of up to $5,000 for 2008 under Code Sec. 402(g)(1)(C).

Employers are generally allowed, but not required, to match the amount of the employee's elective contributions to a 401(k) plan under Reg. §1.401(k)-1(e)(1). Employers can also set up automatic enrollment in a 401(k) plan under Code Sec. 401(k)(13) that automatically contributes a designated portion of the employee's pay (unless the employee opts out) to the plan on his or her behalf.

> **COMMENT**
>
> Code Sec. 401(k)(13), as enacted by the *Pension Protection Act of 2006*, provides an automatic enrollment safe harbor that allows employers to meet the nondiscrimination requirements applied to deferral percentages under Code Sec. 401(k)(3)(A)(ii).

Distributions

Generally, an employer is prohibited by Code Sec. 401(k)(2)(B) from distributing payments from an employee's 401(k) plan until the employee does one of the following:

- Reaches age 50½;
- Dies;
- Becomes disabled; or
- Otherwise severs employment.

Nondiscrimination Requirements for 401(k) Plans

Similar to other qualified retirement plans, a 401(k) plan may not discriminate in favor of more "highly compensated employees." A 401(k) may comply with these nondiscrimination restrictions by satisfying the *actual deferral percentage (ADP) test,* described in Reg. §1.401(k)-2. Plan contributions meet the ADP test if either:

- The percentage of wages deferred by all highly compensated employees for the year is not more than the percentage for all other employees for the year multiplied by 1.25; or
- The excess of the percentage of deferred wages for all highly compensated employees for the year over that for all other employees is not more than two percentage points, and the percentage of deferred wages for highly compensated employees is not more than the percentage for remaining employees, multiplied by two.

EXAMPLE

Fall, LLC, has three different categories of employees, categories A, B, and C, earning $30,000, $15,000, and $10,000, respectively. Fall, LLC, allows employees to contribute up to 10 percent of their compensation to a profit-sharing plan that includes a cash or deferred arrangement (i.e. a 401(k) plan). Employees in category A are highly compensated. For the plan year, employees in category A contribute $1,780, employees in B contribute $750, and employees in C contribute $450 to the 401(k) plan.

As a result, the A employees have an actual deferral ratio of 5.93 percent (1,780 ÷30,000), employees in B have an actual deferral ratio of 5 percent (750 ÷ 15,000), and C employees have an actual deferral ratio of 4.5 percent (450 ÷ 10,000). Although the *actual deferral percentage* for the highly compensated group (employees in category A) is 5.93 percent, the percentage for the nonhighly compensated group is 4.75 percent ((5 percent + 4.5 percent) ÷ 2). Because 5.93 percent is less than 5.94 percent (4.75 percent × 1.25), the first percentage test is satisfied.

The second percentage test is also satisfied because the difference between the deferred wages percentage for the highly compensated group and the other groups is less than two percentage points (5.93 − 4.75 = 1.18) and the percentage for the highly compensated group is not more than twice the percentage of others (5.49 < 4.79 multiplied by 2).

Highly compensated employees, as defined under Code Sections 401(k)(5) and 414(q), include:

- An employee who owned more than 5 percent of the employer (family attribution rules apply) for any time during the year or the preceding years;
- An employee of the company who had annual compensation greater than $105,000 for 2008 (the amount is annually indexed for cost-of-living adjustments); and
- An employee who was in the top-paid group of employees for the preceding year (i.e., the top 20 percent), if the employer elects the application of Code Sec. 414(q)(1)(B)(ii).

A plan that fails to satisfy the ADP test can avoid disqualification by correcting the failure within 12 months after the end of the plan year in which excess contributions were made. But the plan is subject to a Code Sec. 4979 excise tax of 10 percent on any contributions exceeding the nondiscrimination limits if the failure is not corrected within 2.5 months after the end of the plan year. The failure to satisfy the ADP test generally can be corrected by:

- Making qualified nonelective or matching contributions, recharacter- izing the excess contributions so that they are treated as employee con- tributions (and are therefore includable in the employee's gross income) rather than employer contributions; or
- Making a corrective distribution.

EXAMPLE

Excessive contributions by highly compensated employees to a cash or deferred arrangement (a 401(k) plan) allowed by Autumn Manufacturing, Inc., during the plan year result in a violation of the nondiscrimination re- quirements for a qualified retirement plan. The plan year ends on October 1, 2008. If Autumn Manufacturing, Inc., does not remedy this problem by December 15, 2008, it will be subject to the 10 percent Code Sec. 4979 excise tax on the amount by which the contributions exceeded those necessary to meet the ADP test. If the employer does not fix the problem by October 1, 2009, the 401(k) plan will lose its qualification under Code Sec. 401(k)(3) and all tax benefits will end. To fix the problem, Autumn Manufacturing, Inc., could recharacterize some of the highly compensated employees' contributions to the plan as having been contributed by the employees themselves. On the other hand, the corporation could also make more contributions to the plan on behalf of nonhighly compensated employees to meet the ADP test.

Safe Harbor 401(k) Plans

It may be too difficult for some small businesses with a small number of participating employees to fulfill the ADP test. For example, a business having three employees, including the employee-owner, may easily have a qualified retirement plan that fails the ADP test. Although the business owner may perform the majority of the high-level activities, receive a high salary, and expect preferred retirement benefits, the other two employees may perform relatively minor roles in the company and have little concern for retirement benefits. For relief in these instances, Code Sec. 401(k)(12) (B) offers three safe harbors, described here, that automatically allow 401(k) s to fulfill the nondiscrimination requirements.

Contribution requirements. Under the *matching contributions safe harbor,* the employer must make certain matching contributions to the 401(k) on behalf of all nonhighly compensated employees. The amount must match 100 percent of the employee's contributions to the 401(k) plan, up to a maximum of 3 percent of the employee's total compensation, plus 50 percent of the employee's contributions exceeding 3 percent but not more than 5 percent of the employee's compensation.

EXAMPLE

FL Company maintains a cash or deferred arrangement (a 401(k) plan) covering highly compensated employees and others. The highly compensated employees' contributions are excessive and do not meet the ADP test. However, according to the plan agreement, the company provides matching contributions on behalf of all nonhighly compensated employees' elective contributions to the plan. The company contributes amounts to the plan on behalf of nonhighly compensated employees equal to any contributions that are equal to or less than 3 percent of the employee's annual compensation. If the employee contributes amounts exceeding 3 percent, but less than 5 percent, of his annual compensation, the company also contributes half of the amount between 3-5 percent on behalf of the employee. The company does not match contribution amounts exceeding 5 percent of nonhighly compensated employees' income. FL Company has satisfied the safe harbor for the nondiscrimination requirements, even though it violated the ADP test.

Under the *nonelective contributions safe harbor,* 401(k) plans will be deemed to have met the nondiscrimination requirements if the employer simply contributes up to 3 percent of the employees' compensation to the 401(k) plan on behalf of all of its nonhighly compensated employees. No matching *employee* contribution is required.

Finally, a 401(k) plan may also fall within the nondiscrimination safe harbor if the employer makes matching contributions on behalf of the employees using a *formula that is more generous than those previously mentioned.* To qualify, the formula must have a matching rate that does not increase as the participant's rate of contributions increases, and must otherwise be in accordance with the requirements of Code Sec. 401(k)(12)(B)(ii). Also, the matching rate for highly compensated employees must not exceed that for nonhighly compensated employees.

Notice requirements. In addition to the contribution requirements, the Code Sec. 401(k)(12) safe harbor also imposes notice requirements. Participants in a 401(k) safe harbor plan must receive written notice within a reasonable period before any plan year ends, that the employer plans to rely on a safe harbor to fulfill the nondiscrimination requirements. The notice must describe the participants' rights and obligations under the plan.

SIMPLE 401(k) Plans

Small businesses may further reap the advantages of a qualified 401(k) plan with greater flexibility by using a savings incentive match plan (SIMPLE) 401(k), under Code Sec. 401(k)(11). Contributions are deductible by both employer and employee subject to certain limits. Available to employers having 100 or fewer employees, a SIMPLE 401(k) plan is not subject to the nondiscrimination and *top-heavy rules* for qualified plans if all of the following requirements are met:

- Employees can choose to make contributions to the plan as a percentage of their compensation;
- The employer is required to make matching or nonelective contributions to the plan;
- No other contributions can be made to the plan;
- The employer offers no other retirement plans; and
- The employees' rights to benefits vest 100 percent upon contribution.

Similar to a SIMPLE IRA plan, SIMPLE 401(k) plans must meet notification requirements, allow a maximum of $10,500 in annual contributions, and allow a maximum of $2,500 in catch-up contributions (SIMPLE IRAs are discussed later in the chapter.)

Roth 401(k) Plans

Comparison to traditional 401(k)s. Elective employee contributions to a traditional 401(k) plan are generally excluded from gross income at the time they are contributed to the plan. However, employees who make elective contributions to a 401(k) plan can designate some or all of these contributions as Roth contributions under Code Sec. 402A(b), should the employer amend its 401(k) plan to offer this option. *Designated Roth contributions* are includible in gross income at the time they are contributed and when later distributed, are excludable from the recipient's gross income.

> **COMMENT**
>
> Note, however, that contributions to "plain vanilla" (traditional) 401(k) plans and distributions from designated Roth 401(k) plans are both included in the definition of *wages* under Code Sec. 3121(a)(1). Thus, they are both subject to unemployment and Social Security taxes.

Finally, designated Roth contributions must satisfy the basic requirements for contributions made under a traditional 401(k) plan, including the nondiscrimination requirements, and the distributions requirements.

Separate accounting. Employers sponsoring Roth 401(k) plans must maintain a record of the employee's investment in the plan under Reg. §1.402A-2. To accomplish this, Roth contributions and distributions are credited and debited to a designated Roth account maintained for each employee. Gains, losses, and other credits or charges must be separately allocated, on a reasonable and consistent basis, among the designated Roth account and other accounts the employee may have under the retirement plan.

> **COMMENT**
>
> As with contribution limits to traditional 401(k) plans, employees are restricted in their elective contributions to a Roth 401(k) to a maximum of $15,500 for 2008 and up to an additional $5,000 catch-up contribution for employees age 50 or older.

DB/K Plans

The *Pension Protection Act of 2006* created a new type of qualified retirement plan to become available for employers with 500 or fewer employees starting January 1, 2010. The *DB/K plan* (Code Sec. 414(x)) is a combination or hybrid of both the defined benefit and defined contribution concepts. Not only will employees be guaranteed a benefit upon retirement, but also a separate portion of the retirement plan will allow flexibility in contributing to the plan. In addition, the DB/K plan will be exempt from the top-heavy requirements of Code Sec. 416, which should ease the administrative burdens and costs to employers of offering a qualified retirement plan.

Under Code Sec. 414(x), the assets of a DB/K plan must be:

- Held in a single trust;
- Clearly identified; and
- Allocated between the defined benefit and the defined contribution portions of the plan.

> **COMMENT**
>
> In forming a DB/K plan, under Code Sec. 414(x)(7) the defined contribution portion of the plan must have a cash or deferred compensation arrangement.

STUDY QUESTIONS

---

11. Employee elective contributions to a 401(k) plan that are currently included in and not deducted from gross income are:

   a. SIMPLE 401(k) contributions

   b. Traditional 401(k) contributions

   c. Cash-or-deferred arrangement contributions

   d. Designated Roth contributions

12. The _____ is a type of qualified retirement plan that allocates assets between defined benefit and defined contribution portions to enable employers to provide a guaranteed benefit level for employees along with flexibility in making contributions.

   a. Roth 401(k)

   b. DB/K

   c. Safe harbor 401(k)

   d. None of the above is such a hybrid plan

IRA-BASED PLANS

Although employers may successfully add a 401(k) arrangement to defer tax on contributions to a qualified retirement plan, another available type of qualified retirement plan is the individual retirement arrangement (IRA). Available under Code Sec. 408, traditional IRAs are investment accounts or annuities set up to provide tax-deferred returns on investment of employees' retirement savings, similar to 401(k) plans. Contributions to traditional IRAs are fully or partially deductible (based on the employee's income level) and account earnings are not taxed until distributed.

IRAs may comprise the traditional IRA, annuities, bonds, and Roth IRAs. Most accounts are set up by individuals, but employers may also establish and contribute to them for their employees. If an employer sets up IRAs for its employees, it must use a bank to serve as trustee or a nonbank entity or custodial account acceptable to the IRA. The trust is responsible for holding plan contributions in a separate, noncommingled account, investing the funds, and maintaining the accounts/annuities to ensure distributions are available when requested.

Employers can also establish group IRA plans that are treated as IRAs but allow the assets held for many employees to be invested as a single unit. Employers can also offer employees the opportunity to contribute to accounts or annuities maintained by the employer, in addition to the employer's other type of retirement plan. If these accounts satisfy the requirements for traditional IRAs or Roth IRAs, these accounts may be considered "deemed IRAs" under Code Sec. 408(q) (rather than treated as part of the qualified plan) and become subject to most of the IRA rules. Thus, if an employee contributes to a deemed IRA, the amount contributed will reduce the amount that the individual may contribute to his or her own separate IRA not maintained by the employer.

IRA Contributions

Traditional IRAs, similar to other qualified plans, carry many tax advantages. Employee contributions are deductible from gross income, thereby reducing taxable income. The funds may be rolled over into a Roth IRA and other types of retirement plans. Additionally, earnings on these contributions are not taxed until distributed.

> **WARNING**
>
> Rollovers to Roth IRAs from traditional IRAs usually creates recognition of taxable income under Code Sec. 408A.

Until the year in which they reach age $70^1/_2$, individuals can contribute annually and claim deductions up to the lesser of their compensation or an applicable dollar limit ($5,000 for 2008) to a traditional IRA. However, subject to certain gross income restrictions, no such age limitation exists for Roth IRAs.

> **COMMENT**
>
> Employees at least 50 years of age before 2009 may make catch-up contributions for a total of $6,000 to a traditional IRA during 2008, instead of the usual $5,000 maximum contribution applicable to other workers.

Deduction limits. For employees actively participating in other types of qualified retirement plans (such as an employer's retirement plan), Code Sec. 219(g) phases out the traditional IRA deduction as the employee's AGI increases. For 2008, the phaseout range is $53,000 to $63,000 of AGI for individuals and married individuals filing separately. For couples filing jointly with only one spouse participating in a plan, the phaseout range is $159,000 to $169,000, whereas joint filers with two participating spouses are subject to the phaseout between $85,000 and $105,000 of AGI. Married individuals filing separate returns, however, must suffer with a phaseout range of $0 to $10,000 AGI for a right to a traditional IRA deduction.

It should be emphasized that these income caps are keyed to AGI rather than salary so that, for example, someone with large capital gains could be disqualified. Contributions exceeding the annual maximum are subject to an excise tax, unless the employee timely withdraws the excess.

Nondeductible contributions. Individuals who are ineligible to make deductible IRA contributions because they have already participated in an employer's plan and have incomes exceeding the phaseout limits can still make nondeductible contributions to a traditional IRA under Code Sec. 408(o)(2) if the amount they actually contributed is still less than the Code Sec. 219 contribution maximum. Although in these situations the taxpayer claims no deduction, tax is still deferred on the earnings accrued on nondeductible contributions because the original investment was less than the allowed contribution limit. However, should the nondeductible contributions exceed the maximum annual contribution amount, they are subject to the Code Sec. 4973(a) 6 percent excise tax on those excess contributions.

IRA Distributions

Traditional IRAs are subject to restrictions on withdrawals. Generally, account holders can only receive distributions without penalties once they have reached age 59½; otherwise, the Code Sec. 72(t) 10 percent additional tax for early distributions could apply. Yet, under Code Sec. 408(a)(6) and Code Sec. 401(a)(9), distributions must begin when the employee reaches age 70½ under the so-called required minimum distribution (RMD) rules. If less than the minimum required amount (under Code Sec. 401) is distributed, a 50 percent excise tax under Code Sec. 4974 is imposed on the difference between amounts required to be distributed under the RMD rules and amounts actually distributed.

Under Code Sec. 402(c), traditional IRAs may receive rollover distributions directly from other qualified plans. IRA distributions to the participant also can be rolled over into another IRA, and in some situations, into an employer's qualified retirement plan, provided the rollover transactions are completed within 60 days.

COMMENT

Under the newly enacted *Emergency Economic Stabilization Act of 2008*, taxpayers may temporarily make tax-free charitable distributions directly from either a traditional or Roth IRA through December 31, 2009. The maximum contribution limit for 2009 is $100,000. The contribution is generally allowed for organizations described under Code Sec. 170(b)(1)(A), but not for certain private foundations and donor advised funds. Further, no charitable deduction is allowed for any portion of these withdrawals that would have been taxable otherwise. This popular charitable contribution option, created by the *Pension Protection Act of 2006*, had previously expired January 1, 2008.

Simplified Employee Pension (SEP) IRAs

Simplified employee pension (SEP) IRAs, available under Code Sec. 408(k)(1), are highly tax-favorable types of IRAs especially suitable for the small business. SEP IRAs are geared toward smaller employers that may be discouraged by the complexities of establishing a qualified plan or may not have the funds to contribute to qualified plans every year. Under a SEP IRA, the employer agrees to directly contribute to the account of each eligible employee or offer a pretax payroll deduction for contributions to the plan.

Establishing a SEP IRA. A SEP IRA can be established in 2008 as late as the due date of the employer's 2008 federal tax return (including extensions). To establish a SEP IRA, employers must:

- Execute a formal written agreement to provide benefits to all eligible employees;
- Provide certain information about the plan to each eligible employee; and
- Establish a SEP IRA for each eligible employee.

Most employers can use IRS Form 5305-SEP, *Simplified Employee Pension— Individual Retirement Accounts Contribution Agreement,* as the formal written agreement. A copy of the completed form, with its instructions and other information noted in the instructions, must be given to eligible employees. The form requires data regarding the employer as well as the employee, and indicates the tax-free contribution for the year. An employer may draft his or her own SEP form instead of using the prescribed form, although this is rarely done.

Employer funding of the SEP IRA. Unlike a traditional IRA, only employers, not employees, make contributions to an SEP IRA. An employer contributes to a SEP IRA account set up for the individual employee but is not required to make contributions every year under Reg. §1.408-7(c). As with other types of IRAs, tax is deferred on the account's earnings until the employee receives distributions. Any contributions must be allocated among employees according to a written formula and must not discriminate in favor of highly compensated employees. Contributions by an employer in 2008 are limited under Code Sec. 402(h)(2) to the lesser of 25 percent of the employee's compensation or $46,000. Any additional contributions are treated as taxable income but still includible in the SEP IRA.

PLANNING POINTER

Because their contribution limits are differently authorized, SEP IRA contributions are not counted against the annual traditional IRA contribution limit. In other words, a self-employed person could contribute the maximum amounts to both an IRA account and a SEP IRA and claim deductions for the total contributions.

> **COMMENT**
>
> Because they are excluded from the definition of *wages* under Code Sec. 3121(a)(5)(C), contributions to a SEP IRA are generally not subject to Social Security and unemployment taxes. An exception to this rule applies however, if the employee elects to have the employer make a contribution on his or her behalf based upon a percentage of the employee's salary under Code Sec. 408(k)(6). Such an election can only be made for SEP IRAs established prior to 1997.

Savings Incentive Match Plans for Employees (SIMPLE) IRAs

Although an employee elective contribution is not available for SEP IRAs established after 1997, the *savings incentive match plan (SIMPLE) IRA*, available under Code Sec. 408(p), enables employees to elect to have their employers directly make contributions to the employees' accounts by a pre-tax payroll deduction (through a salary-reduction arrangement), rather than funding the plans using after-tax contributions. These plans are even easier to administer than SEP IRAs because they are not subject to nondiscrimination rules or top-heavy rules and involve simplified reporting requirements. Just as with traditional IRAs, the employer is able to immediately deduct its contributions to a SIMPLE account, and income tax for the employee is deferred until contributions and gains are distributed.

Significant size restrictions apply to SIMPLE IRAs, however. The plans are only available to small employers that have 100 or fewer employees (including self-employed individuals) who earned at least $5,000 in compensation during the prior calendar year. Should an employer operate a SIMPLE IRA plan for at least a year but later fail to meet the 100-employee requirement due to a business acquisition, disposition, or similar transaction, a two-calendar-year grace period could apply, during which the employer may continue the plan until it transitions into a more suitable plan structure. The IRS will treat the plan as still meeting the 100-employee participation restriction during the transitional period if coverage under the plan does not change significantly during its duration and the plan would have met the participation limitation had the transaction not occurred.

> **COMMENT**
>
> Similar to a SIMPLE 401(k), the SIMPLE IRA allows employees to defer income tax on earnings in their retirement savings as well as on the actual contributions themselves.

Required employer contributions. However, for all of its ease of administration and welcome tax benefits, unlike funding of traditional IRAs, employers are *required* to make matching contributions of up to 3 percent of the employee's annual compensation or nonelective contributions equal to 2 percent of the employee's annual compensation (the employer must give reasonable notice to employees that it is making an election to use the 2-percent nonelective contribution instead of a matching contribution), under Code Sec. 408(p)(2)(A)(iii)(b). However, as with the traditional IRA, employee contributions to a SIMPLE IRA are limited in amount. For example, for 2008, an employee's contributions may not exceed $10,500.

COMMENT

Catch-up contributions are also available for employees reaching at least age 50 by the end of the year. The maximum catch-up contribution for 2008 is $2,500.

As described in Notice 98-4, the following are contribution deadlines for funding the SIMPLE plan accounts with their financial institutions annually:

- Employers must make salary-reduction contributions before the close of the 30-day period following the last day of the month in which amounts would otherwise have been payable to the employee in cash as compensation; and
- Matching and nonelective employer contributions must be made no later than the due date for filing the employer's income tax return (including extensions) for the tax year that includes the last day of the calendar year for which the contributions are made.

EXAMPLE

FS Corporation, a small manufacturer, sponsors a SIMPLE IRA plan for its employees. FS Corp enters into salary-reduction agreements with its employees, under which contributions will be made on a pretax basis from the employees' compensation. The employees contribute 3 percent of their salary and, according to the SIMPLE IRA arrangement, FS Corp matches these contributions. FS Corporation employees are scheduled to receive their paychecks on March 1, 2009. FS Corp is required to transfer the amounts withheld from this paycheck to the financial institution maintaining the SIMPLE IRA by April 30 (30 days after the end of the March, the month in which the employees would have otherwise received the amounts in cash).

Assume FS Corporation must file its income tax return by April 15, 2010, for the 2009 tax year. It must transfer its matching contributions under the SIMPLE IRA for all employee contributions made during the company's 2009 tax year to the financial institution by April 15, 2010.

Under Code Sec. 408A(f), a SIMPLE IRA may not be *designated* as a Roth IRA, and contributions to a SIMPLE IRA are not taken into account for purposes of determining the Roth IRA contribution limit. Thus, it may be possible to make maximum contributions to *both* types of plans, reaping the tax advantages of both.

Conversion. A SIMPLE IRA may be converted to a Roth IRA on the same terms as a conversion from a traditional IRA. However, any amount distributed from a SIMPLE IRA during the two-year period that begins on the date that the individual first participated in the plan cannot be converted to a Roth IRA under Reg. §1.408A-4 (A-4)(b). A distribution of any amount from an SIMPLE IRA during this two-year period is not eligible to be rolled over into an IRA that is not a SIMPLE IRA. Once an amount in a SIMPLE IRA has been converted to a Roth IRA, however, it is treated as a contribution to a Roth IRA.

> **COMMENT**
>
> Employer matching or nonelective contributions to a SIMPLE IRA are not counted against the annual IRA contribution limit for individuals. Therefore, a self-employed person can contribute the maximum amounts to both an individual IRA account and a SIMPLE IRA (as employer) and claim deductions for the total contributions. Code Sec. 402(g), however, provides that the general contribution annual limit for qualified plans includes the amount of employee salary-reduction contributions to a SIMPLE IRA.

Establishing a SIMPLE IRA. IRS Publication 560 directs taxpayers to use Form 5304-SIMPLE, *Savings Incentive Match Plan for Employees of Small Employers (SIMPLE)—Not for Use with a Financial Institution,* or Form 5305-SIMPLE, *Savings Incentive Match Plan for Employees of Small Employers (SIMPLE)—for Use with a Designated Financial Institution,* to set up a SIMPLE IRA account.

> **COMMENT**
>
> Whether to use the 5304 or 5305 form depends upon whether the employer or the employees will select the financial institution in which to deposit the plan contributions. Form 5304-SIMPLE is used when plan participants choose the financial institution; Form 5305-SIMPLE is used when the employer chooses the financial institution.

Each form is a "model savings incentive match plan for employees" whose completion signifies adoption of the SIMPLE IRA plan. Forms 5304-SIMPLE and 5305-SIMPLE also fulfill the notification requirement employers have to employees and function as records of the plan. IRS Publication 560

(*Notification Requirement*) states that employers are required to notify employees of the following, before the beginning of the plan election period:

- The employee's opportunity to make or change a salary reduction under a SIMPLE IRA plan;
- The employer's choice of either make matching contributions or non-elective contributions;
- A summary description of the plan; and
- Written notice that the employee's balance in the SIMPLE IRA account can be transferred, without cost or penalty, to a designated financial institution.

Roth IRAs

A *Roth IRA* is an IRA that is designated as a Roth IRA at the time it is established under Code Sec. 408A. This variety of IRA is generally subject to the same rules as apply to traditional IRAs. However, Roth IRAs receive reverse tax treatment: contributions to the plan are not deductible from gross income, but most distributions (including contributions and accumulated earnings) are not taxed. As a result, the income earned on the account assets escapes tax, rather than providing a current deduction from income for the initial investment.

Contributions. Roth IRA contributions can be made by taxpayers older than age 70½ under Code Sec. 408A(c)(4), regardless of coverage under an employer's retirement plan, and the original owner is not required to receive distributions during his or her lifetime, as required for the owner of a traditional IRA. Income accrued on Roth contributions is not taxed if it is distributed in a qualified distribution. However, Roth IRA contributions and traditional IRA contributions are limited to a total of $5,000 for 2008.

Rollovers. Prior to December 31, 2007, distributions from qualified plans, other than an IRA plan, could not be rolled over directly to a Roth IRA. A two-step process was required: first qualified distributions were rolled over into a traditional IRA and then the traditional IRA was converted into a Roth IRA.

For tax years beginning after December 31, 2007, thanks to changes to Code Sec. 408A(e) made by the *Pension Protection Act of 2006*, distributions from qualified retirement plans can generally be rolled over directly to a Roth IRA, subject to certain restrictions. This change enables taxpayers to avoid the added cost and hassle of the formerly used two-step process.

> **CAUTION**
>
> For tax years prior to December 31, 2009, a rollover to a Roth IRA will only be allowed if, for the applicable tax year, the taxpayer's AGI does not exceed $100,000 and the taxpayer is not a married individual filing a separate return. But for tax years beginning after December 31, 2009, a taxpayer can convert a traditional IRA to a Roth IRA without regard to his or her income and filing status.

According to Reg. §1.408A-4, Q&A-7, any qualified plan distribution that is converted to a Roth IRA is includable in the taxpayer's gross income, under Code Sec. 408(d), except for any portion that is attributable to a return of basis. The tax on such converted amounts must be paid in tax years in accordance with Code Sec. 408A, as amended. However, pursuant to changes to Code Sec. 408A(d)(3)(a)(iii), as amended by the *Tax Increase Prevention and Reconciliation Act of 2005*, for IRA conversions taking place in 2010, the taxpayer recognizes the conversion amount ratably in AGI in 2011 and 2012, unless the taxpayer elects to recognize it all in 2010.

Table 1 summarizes the features, advantages and drawbacks, and limitations of the major types of qualified retirement plans.

Table 1. Types of Qualified Retirement Plans Compared

Plan Type	Key Features	Advantages	Disadvantages	Limits
Defined Benefit Plans	Required employer contributions according to set formula	Employee is guaranteed benefits	– Requires costly actuarial calculations – Employer bears investment risk – Must meet minimum funding requirements	Maximum contributions of lesser of average compensation over 3 years **or** $185,000
Defined Contribution Plans	Discretionary employer contributions	– Employee bears investment risk – Less administrative costs than defined benefits plans	Must meet non-discrimination and top-heavy rules	Contributions of 100% of annual compensation with a maximum of $46,000
Money purchase plans	Requires fixed and determinable employer contributions	Basis for employer contributions may vary	Same	Same
Profit-sharing plans	Requires recurring and substantial contributions based on profits earned	No required amount of profits to be distributed Contributions must be made per set formula	Same	Same

Plan Type	Key Features	Advantages	Disadvantages	Limits
401(k) Plans	Pretax elective contributions from wages	– Tax is deferred on contributions – and on earnings	Taxable distributions Must meet nondiscrimination requirements through actual deferral percentage test Top-heavy restrictions	$15,500 limit on deferrals $5,000 catch-up contributions for employees aged 50 and older
Safe harbor 401(k)	Required matching employer contributions to 401(k) on behalf of employees	Fulfills nondiscrimination requirements	Additional notice requirements	Same
Savings incentive match plans for employees (SIMPLE) 401(k)	Available to businesses with 100 or fewer employees	Not subject to nondiscrimination or top-heavy rules	Required employer matching contributions	– $10,500 maximum annual contributions – $2,500 maximum catch-up contributions
Roth 401(k)	Election to make taxable contributions to 401(k) with nontaxable distributions	Tax-free distributions	– Nondiscrimination and top-heavy rules – Taxable contributions – Distributions still subject to payroll tax	$15,500 limit on deferrals $5,000 catch-up contributions for employees aged 50 and older
DB/K	Hybrid defined benefits and defined contributions plan	Exempt from top-heavy rules Deferred compensation arrangement allowed	Available after January 1, 2010	Same as defined contributions and defined benefits plans
IRA-Based Plans	Investment accounts or annuities providing tax-deferred return on investments	– Deductions for contributions up to certain limits based upon AGI – Rollovers	– Distributions are generally taxed – Generally subject to top heavy or nondiscrimination rules if employer sponsored	– $5,000 annual contributions until age 70½ – $1,000 catch-up contribution – Required minimum distributions
Simplified employee pension I (SEP) IRAs	Direct employer contributions to employee IRA accounts with no employee contributions	Employer contributions are discretionary and deductible	Same	Employer-only funded
Savings incentive match plans for employees (SIMPLE) IRA	Available to businesses with 100 or fewer employees	– Not subject to nondiscrimination or top-heavy rules – Less paperwork	Required matching employer contributions up to 3% percent of employee compensation	– $10,500 in maximum annual contributions – $2,500 maximum catch-up contributions
Roth IRA	Taxable contributions, tax-exempt distributions with IRA features	– Can make contributions past age 70½ – No required minimum distributions	– Contributions subject to tax – Recognition of income (less basis) on rollovers from traditional IRAs	$5,000 annual contributions past age 70½

STUDY QUESTIONS

13. What is a key difference between a SEP IRA plan and a SIMPLE IRA?

   a. Employers that adopt a SIMPLE plan may have a maximum of 100 employees; there is no size limit for companies sponsoring SEP IRA plans

   b. SEP IRAs require employers to make annual matching contributions; SIMPLE plans do not

   c. SEP IRAs permit deferred vesting of employer contributions; both employer and employee SIMPLE contributions vest 100 percent immediately

   d. None of the above is a difference between the two types of individual retirement arrangement

14. Which of the following is *not* an advantage of Roth IRAs?

   a. Qualified distributions of contributions and earnings are tax-free

   b. Contributions can be made by taxpayers older than age 70½

   c. The original owner of the IRA is not required to receive distributions

   d. All of the above are advantages of Roth IRAs

15. To roll over a traditional IRA account into a Roth IRA in years before 2010, the taxpayer:

   a. May not have an annual adjusted gross income exceeding $15,000

   b. May not use the married, filing separately filing status for federal income tax returns

   c. May not have one or more other qualified retirement plan accounts

   d. All of the above are restrictions on rollovers from traditional to Roth accounts

KEOGH PLANS

Qualified plans for self-employed individuals are known as *Keogh* or *H.R.10 plans*. Individuals who are eligible to establish and participate in these plans are sole proprietors, owners of wholly owned corporations, or partners in a partnership. For purposes of Keogh plans, self-employed individuals do not include "common-law" employees such as corporate officers owning shares of their employer-corporation. Therefore, common-law employees are not allowed to establish Keogh plans.

> **COMMENT**
>
> An important question for determining eligibility to form a qualified retirement plan is, "Who is the employer?" Sole proprietors are treated as their own employer and can sponsor a plan. Sole shareholders of corporations are considered employed by the corporation. In contrast, a shareholder as an employee will not be able to create a Keogh plan.

Because Keogh plans may adopt the structure of any type of qualified retirement plan, such as a defined contribution or defined benefit arrangement, they also adopt the benefits and must meet the same requirements as their specific plan type. However, Keogh plans also have additional restrictions:

- Contributions (also referred to as *annual additions*) to a Keogh plan are subject to the dollar limits of Code Section 415, which are based upon "earned income" as defined under Code Sec. 415(c)(3)(B) and Code Section 401(c)(2);
- Contributions to a Keogh plan must be made from *earned income* as defined under Code Sec. 401(c)(2), which includes the net earnings from compensation received for personal services provided in the self-employed person's trade or business (not investment income); and
- Even if the self-employed individuals can afford contributions to a separate retirement plan established for their employees, the self-employed taxpayers cannot make contributions to their own Keogh plan if they suffer a net self-employment loss.

The owner can receive a lump-sum distribution from the Keogh plan should he or she become disabled. However, the owner cannot receive a lump-sum distribution simply by ceasing to work for the business; either retirement or disability must be the trigger for distribution.

> **COMMENT**
>
> Unlike other employer-sponsored qualified plans, for Keogh plans, contribution limits are based upon compensation that is reduced by any amounts that are deducted for the self-employment tax under Code Sec. 164(f), and by any amounts deducted for employer contributions to a Keogh plan, under Code Sec. 404.

CONCLUSION

As this chapter indicates, there is a plethora of retirement plan options available to smaller employers that are not too difficult or expensive to establish and that offer many tax benefits. Flexibility is the key to minimizing the cost and complexity of creating and maintaining these plans.

Generally, businesses have two options in choosing a qualified retirement plan—a defined benefit plan or a defined contribution plan. Because they do not require actuarial calculations and the investment risk lies mainly upon employees, defined contribution plans are often the choice of businesses. Regardless of which option employers take, plan administrators are responsible for managing the day-to-day affairs of the plan, updating the plan, and correcting plan failures or prohibited transactions.

Of all the available benefit plans, Code Sec. 401 qualified retirement plans are the most tax advantageous and useful for assisting employees in saving for their retirement years. A qualified retirement plan merely requires a written agreement, appropriate disclosures and filings, appropriate administration, and prudent investment of plan assets. Although each of the plan types involves some disadvantages, most plans permit employer deductions of contributions to the plan, within certain limits; many plans permit employees to make pre-tax contributions of deferred compensation up to certain limits; earnings on contributions grow tax-free until distribution; and investments can be rolled over into other types of plans.

Many variations among qualified plan types create flexibility for the small employer. Code Sec. 401(k) plans allow employers to directly withhold pretax contributions to their qualified retirement plan from the employee's paycheck. Beginning in 2010, the new DB/K option will be available to combine defined benefit and defined contribution plans. Alternatively, employers and employees may opt to use one of the types of individual retirement arrangements. The traditional IRA allows investments not only to avoid tax when contributed to the plan but also to provide a return on investment whose tax is also deferred. The Roth IRA, on the other hand, enables an employee to receive tax-free distributions of accumulated plan assets or even to opt never to receive distributions during the contributor's lifetime. Finally, special rules apply to contributions from net earnings for self-employed individuals' Keogh plans.

Because even further options abound within these broad categories, employers are sure to find a retirement plan that will suit both their company's and their employees' needs.

CPE NOTE: When you have completed your study and review of chapters 4 and 5, which comprise Module 2, you may wish to take the Quizzer for this Module.

For your convenience, you can also take this Quizzer online at **www.cchtestingcenter.com.**

Revised Form 990 and Instructions Create New Compliance Challenges for Tax-Exempt Organizations

The IRS has extensively revised Form 990, *Return of Organization Exempt From Income Tax,* the annual information return filed by a majority of tax-exempt organizations. The new Form 990 became effective immediately: organizations will need to fill out the revised form for 2008 (on returns filed in 2009), providing new and enhanced information reporting. This chapter examines the content of the revised Form 990 and its instructions, as well as the disclosure requirements for the new form and other forms filed by exempt organizations. It highlights some of the key reporting areas that have been introduced or changed by the new form and provides insight into the IRS's concerns.

LEARNING OBJECTIVES

Upon completion of this chapter, you will be able to:
- Identify the components of the revised Form 990;
- Contrast features of the previous and revised form;
- Identify key portions of the instructions to the form;
- Describe the requirements for completing various parts and schedules;
- List the filing requirements and transition rules for the revised form; and
- Determine the disclosure requirements for forms and documents filed by tax-exempt organizations.

INTRODUCTION

The nonprofit sector is massive. The IRS has records of approximately 1.3 million public charities (not counting churches), private foundations, and noncharitable exempt organizations. In 2004, organizations filed 364,000 Forms 990 and 142,000 Forms 990-EZ—a total of 506,000 returns. In 2005, exempt organizations owned $2.239 trillion in assets and earned $1.25 trillion in revenue.

Congressional leaders have shown a keen interest in nonprofit organizations in the last several years, sparked by reports of abuses in the nonprofit sector, such as grossly excessive compensation, abusive uses of charitable property, and participation in tax shelters. Also, nonprofits have more frequently placed themselves in competition with for-profit entities that pay taxes on identical services or products. One resulting reform is the redesigned Form 990.

The first draft of the revised Form 990 was released on June 14, 2007. This was followed by a final redesigned form, released December 20, 2007, and a draft of the instructions, released April 7, 2008. The IRS released a revised draft of the instructions on August 19, 2008.

The redesigned form includes an 11-part core form, to be completed by all organizations, and 16 schedules to be completed by different organizations, depending on their category and activities. This is the first significant revision of the form since 1979.

According to the IRS,

> The Form 990 was in need of a major overhaul. It had failed to reflect the changes in the law and the increasing size, diversity, and complexity of the exempt sector. The form no longer adequately served the IRS's tax compliance interests or met the transparency and accountability needs of the states, the public, and communities served by the organizations.

In revising the form, the IRS sought to minimize the burden and enhance transparency while promoting greater compliance and accountability. "The revised form will give the IRS and the public a much better view of how exempt organizations operate," the IRS commissioner said.

COMMENT

Practitioners generally applauded the revision and updating of Form 990. At the same time, filling out the new form will be a huge job. The expanded Form 990 requires much more information than did the prior form. New Form 990 has been met with concern that, in order to show compliance on the new form, organizations first must become compliant with the new requirements. Making new Form 990 effective for tax year 2008 allows organizations that have been casual in their compliance with the technical rules too little time to "get their ducks in a row," some organizations and board members complain.

The IRS also issued detailed instructions for completing the greatly expanded form. The redesigned instructions include line-by-line guidance to the core form and schedules. The IRS explained that it made major changes to the instructions that increase their length but should make it easier for organizations to complete the form. Some of the changes include:

- A glossary of key terms with 176 definitions;
- A sequencing list to help organizations complete the form in order;
- Comprehensive instructions for new reporting requirements, including

governance, foreign activities, hospitals, tax-exempt bonds, and revised reporting of compensation;

■ A compensation table to help organizations determine where and how to report types of compensation; and

■ Appendices with instructions on special topics, such as reporting requirements for group returns.

COMMENT

Due to the large number of changes to the new form and reporting requirements demanded of it, advisors should make sure that their tax-exempt clients are not only aware of the new requirements, but are taking steps immediately to update their systems to capture the information necessary to complete the 2008 returns.

STUDY QUESTION

1. Some exempt organizations object to using the revised Form 990 for their 2008 information returns because:

   a. The updated form will not have detailed instructions available in 2008 for completing Form 990

   b. Making the new Form 990 effective for the 2008 tax year affords the organizations too little time to become compliant

   c. Key terms related to requirements for tax-exempt organization activities are undefined in the new form

   d. Information is lacking for where and how to report types of compensation

REVISED CORE FORM AND SCHEDULES

The following compose the parts and schedules for the revised Form 990:

■ Core Form
  — Part I, Summary
  — Part II, Signature Block
  — Part III, Statement of Program Service Accomplishments
  — Part IV, Checklist of Required Schedules
  — Part V, Statements Regarding Other IRS Filings and Tax Compliance
  — Part VI, Governance, Management, and Disclosure
  — Part VII, Compensation of Officers, Directors, Trustees, Key Employees, Highest Compensated Employees, and Independent Contractors
  — Part VIII, Statement of Revenue
  — Part IX, Statement of Functional Expenses

- Part X, Balance Sheet
- Part XI, Financial Statements and Reporting; and
- Schedules
  - Schedule A, Public Charity Status and Public Support
  - Schedule B, Schedule of Contributors
  - Schedule C, Political Campaign and Lobbying Activities
  - Schedule D, Supplemental Financial Statements
  - Schedule E, Schools
  - Schedule F, Statement of Activities Outside the United States
  - Schedule G, Supplemental Information Regarding Fundraising or Gaming Activities
  - Schedule H, Hospitals
  - Schedule I, Grants and Other Assistance to Organizations, Governments, and Individuals in the United States
  - Schedule J, Compensation Information
  - Schedule K, Supplemental Information for Tax Exempt Bonds
  - Schedule L, Transactions with Interested Persons
  - Schedule M, Non-Cash Contributions
  - Schedule N, Liquidation, Termination, Dissolution or Significant Disposition of Assets
  - Schedule O, Supplemental Information to Form 990
  - Schedule R, Related Organizations and Unrelated Partnerships.

There is no schedule P or Q.

VARIATIONS OF FORM 990

Some organizations may be excepted from filing the new form. For instance, organizations whose annual gross receipts satisfy the dollar threshold amount are not required to file an annual return, but may be required to file an annual electronic notice (e-Postcard). Also, organizations with assets and gross receipts of certain amounts may file Form 990-EZ, *Short Form Return of Organizations Exempt from Income Tax.*

Form 990-N (e-Postcard)

Small tax-exempt organizations having gross receipts of $25,000 or less generally are now required to file Form 990-N, *Electronic Notice (e-Postcard) for Tax-Exempt Organizations Not Required to File Form 990 or 990-EZ.* Small organizations were not required to file annual information return with the IRS before the *Pension Protection Act of 2006* enacted the filing requirement to ensure that the IRS and potential donors have current information about organizations.

> **NOTE**
>
> Starting with the 2010 tax year, the IRS will increase the filing threshold for organizations required to file Form 990-N (the e-Postcard) from $25,000 to $50,000. In 2007, National Taxpayer Advocate Nina Olson called for the threshold to be raised to $50,000 and indexed for inflation because the cost of living has "skyrocketed" since 1982, when the $25,000 amount was established.

Eligibility. Certain organizations are ineligible to file e-Postcards and must file a Form 990 or Form 990-EZ; other nonprofits have no information filing requirement. Ineligible organizations include:

- Private foundations;
- Code Sec. 527 (political) organizations;
- Tax-exempt organizations with annual gross receipts that are normally greater than $25,000; and
- Code Sec. 509(a)(3) supporting organizations that are required to file Form 990 or 990-EZ.

Organizations that are not required to file the e-Postcard include those in a group return, as well as churches, their integrated auxiliaries, and conventions or associations of churches.

Information requested. Each small organization must provide the following information on the e-Postcard:

- Organization's legal name;
- Any other names the organization uses;
- Organization's mailing and website address;
- Organization's employer identification number (EIN);
- Name and address of a principal officer;
- Organization's annual tax year;
- Whether the organization's gross receipts are normally $25,000 or less; and
- Whether the organization terminated operations.

The IRS has created a simple, Internet-based process for filing the e-Postcard, so organization representatives can go to their local library or other public Internet access locales to file the e-Postcard. A completed e-Postcard is filed for free with the IRS by answering a few questions in an online form. There is no paper form. The IRS provides notification of whether an e-Postcard is accepted or rejected.

Failure to file. The first filings for the e-Postcard were due in 2008 for tax years ending on or after December 31, 2007. If an e-Postcard is not filed timely, the IRS will send a reminder notice but impose no penalty. Nevertheless, if an organization fails to file the required e-Postcards for three consecutive years, it will automatically lose its tax-exempt status on the filing due date of the third year. Organizations thus losing their status will have to reapply and pay the appropriate user fee to have their tax-exempt status reinstated.

> **COMMENT**
>
> The new filing requirement for small organizations that previously did not have to file information returns is a mechanism for cleaning up the IRS's master file. Most such organizations the IRS has on file no longer exist or have relocated. The IRS may offer amnesty to small tax-exempts that fail to file an e-Postcard. If an organization can show reasonable cause for failing to file, the IRS has discretion to reinstate the organization's exempt status.

Form 990-EZ

Organizations may file Form 990-EZ, *Short Form—Return of Organization Exempt From Income Tax,* if they meet a profile of having limited gross receipts. The 990-EZ is a four-page form having only seven schedules, which are the same as the schedules from the new Form 990. The form has been slightly revised to incorporate the schedules. Organizations that file the form may have to complete Schedules A, B, C, E, G, L, and N, depending upon the organizations' activities. The form can be filed electronically.

The use of Form 990-EZ will be expanded over a three-year transition period. The form can be used subject to the following conditions:

- For 2008, if gross receipts are less than $1 million and assets are less than $2.5 million;
- For 2009, if gross receipts are less than $500,000 and total assets are less than $1.25 million; and
- For 2010 and later years, if gross receipts are less than $200,000 and total assets are less than $500,000.

STUDY QUESTIONS

> **2.** Small tax-exempt organizations that fail to file the required e-Postcards for three consecutive years will automatically lose their tax-exempt status. ***True or False?***

3. Organizations may use the Form 990-EZ for 2008 if they do not exceed limitations of:

    a. Gross receipts of less than $1 million and assets of less than $2.5 million

    b. Gross receipts of less than $500,000 and total assets of less than $1.25 million

    c. Gross receipts of less than $200,000 and total assets of less than $500,000

    d. Gross receipts of $25,000 and total assets of less than $100,000

DISCLOSURE

Completed Forms 990, 990-EZ, and 990-PF (filed by private foundations) are subject to public scrutiny. Exempt organizations must make Form 990 available to anyone from the general public upon request, whether accessed for charitable giving or general watchdog purposes. Transparency and disclosure are the price organizations pay for tax-exempt status. Without transparency, there is no accountability to the public that nonprofit organizations are serving the public good.

Annual returns for tax years more than three years old do not have to be disclosed. Amended returns must be available for three years after being filed with the IRS. Charities and the IRS must disclose each completed Form 990-T, *Exempt Organization Business Income Tax Return,* filed after August 17, 2006, to report unrelated business income tax (UBIT). This is also a three-year requirement. Form 990-T must be disclosed by organizations, such as churches, that may not have to submit an annual return or an exemption application.

Form 990, Schedule B, Schedule of Contributors, must be disclosed in its entirety by Code Sec. 527 political organizations and by private foundations. For other organizations, the IRS will not disclose names and addresses of contributors. The IRS will not disclose a filer's trade secrets, patents, processes, or styles of work if the organization so requests.

COMMENT

Private foundations are different from public charities because of their narrow base of financial support and control. *Operating foundations,* such as museums, generally conduct their own charitable activities; *nonoperating foundations* provide grants and support to other charities. The majority of foundations are nonoperating. Foundations have income distribution requirements and must pay excise taxes on excess business holdings and other items that do not apply to public charities.

The organization's exemption application on Form 1023, *Application for Recognition of Exemption Under Section 501(c)(3) of the Internal Revenue Code,* used by charities (Code Sec. 501(c)(3) organizations) or Form 1024, *Application for Recognition of Exemption Under Section 501(a),* used for any other tax-exempt status, must be disclosed. The disclosure requirements include any statement or supporting document submitted by the organization or required by the IRS, and any letter issued by the IRS requesting information or approving the organization's tax-exempt status.

The IRS has issued proposed regulations that would require the disclosure of any rulings that deny or revoke an organization's tax-exempt status. The regulations would also require disclosure of IRS technical advice memoranda on the approval of an application, letters that propose to deny exemption where the application is subsequently approved, and letters on an organization's private foundation status.

Appendix D to the core form instructions describes the current requirements for the IRS and the organization to disclose returns and allow their inspection and copying.

CORE FORM: BASIC INFORMATION (PARTS I THROUGH V)

A plethora of information has been incorporated in, deleted from, and moved around on the new Form 990:

- Page 1 is a summary page;
- Activities are described on page 2;
- Pages 3 and 4 consist of questions related to the various schedules;
- Filings of other tax forms are indicated on page 5;
- Governance, policies, and disclosure practices are requested on page 6;
- Pages 7 and 8 discuss compensation;
- Revenue and expenses are recorded on pages 9 and 10; and
- Lastly, page 11 includes a balance sheet.

The core form must be completed by all organizations.

Summary

Part I, Summary, is new and provides certain important information regarding the organization's governance, activities, and current and prior years' financial results. It includes items the IRS wants to analyze first to get a snapshot of the organization. The summary page lists information reported elsewhere on the form, so organizations should defer preparing it until after the other parts of the form are completed.

Signature Block

The signature block in Part II requires the signature of an organization's officer and its paid preparer. The signature block was moved up to the first page to easily determine who signed and prepared the return. Generally, anyone who is paid to prepare the return must sign the return, enter the preparer information, and give a copy of the return to the organization.

Programs

The Statement of Program Service Accomplishments, Part III, records the organization's new, ongoing, and discontinued exempt-purpose accomplishments and related revenue and expenses. The organization's description of its program services was moved to page 2, immediately after the summary and signature. Most of the information required for this part was reported in the old form as well.

Required Schedules

The new Part IV, Checklist of Required Schedules, is a good place to start preparation of the return because it assists reporting organizations in determining which schedules they must submit. The checklist consists of yes or no questions for which each "yes" answer requires the organization to complete the applicable schedule or part of the schedule. All the questions included in the checklist are new.

> **COMMENT**
>
> Organizations are no longer permitted to file freeform attachments; instead, the IRS designates the information it wants by instructing an organization to complete a particular schedule. By eliminating the attachments, the IRS ensures organizations are in compliance with the tax laws.

Other Filings

Part V, Statements Regarding Other IRS Filings and Tax Compliance, considers the reporting organization's compliance with other federal tax reporting and substantiation requirements. It is a compliance list of questions. Many of the questions were included in the previous form, but some are new. For example, there are additional questions pertaining to backup withholding, employment tax, and deductible contributions.

STUDY QUESTIONS

4. Which of the following is **not** required to be available for three years after being filed?
   a. Schedule B, Schedule of Contributors
   b. Form 990-T, *Exempt Organization Business Income Tax Return*
   c. Form 990-PF for private foundations
   d. All of the above are required to be available for three years after filing

5. In which part of the core form would IRS personnel and potential contributors look on an organization's Form 990 to discern what activities a tax-exempt organization conducted and what its accomplishments were for 2008?
   a. Part II
   b. Part III
   c. Part IV
   d. Part V

6. Small tax-exempt organizations filing Form 990 or Form 990-EZ may use freeform attachments for their 2008 returns. **True or False?**

FINANCIAL OPERATIONS

Items on the revised return request detailed information relating to the organization's finances. The IRS wants to ensure that organization funds are appropriately accounted for and that such funds are used to further the organization's exempt purposes.

Revenue (Part VIII, Schedules G and M)

The new form requests information regarding the same types of revenue as the old form did. Revenue amounts are entered in Part VIII, Statement of Revenue. There are different splits of revenue: other revenue, program service revenue, and miscellaneous revenue. In addition, contributions have been broken out into various types, including:

- Fundraising events;
- Membership dues;
- Federated campaigns;
- Related organizations
- Government grants; and
- Any other contributions.

Fundraising or gaming. Schedule G, Supplemental Information Regarding Fundraising or Gaming Activities, collects information about expenses for professional fundraising, as well as revenue from special events and gaming activities. Some of the information in Schedule G was requested in the previous form, but most filers neglected to submit such information. Organizations that have more than $15,000 in fundraising and gaming expenses must file Schedule G. In addition, if an organization had a professional fundraising agreement with an officer, director, trustee, or key employee, it must list the 10 highest-paid individuals or entities that were each paid at least $5,000 by the organization for professional fundraising services.

COMMENT

The IRS has split up the reporting of gaming and fundraising expenses. Gaming activities are of great interest to the state taxing authorities. The IRS is also interested in learning more about gaming activities.

Noncash contributions. Organizations with more than $25,000 of aggregate noncash contributions must complete Schedule M, Non-Cash Contributions. The schedule applies to charities and noncharities. For any contribution received, the organization has to provide the number of contributions and method of determining the properties' revenues.

Functional Expenses (Part IX)

Part IX, Statement of Functional Expenses, gathers information regarding the total expenses of filing organizations. This part looks similar to the previous form, but there are some slight changes. The IRS has further broken out the different services performed by independent contractors. Organizations must record fees charged by outside firms or individuals for management, legal, accounting, lobbying, professional fundraising, investment management, and other services, respectively. Organizations also have to report, among other items, advertising and promotion expenses, as well as amounts for royalties and information technology.

Balance Sheet (Part X, Schedule D)

All organizations must account for their assets, liabilities, and net assets or fund balances in Part X, Balance Sheet.

Part X:

- Separates program related investments from other investments;
- Combines the reporting of land, equipment, and buildings;
- Lists intangible assets as a separate line item; and
- Eliminates the freeform attachments required by the previous form.

> **COMMENT**
>
> Valuation of investments takes place at the close of the tax year; it is not the average investment value throughout the year. For many exempt organizations with calendar years or years closing after August 2008, valuations because of the precipitous drop in the equities markets in the latter months of 2008 must be reflected, irrespective of the organization's otherwise solid portfolio at the start of its 2008 tax year.

Schedule D, Supplemental Financial Statements

The financial information requested in the freeform attachments is now reported in the new Schedule D. It standardizes additional details needed for certain balance sheet information of organizations. There are new disclosure requirements regarding donor advised funds, escrow or custodial arrangements, and uncertain tax positions (FIN 48).

Donor advised funds. The instructions for Schedule D provide criteria for donor advised funds. A donor advised fund is a fund or account: that is separately identified by reference to contributions of a donor or donors; that is owned and controlled by a sponsoring organization; and for which the donor or donor advisor has or reasonably expects to have advisory privileges in the distribution or investment of amounts held in the donor advised funds or accounts because of the donor's status as a donor.

Trust, escrow, and custodial arrangements. An organization that acts as an agent, trustee, custodian, or other intermediary for funds payable to other organizations or individuals, must report the amount of such funds in Schedule D, if not reported elsewhere in the form. Increases or decreases in such accounts must be recorded as well.

> **COMMENT**
>
> Consumer credit counseling agencies and down payment assistance programs tend to have escrow or custodial arrangements that the IRS views as abusive. Organizations that have such arrangements need to pay careful attention to what is reported and provide appropriate disclosures elsewhere in the form.

FIN 48. In Schedule D, organizations are required to account for liabilities for uncertain tax positions under FIN 48 and provide the text of the footnote to its financial statements, if applicable. Any portion of the FIN 48 footnote that addresses only the filing organization's liability must be provided verbatim. Any portion of a footnote that applies to the liability of multiple organizations, including the organization, may be summarized, to describe the filing organization's share of the liability.

> **COMMENT**
>
> The IRS is focused on reviewing the disclosures required by FIN 48. Even though the IRS has received numerous comments regarding the FIN 48 footnote, it is not likely to eliminate the requirement.

Financial Statements and Reporting (Part XI)

Part XI of the form is new and contains questions regarding disclosure of financial statements. The IRS is interested in the filing organization's accounting methods and its compiled, reviewed, or audited financial statements. Organizations must indicate the method of accounting used in preparing the return. Organizations must also indicate whether its financial statements for the reporting period were compiled, reviewed, or audited by an independent accountant or an organizational committee.

> **COMMENT**
>
> The IRS has moved all the financial information to the back of the form and all the disclosures to the front. The accounting method was on the first page of the previous form.

Public Charity Status and Public Support (Schedule A)

The former Schedule A, which asked for information on a variety of subjects, has been revised and separated into various parts of four schedules. Schedule A now addresses reporting by charities of their public charity status (Part I) and public support (Parts II and III). Publicly supported charities must complete Schedule A unless they fall into a specific category such as a church, school, or hospital.

Schedule A modifies the public support test by increasing the testing period from four to five years, including the current year, and allows organizations to report support using their method of accounting, not specifically the cash method. This will require accrual-basis organizations to restate amounts reported for 2007 and prior years on the cash basis. Otherwise, support is calculated in the same manner as it was in prior years.

The IRS has eliminated advance rulings and Form 8734, *Support Schedule for Advance Ruling Period.* Instead, an organization will qualify as a public charity for its first five years if it can show a charitable purpose and that it expects to meet the public support test, regardless of the level of actual support it receives during the five years.

> **COMMENT**
>
> Practitioners welcomed the elimination of the advance ruling process and the IRS's granting of exemption in a final ruling letter for the first five years. After five years, the IRS can use Schedule A to evaluate the organization's support status for subsequent years.

Schedule of Contributors (Schedule B)

The information requested in Schedule B, Schedule of Contributors, is the same information that was requested in the previous form. Schedule B is to be completed by organizations that receive charitable contributions of $5,000 or more from a single contributor and report them as revenues. The special rules are still allowed, which apply to contributions exceeding $1,000 to Code Sec. 501(c)(7), (8), and (10) organizations. One of the biggest changes is that *persons* now includes government contributors, according to the instructions.

Liquidation, Termination, Dissolution, or Significant Disposition of Assets (Schedule N)

Schedule N is used by an organization to report information relating to going out of existence or disposing of more than 25 percent of its net assets. The schedule requests, among other items, identifying information on the:

- Assets distributed or transaction expenses paid;
- Date and fair market value of the distribution or expenditure;
- Fair market value of the asset or expense; and
- Method of valuation.

Also requested on Schedule N is information about the involvement (governing, owning, or working) of an officer, director, trustee, or key employee in a successor or transferee organization.

> **COMMENT**
>
> The previous form required information on a *significant disposition* of assets. This led to uncertainty and inconsistent reporting. The 25-percent threshold should resolve these problems.

STUDY QUESTIONS

---

7. Schedule G of the revised Form 990 requires a nonprofit organization having a professional fundraising agreement with officers, directors, trustees, or key employees to list the _____ highest-paid individuals or entities that the organization paid at least _____for professional fundraising services.

   a. 5; $2,000
   b. 10; $5,000
   c. 20; $10,000
   d. 25; $25,000

8. To qualify as a public charity, an organization obtains an advance ruling from the IRS and uses Form 8734 to assess whether it meets the public support test. *True or False?*

9. Schedule N now requires filers to provide information whenever a disposition of at least _____ of a nonprofit organization's net assets occurs.

   a. 10 percent
   b. 25 percent
   c. 50 percent
   d. 75 percent

PROGRAMS OF EXEMPT ORGANIZATIONS

The revised Form 990 solicits data for a more complete picture of an exempt organization's programs and activities that fulfill its exempt purposes. Every exempt organization must report this information. The description starts with the Summary on the core form, in which organizations briefly describe their mission and most significant activities, and continues with a more complete description on Part III of the core form. Grants and assistance to U.S. and foreign persons must be described, as well as other foreign activities. Conservation contributions and artistic and historical items must be specifically reported.

Statement of Program Service Accomplishments (Core Form, Part III)

Part III requires a description, in a narrative format, of mission, program services and accomplishments, and changes in program services. A *program service* is an activity that accomplishes the organization's exempt purpose. This part generally requests information that was on the 2007 form, although it was moved forward to page 2 of the 2008 form. Part III requires a description of the organization's three largest program services, based on expenses. Organizations may report additional activities on Schedule O, Supplemental Information to Form 990, that they consider of comparable or greater importance, even if expenses are smaller.

The revised form expands the 2007 form by asking for a description of significant changes in activities: new and discontinued programs, and changes in the conduct of programs.

Charities, social welfare organizations, and trusts must also report revenue from the activity that is included on Part VIII, Statement of Revenue, and grants and other assistance made because of the activity. Grants received are not counted as revenues. Expenses and grants should also be entered on Part IX, Statement of Functional Expenses. Total program service expenses must be included on Part III. The form asks for an activity code, but this code is not being used for 2008. The IRS may amend the instructions to require activity codes for later years.

> **COMMENT**
>
> The IRS asked for details of program services, including specific measurements such as clients served or days of care provided. The instructions say to be concise *and* complete. However, a public interest law firm exempt as a charity or social welfare organization is required to include a list of all cases litigated during the year, a description of the matters in dispute, and an explanation of the benefit of the cases to the public.

Conservation Easements, Art Collections (Schedule D, Schedule M)

Schedule D, Supplemental Financial Statements, requires reporting by conservation organizations that hold easements and by museums and other organizations that maintain art collections, historical treasures, or similar assets. Easements can be for open space, recreation, the environment, historic lands, or historic structures (facades). An easement must be in perpetuity.

The reporting of conservation easements has been revised from 2007. Part II of Schedule D asks for information on the bona fides of the easements:

- Number of easements and total acreage;
- Number of easements modified, transferred, or terminated;
- Number of states where easements are located; and
- Policies and actions to monitor, inspect, and enforce easements.

The reporting of collections in Part III of Schedule D is new. Organizations must separately report assets and revenues of art and treasure that are held for public exhibition, education, or research and those that are held for financial gain. Alternatively, as allowed by accounting practice, items held for exhibition, education, or research may be reported as a footnote to the financial statement and reiterated on Schedule D. Organizations must describe their collections and explain how the collections contribute to their exempt purpose. Part III also asks whether items are solicited or donated to raise funds.

> **COMMENT**
>
> The IRS reported that items in Parts II and III will increase the record-keeping and reporting burden for organizations significantly involved in these activities. Both conservation easements and art valuation for tax purposes have been hotbeds of abuse, according to various IRS reports. The Senate Finance Committee revealed extensive abuses of conservation easement donations, including easements that lacked substance and easement-encumbered property being sold at a discount to favored purchasers. Recent legislation has tried to rein in façade easement abuses and overvaluation of charitable contributions of art works, among other abuses. The IRS is intent on attacking these issues on both sides of the transactions: on the donor end and from the perspective of the exempt organizations that facilitate them.

Part VIII of Schedule D reports Program-Related Investments. These are investments to accomplish the organization's exempt purpose, such as student loans, rather than produce income. Part VIII asks for listings of each type of program-related investment, its book value, and the organization's method of valuation (cost or end-of-year market value).

Schedule M, Non-Cash Contributions, is new. It must be completed if the organization received more than $25,000 in noncash contributions during the tax year, as reported on its Statement of Revenue (Core Form, Part VIII) or if it received any contributions of art, historical treasures, or qualified conservation items. Historical artifacts, scientific specimens, and archaeological artifacts are also reported. The instructions define *art, historic treasures,* and other terms. *Qualified conservation contributions* include easements and other interests in real property. *Nonqualified easements* are reported separately as "other property."

The form requires reporting of the number of contributions, the revenue included on the organization's statement of revenue, and the method of determining the revenue. Organizations can report the number of items instead of the number of contributions. A gift of stock is one item. No revenue has to be reported for museum-type collections and conservation contributions.

STUDY QUESTIONS

---

10. All of the following data-gathering tools related to reporting programs and activities of exempt organizations were created for the revised Form 990 *except:*

   a. Part III of Schedule D for reporting collections

   b. Part III of the core form for reporting the organization's program services

   c. Schedule M, Non-Cash Contributions

   d. All of the above are new parts of the core form or a schedule

11. Nonqualified conservation easements are reported:

   a. Separately as "other property" on Schedule M of Form 990

   b. Together with qualified conservation contributions on Schedule M of Form 990

   c. On Part VIII of Schedule D of Form 990

   d. None of the above is the part of the core form or schedule on which nonqualified easements are reported

---

Statement of Activities Outside the United States (Schedule F)

Schedule F is new. The 2007 form did not request much information about foreign activities. The focus is on grant making, although organizations that raise funds, operate a business, and conduct program activities must also file Schedule F. Grants include awards, stipends, scholarships, fellowships, research grants, and noncash assistance.

Requirements include the following:

- Any organization with more than $10,000 in revenue or expenses from foreign activities must complete Part I of Schedule F;
- Ones having more than $5,000 in grants or assistance to any foreign organization or entity (including governments) must complete Part II; and
- Organizations having more than $5,000 in total grants or assistance to individuals must complete Part III.

Foreign individuals include U.S. citizens and residents living outside the United States when the grant is paid. Branches and employees of the organization located outside the United States are not foreign, but an affiliate that is a separate legal entity is foreign. U.S. commonwealths and territories are not foreign.

Part I asks organizations to report foreign activities, including the number of offices and employees, as well as activities and total expenditures. Part I also asks whether the organization has records of its grants, including selection criteria. Parts II and III inquire about each grant by recipient. The form asks for a description in Part IV of how the organization monitors the use of expenditures and grants. To preserve security, names of foreign entities and individuals do not have to be disclosed.

Each part asks for the region in which the activity occurred. The instructions divide the world into nine regions.

> **COMMENT**
>
> Large organizations have complained about the burden of the new Schedule F reporting requirements. The IRS responded that the $10,000 threshold may eliminate the need for small organizations to report their activities in Part I.

STUDY QUESTION

> **12.** For purposes of Schedule F's Statement of Activities Outside the United States, which of the following is *not* considered to be a grant?
>
> **a.** Noncash assistance
> **b.** Scholarships
> **c.** Stipends
> **d.** All of the above are included in the definition of *grants* for new Schedule F

Grants and Assistance (Domestic)
(Schedule I; Core Form, Parts I, IX)

Schedule I continues the reporting of grants and assistance from the 2007 form. The reporting of these payments has been extended to Line 14 of Part I (Summary) of the core form and continues on Lines 1 through 3 of Part IX of the core form. Part IX, the Statement of Functional Expenses, asks for grants and other assistance to:

- U.S. governments and organizations;
- U.S. individuals; and
- Any of these recipients outside the United States.

All organizations must report total expenses in Part IX for each category. Charities and social welfare organizations also must report program service expenses. Program services are mainly those activities that further the organization's exempt purposes. Program services can also be part of the organization's unrelated trade or business activities, such as articles in a magazine that also contains advertising.

Parts II and III of Schedule I are similar to those of the 2007 form. They require information on cash grants and noncash assistance to governments, organizations, and individuals in the United States. Amounts to organizations and governments only have to be reported if they exceed $5,000 per recipient. Amounts to individuals are reportable if the total for all recipients exceeds $5,000. Like Schedule F, the form asks whether the organization has records of its grant making and requests a description of its procedures to monitor the use of grant funds. Unlike Schedule F, organization and government-funded recipients must be identified.

GOVERNANCE (CORE FORM, PART VI)

The IRS believes that a well-governed organization is more likely to obey the tax laws, safeguard charitable assets, and serve charitable interests than an organization with poor governance. Although federal tax law generally does not mandate particular management structures, operational policies, or administrative practices, it is important that each organization be thoughtful about the governance practices that are most appropriate for it in ensuring sound operations and compliance with the tax law. With this bar in mind, the IRS created Part VI, Governance, Management, and Disclosure, which records information regarding the organization's governing body and management, policies, and disclosure practices.

> **COMMENT**
>
> Federal tax law does not mandate governance requirements. As a result, some organizations may feel they do not have to expend effort in governance or spend limited resources filling out the questions. However, many donors will examine these questions, because the return is a public document, and donors may stop contributing if an organization omits the requested information. Board members, especially those who volunteer their services, are also becoming more concerned that governance reporting will eventually result in increased liability on their part.

Governing Body

According to the IRS, governing boards should be composed of persons who are informed and active in overseeing an organization's operations and finances. Successful governing boards include individuals who are engaged and knowledgeable. The IRS emphasizes that the size of the board should be appropriate to ensure that the organization conducts itself properly. Regardless of size, the IRS believes a governing board should include independent members.

Number of voting members. Organizations must indicate the number of board members with the power to vote on all matters as of the end of the organization's tax year. If members of the board do not all have the same voting rights, material differences must be explained. In addition, the number of independent voting members of the organization's board must be reported. For members to be independent, they cannot:

- Be compensated as an officer or employee of the organization or a related organization;
- Receive more than $10,000 in their capacity as independent contractors from the organization or a related organization; and
- Have transactions reported on Schedule L from/for the organization or a related organization.

> **COMMENT**
>
> The governance section asks whether a copy of the form (including schedules) as filed with the IRS was provided to each voting member of the organization's board, prior to being submitted. It also requests that an organization describe the process, if any, by which any of the organization's officers, directors, trustees, board committee members, or management reviewed the form, including specific details about the review.

Relationships. Family or business relationships among officers, directors, trustees, or key employees must be disclosed. The instructions explain what are business and family relationships. Adopted children are included in the definition of family and three criteria are used in determining whether there is a business relationship.

> **COMMENT**
>
> *Reasonable efforts* is the phrase being used by the IRS in response to questions from organizations about how to determine the independence of board members. The IRS has informed organizations that they need not engage in more than a reasonable effort to obtain the necessary information. Organizations are expected to send out an annual questionnaire to their members and may rely on the information provided by the members. An organization is not required to provide information about a family or business relationship if it is unable to secure the information. However, the failure to provide such information could be a basis for dismissal of a board member.

Outsourcing management. The IRS wants to know whether the board is actually managing the organization or has hired an outside management company to take on such duties. Organizations have to disclose whether they have an absentee board of governors. Donors are interested in this information as well.

Management Policies

An organization's information return will be reviewed by the IRS to determine whether it has implemented various policies. The agency asks whether an organization has whistleblower, joint venture, document and destruction, and conflict of interest policies, as well as policies governing the organization's chapters, branches, or affiliates.

Organizations that have implemented a conflict of interest policy must describe how the policy is monitored and enforced. The organization must indicate whether the policy requires the organization to evaluate joint ventures to ensure the organization's tax-exempt status is protected, and whether the organization has taken steps to protect its status.

Transparency

The IRS encourages organizations to make publicly available its mission, activities, and finances to provide transparency and accountability to it constituents. Filing organizations must state how they publicize certain documents whose disclosures are required by law. An organization must also state whether and how it makes other documents (not required to be disclosed) available to the public.

STUDY QUESTION

13. Schedule M for Form 990 is required for the 2008 reporting period if organizations:

  a. Received more than $10,000 total cash contributions during the 2008 period
  b. Received more than $25,000 in noncash contributions during the 2008 reporting period
  c. Are accountable for than $5,000 in unrelated business income tax (UBIT) for 2008
  d. Are subject to all of the above thresholds

COMPENSATION (CORE FORM, PART VII, SCHEDULES J, L, R)

As the charitable and nonprofit sector grows, the funds it controls and income generated annually have mushroomed into trillions of dollars. Charitable organizations are making large payments of compensation and providing huge benefits to their top employees. Congress has focused a spotlight on these compensation arrangements as a device for using charitable dollars to benefit the organizations' top officials and contributors.

> **COMMENT**
>
> The IRS has picked up on this concern. "Accurate and complete reporting of executive compensation by exempt organizations has been a concern of the IRS and the public," the IRS stated in its Background Paper discussing the changes to Form 990. "In the past, there has been a lack of uniformity and considerable confusion regarding how, when, and where to report various types of compensation."

The IRS has revised and expanded the reporting of compensation and benefits. The IRS stated that "additional compensation information is needed to more effectively administer the laws regarding inurement, exempt purpose, and private benefit." The form also requires separate reporting of transactions between the organization and its top officials.

> **COMMENT**
>
> "There is no more sensitive topic than the disclosure of compensation on the 990," explained Sarah Elizabeth Hyre, a CPA specializing in nonprofit organizations with Clark Nuber P.S., at a July 2008 CCH seminar.

Expanded Compensation Reporting

"The new form [990] dramatically changes the reporting of executive compensation by exempt organizations and their related organizations," the IRS stated. Reporting of compensation paid to the five highest compensated employees (HCEs) and five independent contractors has been extended from Code Sec. 501(c)(3) charities to all tax-exempt organizations that file the annual Form 990, such as social welfare organizations, business leagues, trade associations, and social clubs. The information must be reported on Part VII of the core form. The definitions and requirements for who must be reported have been substantially revised. More detailed compensation information must be reported on new form Schedule J, Compensation Information, to Form 990, as well as information on the organization's compensation practices and arrangements.

Other compensation matters are reported on Part VI and Schedule L. Part VI of the core form, Governance, Management and Disclosure, considers whether members of the board (the *governing body*) are independent. One factor is whether the person or a family member has an employment or independent contractor relationship with the organization or a related organization. Another factor is whether the board member is involved in a transaction or relationship that would be reportable on Schedule L, Transactions with Interested Persons. Other questions on Part VI ask about the possible misuse of assets.

> **COMMENT**
>
> One practitioner told CCH that it will be "essential" to use a flowchart approach to determine what is reported on different forms. There will be a learning curve for reporting organizations that will become critical for accurate and consistent reporting across the tax-exempt sector.

The IRS aimed, in the compensation instructions, to provide more certainty and objectivity in reporting executive compensation. For example, the instructions define *key employee* uniformly for:

- Reporting compensation on Part VII of the core form and Schedule J;
- Reporting loans, grants, and business transactions on Schedule L; and
- Part VI, Governance, on the core form.

Who and What?

The key compensation questions asked by the revised form are who and what, practitioners say. To begin ascertaining *who* must be reported, organizations should make determinations under Schedule R, Related Organizations and Unrelated Partnerships, and cross-reference the results with Part VII, Section A, of the core form. Compensation to a reporting organization's employees for services to that organization includes compensation paid by a related organization.

Related organizations include organizations that are more than 50-percent owned by the taxpayer organization, parent-subsidiaries, brother-sister, and supporting-supported organizations. If the organizations do not have owners, control in a *parent-subsidiary relationship* means the power to remove and replace a majority of the other organization's directors or trustees, or an overlap in which a majority of the subsidiary's directors/trustees are directors, trustees, officers, employees, or agents of the parent organization. A *brother-sister relationship* requires that the same persons be a majority of the governing body of both organizations.

> **COMMENT**
>
> A disregarded entity that is 100-percent owned, although reported separately on Schedule R, is treated as part of the reporting organization and not as a separate, related entity on other parts of Form 990.

ODTKEs on Part VII

The reporting of compensation on Section A has led to a new acronym—ODTKE: officers, directors, trustees, and key employees. Reporting is required of the ODTKE, the five highest compensated employees (HCEs), the five highest paid independent contractors, and individuals who were an ODTKE or HCE in any of the five previous years.

The instructions define who is an ODTKE. One category is an officer, whether elected or appointed, that manages the organization's daily operations. Top management officials who are not identified as officers must be treated as officers, including the top executive official and the top financial official.

Advisory board members are not officers or trustees unless they have governing powers. A trustee can be an institution, and employees of an institutional trustee can include key employees.

Key employees. Key employees are individuals who are not officers, directors, or trustees and who satisfy three criteria:

- Compensation test: They receive "reportable compensation" (Form W-2) from the organization and related organizations exceeding $150,000 for the calendar year;
- Responsibility test: They have power similar to an officer or director; manage a discrete activity that is 10 percent or more of the organization's activities, assets, income, or expenses; or have (or share) authority to control or determine at least 10 percent of the capital or operating budget or employee compensation; and
- They are among the organization's 20 highest-paid persons (aside from an HCE).

COMMENT

The revised definition of *key employee* will narrow the number of reportable employees by requiring organization-wide control or influence, or control of at least 10 percent of the organization, although some practitioners had asked that the standard be raised to 15 or 20 percent.

COMMENT

The 20-person limitation for key employees is a helpful cutoff, practitioners said.

STUDY QUESTION

14. All of the following are criteria determining who qualifies as a key employee for Form 990 reporting purposes *except:*

   a. Being one of the 20 highest paid persons other than highly compensated employees (HCEs) of the organization
   b. Powers and management authority under the responsibility test
   c. Reportable calendar year compensation exceeding $150,000
   d. All three are criteria of key employees

Others reportable. Other categories are the top five HCEs and the top five independent contractors (ICs) who are not ODTKEs. These are new reporting requirements for noncharities. An HCE or top IC has to be paid more than $100,000 in reportable compensation or fees. In previous years, the threshold for HCEs and ICs was $50,000. An IC can be an organization as well as an individual and must be listed on Part VII, Section B.

Individuals who were formerly in one of these categories (except for independent contractors) in the last five years must also be reported in Section A of Part VII. A former director or trustee must have earned over $10,000. Under a transition rule for 2008, noncharities do not have to report former HCEs.

Compensation. The instructions have a multipage table that lists whether various types of compensation should be treated as base compensation or other compensation, which must each be reported separately on Part VII and Schedule J. A helpful matrix identifies which categories of employees and other service providers must be reported on Part VII and Schedule J. Compensation from related organizations must be reported separately for Part VII and Schedule J.

> **COMMENT**
>
> The Schedule J instructions provide extensive clarification of reportable compensation (that is, wages) and other compensation, practitioners said. All compensation should be reported for the individual. The employer should not separate officer compensation from employee compensation. The amounts should be explained on Schedule O.

Part VII details. Section A requires that ODTKEs and HCEs be listed in a specific order: directors and trustees, officers, key employees, HCEs, and former such persons.

> **COMMENT**
>
> Tracking "formers" will be difficult, practitioners say. Individuals may drop off the current list but still be reportable as a former, such as a former board member.

To preserve privacy, Column A requires name and title but no address for those listed. Column D, reportable compensation, comprises Medicare wages on Box 5 of Form W-2 or Box 7 of Form 1099-MISC. Reportable compensation of less than $10,000 from a related organization does not have to be reported. Fiscal year taxpayers can no longer elect to use amounts paid during the fiscal year. Instead, all taxpayers must use the Forms W-2 or 1099 for the calendar year that ends with or within the fiscal year.

> **COMMENT**
>
> The wage compensation reported on Part VII may not match amounts reported on the functional expense statement (Core Form, Part IX) for ODTKEs or disqualified persons, but there is no requirement to reconcile them. Fiscal year organizations do not favor using Form W-2, because the employee's year and the organization's tax year do not line up, practitioners said. The IRS commented that the use of annual reporting forms would simplify reporting and make it more objective.

Other compensation reported in Column F includes nontaxable fringe benefits, the actuarial increase in value of a qualified or nonqualified defined benefit plan (even if unfunded or nonvested), and the value of health benefits. Other compensation from either the reporting organization or a related organization does not have to be reported if it is under $10,000. However, deferred compensation and health benefits must be reported even if they total less than $10,000.

Compensation Information (Schedule J)

Schedule J, Part I, asks questions about compensation practices. Question 2, concerning substantiation before reimbursement, is a "best practice" that should be instituted by organizations, ideally by the end of 2008. Question 3 asks how compensation was set for the organization's head. Although it lists an independent compensation consultant, this is not required, practitioners say. Questions 5 through 8 ask for descriptions of potential excess benefits subject to intermediate sanctions.

Part VI of the core form (Governance, Management, and Disclosure) also asks questions about compensation practices, among other issues. Question 15 asks whether the organization used practices that are necessary to establish a rebuttable presumption of reasonableness under Code Sec. 4958. It overlaps with Question 3 of Schedule J.

Part VII of the core form has trigger questions that require reporting on Schedule J. Filing Schedule J is required for the former ODTKEs and HCEs, for anyone with total compensation greater than $150,000 on Schedule A, and for persons receiving compensation from an unrelated organization for services to the reporting organization.

> **COMMENT**
>
> The IRS stated that exempt organizations have arranged for compensation from unrelated organizations to avoid reporting thresholds on the Form 990. The revised Form 990 requires reporting of any compensation from an unrelated organization.

Schedule J, Part II, asks for details of amounts included on the Form W-2. Column D is looking for nontaxable benefits such as dependent care assistance or educational assistance. Column F asks for the prior year's compensation reported for a discrete ODTKE, not just amounts in functional expenses. Columns E and F compare current and prior year compensation.

> **COMMENT**
>
> Organizations should consider explaining any large differences, practitioners say.

Transactions with Interested Persons (Schedule L)

The new form revises the reporting of transactions between an exempt organization and *interested persons,* as defined in the instructions. The information must be described in new Schedule L, Transactions with Interested Persons. Loans, grants, and other financial assistance, and business transactions involving interested persons also must be reported. The instructions define business transactions as a sale, lease, license, or performance of services. Schedule L requires information to be listed for 2008 that in 2007 was reported on freeform (unstructured) attachments.

Excess benefit transactions. Schedule L also requires reporting of excess benefit transactions with disqualified persons subject to Code Sec. 4958. Charities and social welfare organizations must report excess benefit transactions on Part I of Schedule L. The 2008 Form 990 requires the same information for such transactions as in prior years. The instructions have a separate appendix for Code Sec. 4958 excess benefit transactions. The appendix explains who qualifies as a disqualified person. The IRS claimed that most employees and contractors will not be reportable. But a person with "substantial influence" at any time during a five-year period must be tested for these transactions. The instructions list 12 facts and circumstances that tend to show whether an individual has substantial influence over the organization. The new form requires that the identity of the disqualified person be reported, not just the person's office or status.

An organization that has excess benefit transactions must pay excise taxes on Schedule I of Form 4720, *Return of Certain Excise Taxes Under Chapters 41 and 42 of the Internal Revenue Code.* Most of the taxes paid on Form 4720 apply to private foundations, but the form also must be used by a party to a prohibited tax shelter transaction.

Loans, grants, and business transactions. Parts II through IV require reporting of transactions with interested persons: loans, grants and assistance, and business transactions, respectively. Filing Part IV is new for noncharitable organizations.

COMMENT

"There are three categories of transactions with 'interested persons' that must be reported on Schedule L, and each category uses a different definition of *interested persons*," one practitioner noted. This illustrates the complexity of the revised Form 990.

Loans, grants, and assistance must be reported regardless of amount; there is no de minimis threshold. Loans must be reported by all organizations if made to individuals listed on Part VII—current or former ODTKEs and the five HCEs. Disqualified persons of Code Sec. 501(c)(3) charities, 501(c)(4) social welfare organizations, and Code Sec. 509(a)(3) supporting organizations are interested persons. There is an "ordinary course of business" exception for receivables and exceptions for credit union loans, unpaid compensation, charitable pledges, and advances under an accountable plan.

Grants and assistance must be reported if paid to a current or former ODTKE, a substantial contributor, or a related person. Grants include scholarships, internships, prizes, and awards. There are exceptions for nondiscriminatory grants and grants or assistance to a member of a charitable class benefited by the organization. A *substantial contributor* is a person reported on Schedule B, Schedule of Contributors, who contributed at least $5,000. A *related person* includes:

- A member of the organization's grant selection committee, ODTKE, or a substantial contributor;
- A family member of a person in any of these three categories;
- A 35-percent controlled entity of a person in one of the three categories; or
- An employee or child of a substantial contributor or controlled entity of a substantial contributor.

Business transactions must meet any of the following financial thresholds for reporting purposes:

- All payments during the year exceed $100,000;
- Payments from a single transaction exceed the greater of $10,000 or 1 percent of the organization's revenues; or
- Compensation paid to a family member of certain persons exceeds $10,000.

Business transactions include (but are not limited to) a sale, lease, license, or performance of services, or a joint venture in which the individual and the organization each own an interest exceeding 10 percent.

> **COMMENT**
>
> The IRS stated that the new financial threshold should reduce the reporting burden.

Interested persons include:

- Current and former ODTKEs and their family members;
- A greater-than-35-percent controlled entity; and
- Certain organizations with common ODTKEs or with ownership exceeding 5 percent by an ODTKE.

There are reporting exceptions for nondiscriminatory awards and awards to a member of the group intended to benefit from the program.

HOSPITALS (SCHEDULE H)

In 2006, the IRS sent surveys to more than 500 tax-exempt hospitals as part of a compliance project. The survey asked detailed questions about the facilities' community benefits and executive compensation. Based on the information provided in the surveys, the IRS decided to require a separate schedule for hospitals: Schedule H.

> **COMMENT**
>
> Nonprofit hospitals constitute one of the largest components of the tax-exempt sector. The purpose of the hospital compliance project was to provide the IRS with a better picture of how tax-exempt hospitals operate. The IRS received responses from almost all of the survey recipients.

The information requested in the new Schedule H, Hospitals, must be completed by any organization that operates at least one facility that is, or is required to be, licensed, registered, or similarly recognized by a state as a hospital, regardless of whether the facility is operated directly by the organization or indirectly through a disregarded entity or joint venture taxed as a partnership. For 2008, organizations are only required to complete Part V of Schedule H, Facility Information. Parts I through IV and VI are optional for 2008 returns, but organizations will be required to complete these parts about operations in returns filed for the 2009 year.

Facility Information

The identifying information that must be provided in Part V includes the name, address, and type of each of the organization's facilities that was recognized as a healthcare facility at any time during the tax year. The instructions define various types of facilities, such as a children's hospital, critical access hospital, teaching hospital, research facility, emergency room, and general medical and surgical hospitals. Organizations must also identify other facilities (for example, outpatient physician clinics, long-term acute care facilities, diagnostic centers, rehabilitation clinics, and skilled nursing facilities) that are not explicitly listed. The instructions clarify that physician clinics and skilled nursing facilities are treated as subsidized health services.

Charity Care and Community Benefits

Part I of Schedule H requires reporting of charity care policies, the existence and availability of community benefit reports, and the cost of certain charity care and other community benefit programs. A charity care policy, according to the instructions, describes how the organization provides free or discounted health services (charity care) to patients who need financial assistance. Worksheets and accompanying instructions are provided to assist organizations in completing this part.

> **COMMENT**
>
> The IRS has stated that the lack of consistency in classifying and reporting charity care and various types of community benefits makes it difficult to determine whether a hospital is in compliance with the tax law. The IRS will analyze the information reported in Part I to assess whether the tax-exempt hospital is in compliance.

Other Parts of Schedule H

The costs of activities that an organization engaged in to protect or improve the community's health or safety (and that are not reported elsewhere in the form/schedule) are recorded in Part II. Part III asks questions pertaining to bad debt, Medicare, and collection practices. Part IV considers information regarding the organization's involvement with management companies and joint ventures or other separate entities. Supplemental information is requested in Part VI, such as descriptions of how patients are educated about their eligibility for financial assistance and how the organization assesses the healthcare needs of the community it serves.

> **COMMENT**
>
> Although one of the its goals was to reduce the reporting burden on exempt organizations, the IRS conceded that most of the information requested in Schedule H could be a substantial burden for many hospitals, particularly in the first year of reporting.

SUPPLEMENTAL INFORMATION ON TAX-EXEMPT BONDS (SCHEDULE K)

Schedule K must be filled out by any tax-exempt organization that has outstanding liabilities arising from the issuance of tax-exempt bonds. Schedule K is a new form that replaces the requirement on the 2007 Form 990 to provide a freeform attachment that described the purpose and amount of the issue, the unexpended bond proceeds, and whether a third party uses a bond-financed facility. The new schedule requires additional information and is divided into four parts:

1. Bond Issues;
2. Proceeds;
3. Private Business Use; and
4. Arbitrage.

An organization does not have to report bonds issued before 2003 or bonds with outstanding principal amounts of $100,000 or less for the current year or the year chosen by the organization. Reporting a bond issue may be done for any 12-month period selected and used consistently by the organization; thus, an organization may use a different reporting period for different bond issues, as long as it identifies the period on a separate Schedule O.

Part III, Private Business Use, does not have to be filled out for any refunding bond issued after 2002 to refund bonds issued before 2003. The instructions provide examples that explain this exception. Part III asks about membership in an organization owning the bond-financed property, as well as lease arrangements, management or service contracts, and research agreements that may result in private business use.

> **COMMENT**
>
> Practitioners say these exceptions will help to reduce their reporting burden, especially for older bond issues for which the records may not contain the required information.

Except for the listing of bond issues in Part I, completion of Schedule K is not required for 2008. The form has space for five bond issues, but additional forms must be used to report all outstanding issues. The other parts are optional for 2008 returns. All parts must be completed for the 2009 reporting period.

The information provided on Part I, columns (a) through (e), including issuer name, date issued, and issue price, should be consistent with Form 8038, *Information Return for Tax-Exempt Private Activity Bond Issues*. If the issue price is not identical, the organization must explain the difference on Schedule O. Column (f) describes the purpose of the bond issue, including bonds that are used for multiple purposes, for a single facility, or to refund a prior issue.

With post-issuance compliance becoming a growing concern of the IRS, Schedule K asks for information about recordkeeping and record retention requirements. For example, Part II, Question 12 asks whether the organization maintains adequate books and records to support the final allocation of proceeds. Question 7 of Part III asks whether the organization has adopted management practices to ensure post-issuance compliance.

> ### COMMENT
>
> The core form also asks filers to provide information on tax-exempt bonds. For example, Part VIII of the core form, Question 4, asks about investment income from tax-exempt bond issues. Line 20 of Part X, Balance Sheet, requires the listing of tax-exempt bond liabilities.

CAMPAIGN ACTIVITIES (SCHEDULE C)

Enhanced reporting of political campaigning or lobbying activities by tax-exempt organizations is solicited on Schedule C, Political Campaign and Lobbying Activities. In Part I-A of the schedule, Code Sec. 501(c) organizations should provide a detailed description of their direct and indirect political campaign activities and the total amount spent conducting the activities. If an organization uses volunteer labor for its political campaign activities or Code Sec. 527 exempt function activities, the total number of volunteers' hours should be provided.

Noncharities must enter the amount of funds that were expended for exempt function activities as well as funds transferred to other organizations, including any separate segregated funds created by the organization, in Part I-C. Parts I-B (excise tax), II-A (lobbying activities if the Code Sec. 501(h) election was made), II-B (lobbying activities if the Code Sec. 501(h) election was not made), and III (Code Sec. 6033(e) requirements) request information that was required on the previous form.

SCHOOLS (SCHEDULE E)

In Schedule E, Schools, the IRS asks for information regarding private schools. The questions relate almost exclusively to nondiscrimination issues. The threshold requirements and requested information are the same as on the previous form.

STUDY QUESTION

15. Which of the following is a required filing for all tax-exempt bond issues in 2008?

   a. Private Business Use, Part III of Schedule K

   b. Schedule O

   c. Proceeds, Part II of Schedule K

   d. None of the above is required for 2008 bond issue filings

CONCLUSION

Organizations filing Form 990 for 2008 have a big job. Without much time to digest the new form and instructions, they must fill out the form in 2009 to report their 2008 operations. One practitioner asked that the IRS take a lenient view and not impose penalties for incomplete forms. Organizations may want to practice filling out the form so they will understand what information is needed. New recordkeeping and accounting systems will be necessary to record and gather this information. Finally, avoiding penalties for filing an incomplete new Form 990, although a major concern for many exempt organizations, may prove relatively minor for those that discover in filling out the new form, that they have not been following all the rules required for their tax-exempt status. These groups will discover that even more hefty penalties may be imposed for noncompliance with the rules that the new Form 990 is intended to police.

MODULE 3: TAX REPORTING IN TRANSITION — CHAPTER 7

Worker Classification

This chapter explores the continuing and escalating controversy over the classification of workers as employees or independent contractors. The distinction has significant federal tax consequences.

LEARNING OBJECTIVES

Upon completion of this chapter, you will be able to:

■ Identify the traditional distinctions between employees and independent contractors;

■ Describe the factors the IRS uses to determine whether an individual is classified as an employee or independent contractor;

■ Understand the employment tax obligations of employers vis-à-vis employees and independent contractors;

■ Describe IRS activities to counter employment tax evasion;

■ Understand the consequences of misclassifying employees as independent contractors; and

■ Identify pending legislation addressing the controversy concerning classification of employees and independent contractors.

INTRODUCTION

Under pressure from Congress, the IRS has been aggressively attempting to reduce the $345 billion *tax gap*—the difference between what taxpayers owe and what they actually pay. Nonpayment and underpayment of employment taxes have been identified by the IRS and other federal agencies as contributing at least $45 billion to the tax gap. By misclassifying employees as independent contractors, employers contribute to the tax gap principally by evading federal payroll taxes. By focusing on finding more cases of misclassification, the IRS lately has begun to realize a relatively easy way to collect more revenue. The taxes to be collected from misclassification of employees as independent contractors represent relatively "low-hanging fruit" for the IRS. This is the principal reason why employee misclassification has become such a hot tax issue.

Many employers unintentionally misclassify employees simply because they are confused by the conflicting worker classification rules. The confusion is understandable because federal and state laws may define the term *employee* differently and use varying tests to differentiate between employees and independent contractors. However, if an employer–employee relationship exists, the terminology used to describe it is inconsequential; payroll taxes are required. An employee for federal tax purposes may be called an *agent* or *independent contractor*. It also does not matter to the IRS how payments are measured or paid, what they are called, or whether the employee works full or part-time.

In addition to employment tax issues, classification as an employee or independent contractor also can directly affect the allocation of and right of participation in tax-free fringe benefits and tax-deferred qualified retirement plans. Compliance with *nondiscrimination provisions* within the employee benefits area is directly determined by counting all employees (and generally excluding all independent contractors). Noncompliance can mean penalties for the employer and, in some cases, even complete termination of the benefits plan itself.

CLASSIFICATION AS AN EMPLOYEE OR INDEPENDENT CONTRACTOR

To properly treat compensation for services rendered, a business must determine the relationship it develops with an individual engaged to perform the services. The worker performing services must be classified either as an employee or an independent contractor; there is no middle ground or "hybrid" classification, even though determining whether a worker falls into one or the other classification may be a close call. Additionally, individuals who would not normally be considered employees may be considered employees by law (and under the Tax Code). These workers are referred to as *statutory employees*. This chapter first looks at who qualifies as an employee for federal tax purposes.

> **REMINDER**
>
> Worker classification rules for federal tax purposes apply to all employers, including not-for-profit employers. However, there are exceptions for some clergy and religious workers.

Employees

An individual who performs services for a business is an employee, if the business has the right to control and direct the individual, regardless of whether that right is exercised. This is the key test of who is an employee. The employer of an employee must have control over the *result* to be accomplished and *how* it is accomplished. The business need not set the employee's hours or supervise every detail of his or her work to control the employee. There is no distinction between classes of employees.

EXAMPLE

Brittany Howe is a reporter for a daily newspaper. Brittany works five days a week, and is on duty certain assigned days and times. She covers breaking news stories and writes feature articles for the newspaper. Her articles are reviewed by her editor before they are published. Brittany also has to develop news stories. Because of her experience, Brittany requires only minimal assistance in her work. Brittany is paid a weekly salary and is eligible for bonuses offered by the newspaper. The newspaper also pays the cost of health insurance and group-term life insurance for her. Brittany is an employee of the newspaper.

COMMENT

An *employee for tax purposes* may be different from an employee for other purposes. For example, differences may include classifying certain workers as employees for Department of Labor purposes, even though the workers do not fit the tax law definition of employees.

Statutory Employees

Statutory employees are workers who may appear to be independent contractors but under federal tax law qualify as employees. Generally, workers of the type covered as statutory employees (or statutory nonemployees) at one time were the focus of some controversy over whether they were employees or independent contractors. A statute was then enacted to settle the question unequivocally, either in favor of employee status even where certain factors might otherwise point to independent contractor status (the so-called statutory employee) or in favor of independent contractor status despite some clear employee characteristics (the so-called statutory nonemployee).

Life insurance salespersons. Any individual whose entire or principal business activity consists of the solicitation of life insurance and or annuity contracts for a single life insurance company is a statutory employee. In general, these salespersons are furnished with forms, rate books, office space, telephone facilities, and advertising materials by the company or its general agent. The employer of the salespersons may be either the company or the general agent.

COMMENT

The salesperson may occasionally sell other types of insurance but still qualify as a life insurance salesperson for this classification.

Agent- or commission-drivers. An agent- or commission-driver can be a statutory employee if he or she distributes for his or her principal/business owner, meat or meat products, vegetables or vegetable products, fruit or fruit products, bakery products, beverages (other than milk), or laundry or dry cleaning services. Such drivers include individuals:

- Who operate their own vehicle or the vehicle of their principal;
- Who service customers selected by their principal and those solicited by them; and
- Whose compensation is a commission on sales or the difference between the price they charge their customers and the price they pay the principal for the products.

A driver may sell at wholesale or retail, and his or her manner of compensation is irrelevant. The individual may distribute other products also as long as such distribution is incidental to the handling of the specified products.

Traveling and city sales representatives. Full-time traveling or city sales representatives (except agent- or commission-drivers) are statutory employees if their entire or principal activity is the solicitation of orders for merchandise on behalf of their company and submission of the orders to the company, and they obtain orders from wholesalers and other customers for merchandise for resale or supply use in their business. A representative's principal activity is soliciting orders on behalf of one company, but if he or she solicits incidental orders for another, he or she is a full-time representative with respect to the primary company's orders only. If a traveling or city sales representative devotes 80 percent or more of work time to soliciting orders for one principal in a calendar year he or she satisfies the principal business activity test.

Homeworkers. An individual meeting the definition of a homeworker is also a statutory employee for federal tax purposes. A homeworker is an individual who works at his or her home on materials or goods that:

- Are supplied by an employer; and
- Must be returned to the employer or an individual specified by the employer.

It is irrelevant whether the employer picks up the work or the individual delivers it to the employer.

An employer must withhold Social Security and Medicare taxes from the wages of these statutory employees if:

- The services are performed on a continuing basis for the same payer;
- The service contract states or implies that substantially all the services are to be performed personally by them; and
- They do not have a substantial investment in the equipment and property used to perform the services (other than an investment in transportation facilities).

STUDY QUESTIONS

1. The key test of who is classified by the IRS as an employee is a worker:
   a. Whose business has the right to control and direct the individual's work result and how it is accomplished
   b. Who is paid by the hour or a flat salary but who retains the right to set his or her hours of work
   c. Whose employment-related costs, such as work attire and mobile telephone services, are established by the employer and are tax deductible by the worker
   d. Who is limited to distributing products or services only to the principal

2. A commission-based salesperson whose office is at an off-site location offers annuity contracts for one insurance company. He is classified as a(n):
   a. Common law employee
   b. Statutory employee
   c. Independent contractor
   d. Contract agent

Statutory Nonemployees

Federal tax law treats two categories of workers—real estate agents and direct sellers—as nonemployees. These *statutory nonemployees* are treated as self-employed for all federal tax purposes. Payments made to such individuals are not subject to employment taxes; instead, these workers are required to pay self-employment taxes.

Real estate agents. A qualified real estate agent is an individual who satisfies the following requirements:
- An individual who is licensed and engaged in real estate sales;
- Substantially all of the compensation for services performed by the individual is directly related to sales or other output, including the performance of services; and
- The services performed by the individual are pursuant to a written contract that states the individual will not be treated as an employee for employment tax purposes.

Direct sellers. A direct seller is a person who is engaged in the trade or business of:
- Selling or soliciting the sale of consumer products to a buyer in the home for resale by the buyer or any other person in some place other than a permanent retail establishment;

- Selling or soliciting the sale of consumer products in the home or business (other than a permanent retail establishment); or
- Delivering or distributing newspapers or shopping news, including any services directly related to the trade or business.

Consumer products include consumer goods and intangible services. Individuals are not treated as direct sellers unless their services are performed under a contract that states the individuals will not be treated as employees for employment tax purposes. Substantially all compensation received for services performed as a direct seller must be directly related to sales or other output rather than to the number of hours worked.

> **COMMENT**
>
> Sometimes, companion sitters (also known as home care workers) are treated as self-employed unless they are paid by a placement agency for their services. Companion sitters provide companionship, personal attendance, and household care services to the elderly, disabled, and children.

Independent Contractors

Generally, an individual is an *independent contractor* if the person engaging his or her services has the right to the result of the work and not also the right to control or direct the means and methods of accomplishing the result. Facts that demonstrate independent contractor situations are, among others:

- Providing services part-time while working for others;
- Payment by the job or based on invoices submitted; and
- Reimbursement of business expenses pursuant to a contract.

If the individual is not an employee (either by statute or under common law criteria), then he or she is an independent contractor.

> **COMMENT**
>
> Because a worker is only either an employee or an independent contractor, another logical definition of an *independent contractor* is "any worker who is not an employee." In the "real tax world," however, that begs the question; the tests for either category are reciprocals of one another. Factors that tend to prove independent contractor status also tend to disprove employee status. It is the weighing of each factor, and the nuances that each real-world situation brings to that task, that creates the real difficulty in separating one category from the other.

EXAMPLE

Kyle Jantz is a licensed electrician. A school in his town is seeking bids for electrical work. Kyle bids on the project using a contract and the school accepts his bid. Kyle is to receive a lump sum payment of $1,500 for the job. The contract states the type of electrical work that must be performed (installing new wiring and lighting fixtures in various classrooms) and the business expenses that will be reimbursed to Kyle. Kyle will perform the work on a part-time basis because he has other projects. The school may set the times when the work is to be performed but not the means or methods of accomplishing the work. Kyle is an independent contractor and not an employee of the school.

STUDY QUESTIONS

3. Which of the following workers is considered a statutory nonemployee?

    a. A seamstress using a company-provided machine to sew aprons for $7.50 each for a textile company

    b. A long-haul truck driver who picks up bulk lettuce and tomatoes from a farm to deliver to three vendors at an outdoor market in St. Louis

    c. A sales representative who works from a home office and travels statewide to solicit wholesale orders for video camera parts

    d. An individual who delivers newspapers to private residences and stores each morning.

4. Workers are not considered direct sellers unless:

    a. They are not self-employed

    b. They are subject to contracts that specify they are not employees for employment tax purposes

    c. Their work involves selling tangible products, such as consumer goods

    d. Their sales are limited to wholesale transactions

IRS FACTORS FOR CONTROL OF SERVICES BY EMPLOYEES VERSUS INDEPENDENT CONTRACTORS

The IRS generally considers three aspects of control when determining whether an employer–employee relationship exists:

- Behavioral control;
- Financial control; and
- Nature of the parties' relationship.

> **COMMENT**
>
> The entire business relationship is examined to determine the extent of the right to direct or control the work efforts of the individual rendering services. A business should document each of the factors considered in determining the worker's classification.

Behavioral Control

Behavioral control is generally shown by facts that illustrate whether the service recipient has a right to direct or control the particulars of how the worker performs the specific tasks for which he or she is hired. Facts that show whether there is a right to control how a worker performs a task include the provision of training or instruction. Specifying by contract the particulars of a job that address the quality of the results is not by itself an earmark of an employer–employee relationship (for example, the outside of the house shall be hand- and not machine-sanded before painting). However, visiting the job site and giving ongoing instructions on how the hand sanding should be done would indicate a control characteristic of an employer–employee relationship.

The extent to which the individual has to be trained or instructed in performing the job is an essential element. An employee is generally subject to business instruction about when, where, and how to work. Examples of business instructions include:

- The timing and location for performing the work;
- The tools or equipment to use;
- What workers to hire or to assist with the work;
- Where to purchase supplies and services;
- Which work must be performed by a specified individual; and
- The order or sequence of steps to follow.

Table 1 provides examples of the degree of behavioral control the service recipient exercises for employees versus independent contractors.

Table 1. Examples of Behavioral Control for Employees Versus Independent Contractors

Employees	Independent Contractors
Crab-meat pickers who were unsupervised in the details of their work and who could be dismissed if their work was consistently noncompliant (**Breaux and Daigle, Inc. v US,** CA-5, 90-2 USTC ¶50,491, 900 F2d 49)	An unsupervised grocery bagger who worked only for tips, purchased a uniform smock, paid for his damages to groceries, and could work elsewhere (IRS Letter Ruling 200129004)
Drivers for a trucking company that required them to call in daily to report their location and progress and determined which loads the drivers would haul and the prices charged, as well as determining whether truck repairs should be performed on the road or deferred until the drivers returned (**R.P. Day v Commr,** Dec. 54,150(M), TC Memo. 2000-375)	Disabled individuals who participated for a limited time in a program that used work samples, simulated job stations, paper or pencil tests, and other methods to obtain job prospects based on the individuals' skills, abilities, aptitudes, etc. (IRS Letter Ruling 9801003)

Financial Control

Financial control is generally shown by facts that illustrate whether the service recipient has a right to direct or control the financial aspects of the worker's activities. These aspects include:

- Significant investment;
- Unreimbursed expenses;
- Making services available to the relevant market;
- The method of payment; and
- The opportunity for profit or loss.

An individual who makes a substantial financial investment in tools, equipment, or the facility at which he or she works is more likely to be considered by the IRS as an independent contractor than is an individual for whom such resources are furnished. In addition, if an individual assumes some entrepreneurial risks, he or she is more likely to be considered an independent contractor. Two indicators of entrepreneurial risk are the dependence on more than one client and the possibility of a profit or loss through the exercise of managerial skill.

COMMENT

Certain facilities, such as home offices, are scrutinized more closely and frequently by the IRS than are other facilities that are more readily recognized as places of business.

Table 2 provides examples of the degree of financial control the service recipient exercises for employees versus independent contractors.

Table 2. Examples of Financial Control for Employees Versus Independent Contractors

Employees	Independent Contractors
Telephone solicitors who worked on the company's premises (Rev. Rul. 74-333)	A newspaper columnist who was not required to work on the company's premises and used his own equipment and supplies in writing columns for the paper (Rev. Rul. 65-312)
Drivers who owned their own mechanical tools, but not the trucks they drove (*R.P. Day*)	An ice cream salesman who purchased gasoline for use in a rental truck, owned by the distributor, from which he worked (Rev. Rul. 57-63)
A full-time messenger who received a certain fee for each delivery made in his own car and who was reimbursed for mileage (*K.W. Frische v Commr*, Dec. 53,979(M), TC Memo. 2000-237)	A watch repairperson who used his own equipment to perform services in a jewelry store and paid the owner a percentage of the profits (Rev. Rul. 55-248)

Nature of Relationship of the Parties

The relationship of the parties is generally shown by examining the parties' agreements and actions with respect to each other, paying close attention to facts that show not only how they perceive their own relationship but also how they represent their relationship to others. Facts that illustrate how the parties perceive their relationship include:

- The intent of the parties, as expressed in written contracts;
- The provision or lack of employee benefits;
- The right of the parties to terminate the relationship;
- The permanency of the relationship; and
- Whether the services performed are part of the service recipient's regular business activities.

Table 3 provides examples of the relationship between employers and employees versus employers or service recipients using independent contractors.

Table 3. Examples of Employer–Employee Relationship Versus Service Recipient–Independent Contractor Relationship

Employees	Independent Contractors
Models who were free to refuse assignments but could be discharged for refusing too many (Rev. Rul. 74-332)	Home demonstration workers who sold products on a commission basis under a contract, which could be terminated if the workers failed to average a specified sales amount each week (Rev. Rul. 70-601)
Associate physicians who could be fired for failing to meet hospital standards of performance (Rev. Rul. 72-203)	A trade consultant whose services were publicly available and who was compensated on a fee or retainer basis (Rev. Rul. 54-586)
An architect who performed services essential to the business and was paid according to the difficulty of the job (Rev. Rul. 74-412)	
The sole shareholder of an S corporation who performed the corporation's accounting services for its clients, was the firm's central worker and had not performed similar services for other corporations (*Spicer Accounting, Inc. v US,* CA-9, 91-1 USTC ¶50,103, 918 F2d 90)	

COMMENT

An individual who performs services for a former employer under a contract may still be an employee if the relevant factors apply. This employer–employee relationship persists even if the contract requires the individual to train his or her replacement and designates the individual as an independent contractor.

CAUTION

The IRS is suspicious of the degree of worker independence when a worker retires, then quickly returns to the business as an independent contractor and performs the same services he or she did as an employee. A business should document the factors that demonstrate it has little enough control over the worker to permit his or her classification as an independent contractor. This issue can take on added tax significance if a pension plan payout is involved because full retirement generally must take place for tax-favored distributions to begin (although "partial retirement" provisions soon may be allowed by Congress).

Traditional 20 Factors List

Before it consolidated its focus on behavioral control, financial control, and the nature of the parties' relationship, the IRS identified 20 factors traditionally considered to help determine whether an individual is an independent contractor or an employee. These factors were derived from court decisions and IRS rulings. They are similar to the factors identified under behavioral control, financial control, and the nature of the parties' relationship and continue in use by both the IRS and taxpayers in arguments supporting their respective positions. The 20 factors remain relevant both as a subset for proving IRS's condensed three-factor test and as a more detailed test upon which many courts continue to rely in close situations. The 20 factors are described here.

Control of when, where, and how the worker performs services. Provision of instructions regarding when, where, and how the worker is to work is indicative of an employer–employee relationship. Independent contractors tend to exercise control of the time, place, and method at and by which the workers perform job obligations.

Training. Training, requiring services to be performed with other workers, and requiring the worker to attend meetings, are indicative of an employer–employee relationship.

Integration into firm operations. The integration of a worker's services into the operations of the business indicates the direction and control generally found in an employer–employee relationship.

Requirement that services be personally performed. Limited identity of the service provider is indicative of an employer–employee relationship. Independent contractors are often not required to personally perform the services. However, there are exceptions and this factor alone is often not determinative.

Control over assistants. An employer–employee relationship is indicated when the firm has the right to hire, supervise, and pay the worker's assistants.

Length of relationship. A long-term, continuing relationship indicates an employer–employee relationship.

Work schedule. A worker given a set work schedule indicates the control of an employer in an employer–employee relationship.

Number of hours of service required. The amount of time the worker is required to provide services to the employer is indicative of the worker's status. Full-time employment and firm control over time spent working are indicative of an employer–employee relationship.

Location where services are performed. The requirement that services be provided on the firm's premises suggests an employer–employee relationship. However, some types of services or work cannot be performed elsewhere, such as improvements to the firm's facilities.

Control over technique or sequence. Control of the order or sequence in which the worker performs required tasks suggests that an employer–employee relationship exists. When the worker determines how and in what order tasks will be performed, it is less indicative of an employer–employee relationship.

Reports to firm. Submission of regular or periodic oral or written reports suggests that there is a degree of control indicative of an employer–employee relationship.

Payment method. The interval of payment may be indicative of an employer–employee relationship. Payments by the hour, week, or month suggest that an employer–employee relationship may exist. Payment by the job or based on invoices submitted by the worker are indicative of an independent contractor relationship.

Work-related expenses. Payment of the worker's business and travel expenses suggests an employer–employee relationship.

Tools. Whether the worker is required to furnish his or her own tools is an important consideration in determining whether an employer–employee relationship or independent contractor relationship exists. Provision of necessary tools and equipment by the firm suggests that there is an employer–employee relationship. However, the fact that a worker supplies or is required to supply tools and equipment is not necessarily determinative.

Work facilities. Investment in and provision of work facilities by the worker, especially if of a type not generally maintained by employees, indicates an independent contractor relationship.

Profit and loss potential. Workers likely to profit from the success of an enterprise and at risk of experiencing a loss on its failure are usually independent contractors. Workers paid a fixed rate based on time with no possibility of loss are more likely to be considered employees.

Multiple employers. The presence of multiple employers, rather than employment by a single firm, is indicative of a worker having an independent contractor status.

Restrictions on customers and clients. Workers who offer their services to the public on a regular, consistent basis are less likely to be considered employees than those with a single employer. Workers significantly restricted as to the identity of those for whom they can work are probably employees.

Termination of worker. The firm's ability to terminate its relationship with the worker for any reason without penalty indicates an employer-employee relationship.

Termination of relationship by worker. The worker's ability to end the relationship at any time without penalty is indicative of an employer–employee relationship. Liability to the worker for terminating the relationship without cause or for reasons not permitted by the agreement may indicate an independent contractor relationship.

Figure 1 provides a checklist for distinguishing whether an employer has properly classified a worker as an independent contractor or an employee based upon IRS criteria.

Figure 1. Checklist: Independent Contractor or Employee

The following can help determine whether an individual is an independent contractor or an employee. This list should be used in conjunction with the IRS 20 factors. Check each statement that is true, remembering that the final determination depends on all the facts and circumstances and that no single issue is dispositive. Checking off any of the statements below may indicate an employer-employee relationship.

☐ The employer controls the time, place, and manner of the work.

☐ The employer provides or requires training, or requires attendance at training meetings.

☐ The employer integrates the worker into regular operations.

☐ The employer requires that the worker specifically perform the work.

☐ The employer hires and controls the worker's assistants.

☐ The employer and the worker have a long-term working relationship.

☐ The employer requires the worker to work certain hours or a certain schedule.

☐ The employer requires a certain number of hours.

☐ The employer requires work at a specific location.

☐ The employer controls the order of the work or the technique used.

☐ The employer requires reports from the worker.

- ☐ The employer pays on a regular basis, rather than on receipt of invoices.

- ☐ The employer pays the worker's work-related expenses.

- ☐ The employer furnishes tools or other needed equipment for the job.

- ☐ The employer provides work facilities, rather than the worker maintaining separate space.

- ☐ The worker does not risk loss through completion of the job.

- ☐ The worker works only for the employer or for the employer's customers.

- ☐ The employer may terminate the worker's services or the worker may quit at any time.

COMMENT

The U.S. Tax Court has also identified factors to help determine the nature of an employment relationship. The Tax Court has traditionally looked to: (a) The degree of control exercised by the principal over the details of the work; (b) which party invests in the facilities used in the work; (c) the opportunity of the individual for profit or loss; (d) whether the principal has the right to discharge the individual; (e) whether the work is part of the principal's regular business; (f) the permanency of the relationship; and (g) the relationship the parties believe they are creating.

Facts and Circumstances

Notwithstanding all of the factors used by the IRS and the courts, every situation is different and to a great extent the final determination of whether an individual is an employee or an independent contractor is largely based on how the particular facts and circumstances of that case fit together. Businesses must weigh all the factors. Certain factors may indicate that the individual is an employee; others may suggest that the individual is an independent contractor. No one factor is determinative. Depending on the occupation being considered, factors which are relevant in one employee situation may not be relevant in another and the same is true for situations involving independent contractors. The entire relationship should be considered when a service recipient and worker are determining the extent of the right to direct and control.

> **COMMENT**
>
> Individuals employed by temporary employment agencies may be employees of the agencies' clients or of the employment agencies. The control factors are used in determining which of the potential multiple employers will be treated as the employer for employment tax purposes.

STUDY QUESTIONS

5. According to the IRS 20 factors list, which factor does **not** indicate that a worker is an employee?

a. Requiring that services be performed with other workers
b. Requiring submission of periodic oral or written reports
c. Restricting employers for whom work is performed
d. All of the above are factors indicating an employer–employee relationship

6. Under the 20 control factors, liability for payment to a worker when an employer ends a relationship without cause indicates which of the following to the IRS?

a. An independent contractor relationship
b. An employer–employee relationship
c. A customer–supplier relationship
d. None of the above is indicated by the termination

EMPLOYMENT TAX OBLIGATIONS

It is critically important that businesses correctly determine whether individuals providing services are employees or independent contractors. The Internal Revenue Code requires an employer to withhold income and *Federal Insurance Contributions Act* (FICA) taxes, as well as pay the employer's share of FICA taxes on the wages of an individual who is an employee. The employer must also pay *Federal Unemployment Tax Act* (FUTA) taxes on wages paid to an employee. A business does not have to withhold or pay any taxes on fees charged by independent contractors. An independent contractor is solely responsible for the payment of self-employment and income taxes on his or her earnings.

> **CAUTION**
>
> Employers may want to inquire of the IRS whether individuals would be considered employees or independent contractors. However, the IRS does not issue determination letters on whether an individual is an employee or an independent contractor in proposed or hypothetical situations.

> **COMMENT**
>
> The U.S. Government Accountability Office estimates that misclassification results in a federal income tax loss of $4.7 billion annually.

Federal Income, Social Security, and Medicare Taxes

Generally an employer must withhold federal income, Social Security, and Medicare taxes from an employee's wages. Social Security and Medicare taxes pay for benefits that workers and families receive under FICA. Employers withhold an employee's part of these taxes from the employee's wages and pay a matching amount from its funds.

Tax-exempts. Payments received by employees of nonprofit organizations are subject to FICA taxes unless the employees earn less than $100 in a tax year. However, church or church-controlled 501(c)(3) organizations, in opposition to the payment of such taxes based on religious reasons, may file for exemption. To obtain the exemption, both the employer and the employee must file. Section 501(c)(3) organizations exempt from federal income tax are also exempt from FUTA. Nonprofit organizations other than 501(c)(3)s are subject to FUTA for employees whose wages are $50 or more in a calendar quarter.

Differential pay/continuation payments. When a military reservist is called to active duty, his or her civilian job and salary is placed on hiatus while he or she receives military pay. Some civilian employers voluntarily pay the difference between the reservist's regular pay and his or her military pay, if the regular pay is higher. The *Heroes Earnings Assistance and Relief Tax Act of 2008* treats this so-called differential pay as wages subject to employment taxes. This treatment allows reservists to contribute more to their retirement accounts and makes it easier for employers to contribute to the reservist's employer-sponsored retirement plans.

> **PLANNING POINTER**
>
> Effective June 18, 2008, qualifying small employers can claim a temporary tax credit for the differential pay for reservists called to active duty. The credit is worth 20 percent of differential pay up to $20,000. A *small employer* is one that employs an average of fewer than 50 individuals annually and provides differential pay to qualified employees under a written plan.

Summer jobs. Students working for the summer do not pay income tax withholding if they do not owe any tax for the previous year and do not expect to owe tax in the current year. A student who can be claimed by someone else as a dependent may be exempt from income tax withholding, if his or her unearned income is $300 or less and total income for the year is not more than $5,450. However, if the student's investment income is more than $300, his or her total income cannot exceed $500 without paying income tax withholding.

Federal Unemployment Tax (FUTA) Taxes

FUTA taxes pay unemployment compensation to workers who lose their jobs. Employers do not withhold FUTA taxes from employees' wages, but report and pay the tax from their own funds. FUTA taxes are reported on Form 940, *Employer's Annual Federal Unemployment (FUTA) Tax Return.*

Family employees. A child who performs services for his or her parent(s) in a trade or business generally does not pay Social Security and Medicare taxes, if the child is younger than age 18. The trade or business must be a sole proprietorship or a partnership in which each partner is a parent of the child. On the other hand, compensation for domestic work performed by a child is not subject to Social Security and Medicare taxes until the child reaches 21 years old.

COMMENT

Similarly, FUTA tax does not apply until the child reaches age 21 if the child works for his or her parents, regardless of whether the work performed is domestic or in a trade or business.

For services performed in a trade or business, the wages of an individual who works for his or her spouse are subject to income tax withholding and FICA, but not FUTA taxes. However, compensation for other services performed by one spouse employed by the other spouse is not subject to FICA or FUTA taxes.

FICA taxes do not apply in certain situations in which a parent performs domestic services for his or her child. Wages paid to a parent employed by his or her child are not subject to FUTA taxes, regardless of the type of work provided.

Despite these general rules, payments to a child may be subject to FICA and FUTA taxes if the child works for a corporation, even if it is controlled by the child's parent, or a partnership, even if the child's parent is a partner, unless each partner is a parent of the child. Similarly, FICA and FUTA taxes apply if the child is performing services for the estate of a deceased parent.

An individual may be employed by his or her spouse. If the employed spouse is engaged in a trade or business, his or her wages are generally subject to FICA taxes, but not FUTA taxes. However, if the employed spouse is not engaged in a trade or business (for example, domestic service), his or her wages are not subject to FICA and FUTA taxes. Additionally, the spouse's wages are subject to FICA and FUTA taxes if he or she works for a corporation, even if it is controlled by the individual's spouse, or for a partnership, even if the individual's spouse is a partner.

Statutory employees. A worker who is statutorily exempt from FICA and FUTA taxes may nonetheless be subject to federal income tax withholding on his or her compensation. For example, an agent-driver is a statutory employee for FICA and FUTA purposes. The same worker may be an independent contractor for income tax withholding purposes if the employer does not control the driver's work.

For FICA and FUTA tax purposes, full-time traveling or city sales representatives and agent- or commission-drivers are considered statutory employees. However, life insurance sales representatives and homeworkers are considered statutory employees for FICA tax purposes only. A homeworker who is a statutory employee subject to FICA taxes must have earned at least $100 in cash wages for the year in order to be subject to such taxes.

Form W-2, *Wage and Tax Statement*

Employers are required to furnish two copies of the Form W-2, *Wage and Tax Statement*, to each employee for whom during the previous calendar year the employer:

- Would have withheld income tax;
- Withheld income tax or Social Security tax;
- Paid total wages and other compensation, including compensation not subject to withholding, of $600 or more; or
- Paid any amount for services performed (if the employer is engaged in a trade or business).

COMMENT

Wages must be reported on the Form W-2. Other nonwage compensation must be reported on the Form W-2 if the total of the compensation payments and the amount of wages paid, if any, is $600 or more in a calendar year. For example, if a payment of $800 is made to an employee and $500 of the payment is wages subject to withholding and the remaining $300 represents compensation not subject to withholding, such wages and compensation must both be reported on Form W-2. Certain business expense reimbursements and taxable payments for health or insurance plans are examples of compensation not subject to withholding.

FormW-2 must be provided to a member of the U.S. Armed Forces only if income tax or Social Security was withheld or if the individual received wages includible in gross income. In general, employers issue only one Form W-2 to an employee for a calendar year.

At the end of the year, the employer must complete Form W-2. A copy of this form must be given to the employee by January 31 after the end of the year. If the employee terminates employment before the end of the year, the employer must furnish the Form W-2 within 30 days of the former employee's request for a copy of his or her W-2. A copy must also be sent to the Social Security Administration by February 28 unless it is filed electronically. Forms filed electronically are due on March 31.

Form 1099-MISC, *Miscellaneous Income*

A business is responsible for issuing Form 1099-MISC, *Miscellaneous Income,* to report compensation paid to individuals who are considered independent contractors. The form is most commonly used by employers to report payments of $600 or more made to independent contractors during the year. The business must provide a copy of Form 1099-MISC to the independent contractor by January 31 of the year following compensation and must send a copy to the IRS by February 28 as well. Once an independent contractor receives Form 1099-MISC for services provided, the contractor must report the income on Form 1040 Schedule C, *Profit or Loss from Business (Sole Proprietorship)* and pay self-employment tax on the net profit using Form 1040 Schedule SE, *Self-Employment Tax.*

> **CAUTION**
>
> If a business provides Form W-2 and Form 1099-MISC to the same individual in one year, the business is more likely to be scrutinized by the IRS. The IRS views it as a potential worker classification issue.

Self-Employment Tax

Under the *Self-Employment Contributions Act,* individuals engaged in a trade or business as sole proprietors or partners must pay self-employment tax on self-employment income. *Self-employment income* is income an individual earns from a trade or business as a sole proprietor or partner, minus the deductions attributable to the trade or business. The tax has two components: old age, survivors and disability insurance and hospital insurance, which are the equivalents of Social Security and Medicare under FICA.

No tax is due if self-employment income for the year is less than $400.

COMMENT

The contributions of small business owners to one-person 401(k) plans are not subject to self-employment tax. Instead, the tax is calculated after the 401(k) contributions are subtracted from the individual's income. Such plans allow proprietors to contribute as much as $15,500 and the business can contribute as much as 20 percent of net earnings from self-employment. Employees pay FICA taxes on contributions and receive an income tax exclusion.

REMINDER

Independent contractors may have their own employees or may hire other independent contractors (subcontractors) for which they have tax responsibilities, including filing and reporting requirements.

COMMENT

A business should have an independent contractor complete Form W-9, *Request for Taxpayer Identification Number (TIN) and Certification,* to request the correct name and TIN of the contractor. The IRS randomly checks backup withholding required of businesses that are notified of mismatched employee names and TINs. Employers that receive such notices are obligated to immediately start withholding tax at a 28 percent rate and to continue to do so until the problem is resolved.

ENFORCEMENT EFFORTS

The IRS is increasingly vigilant in its attack on businesses that violate the worker classification rules. The agency has developed Form SS-8, *Determination of Worker Status for Purposes of Federal Employment Taxes and Income Tax Withholding,* and Form 8919, *Uncollected Social Security and Medicare Tax on Wages,* to assist in identifying employers that are misclassifying workers. It has also launched an initiative, the Questionable Employment Tax Program (QETP), to prevent employers from evading employment taxes. There is likely to be a significant increase in examinations as the agency generates leads from SS-8 inquiries, 8919 reports, and the QETP.

Form SS-8, Determination of Worker Status

To request the IRS to determine whether an individual is an employee, the employer can file Form SS-8, *Determination of Worker Status for Purposes of*

Federal Employment Taxes and Income Tax Withholding. The IRS requires an individual to be currently performing services or to have already completed performing services for the employer.

If a business or worker is unable to clearly determine the proper classification of the worker, either can petition the IRS to determine the individual's status by filing Form SS-8. The IRS will review the information provided and officially determine the individual's status.

> **COMMENT**
>
> An individual who is unsure whether he or she is an independent contractor may also use Form SS-8 to ask the IRS to make an official status determination. In this case, the IRS will also request that the firm complete Form SS-8. If the firm fails to respond, the IRS will nonetheless issue a determination.

Form SS-8 requires detailed Information about the services performed by the individual, including:

- How the worker obtained the job;
- A description of the firm's business; and
- An explanation of why the filer believes the individual is an employee or an independent contractor.

Form SS-8 also requires the filer to answer questions describing behavioral control, financial control, and the parties' relationship.

> **PLANNING POINTER**
>
> A business that continuously hires the same types of workers to perform certain services should consider filing Form SS-8.

> **COMMENT**
>
> The IRS has advised it may take up to six months for it to make a determination after an employer files Form SS-8. The IRS also may ask for additional information beyond what is provided on Form SS-8.

Information must be provided concerning the services the individual performed. The determination made with respect to such individual also applies to other workers in the same class, if the facts concerning the other workers do not differ significantly from the facts applicable to the individual whose status was determined. A business can request a determination of a class of workers as long as a separate statement is provided for one individual whose services most closely represent those of the class.

> **COMMENT**
>
> Although the IRS issues rulings regarding prior employment, it does not issue advance rulings as to whether an individual is an employee or an independent contractor for purposes of determining prospective employment status.

In 2007, the IRS issued a new form for employees who were misclassified as independent contractors. Form 8919, *Uncollected Social Security and Medicare Tax on Wages*, is used to calculate and report the filer's share of uncollected Social Security and Medicare taxes due on his or her wages.

Form 8919, *Uncollected Social Security and Medicare Tax on Wages*

Beginning with the 2007 tax year, employees who believed that their employers incorrectly classified them as independent contractors submitted a new form to the IRS. These employees filed Form 8919, *Uncollected Social Security and Medicare Tax on Wages,* which is used to calculate and report an employee's share of unpaid Social Security and Medicare taxes due on their wages. The IRS shares the data on Form 8919 with the Social Security Administration so that the Social Security and Medicare taxes are credited to the employee's Social Security records.

The business or the worker may be contacted by the IRS for additional information, depending on the reasons for filing Form 8919. If the IRS does not agree with classifying the worker as an employee, he or she may be billed for additional tax, penalties, and interest. Employers are responsible for all FICA taxes on wages paid to its employees even if the taxes are not collected from the employee.

> **COMMENT**
>
> Previously, misclassified employees were required to file Form 4137, *Social Security and Medicare Tax on Unreported Tip Income,* to report their share of the taxes. Now Form 4137 is only used by certain tipped employees to report Social Security and Medicare taxes on allocated tips and tips not reported to their employers.

An individual must file Form 8919 if *all* of the following apply:

- He or she performed services for a firm;
- The firm did not withhold his or her share of Social Security and Medicare taxes;
- The individual's pay from the firm was not for services as an independent contractor; and
- The individual meets one of seven other, additional criteria.

The seven additional criteria are:

- The individual has filed Form SS-8 and received a determination that he or she is an employee of the firm;
- The individual filed Form SS-8 but has not yet received a reply from the IRS;
- The individual was designated a "Section 530 employee" by his or her employer;
- The individual received other correspondence from the IRS stating that he or she is an employee;
- The individual was previously treated as an employee by the company and is performing the same or similar services;
- Coworkers performing substantially similar services under substantially similar direction and control are treated as employees; and
- The individual's coworkers are performing similar services and filed Form SS-8 and received a determination that they were employees.

Questionable Employment Tax Program (QETP)

A new IRS compliance initiative, QETP, is intended to deter employers from evading employment tax liabilities by misclassifying employees. At the heart of the program is cooperation between the IRS and state workforce agencies to identify employment tax evasion. The IRS has entered into agreements with Arizona, Arkansas, California, Colorado, Connecticut, Hawaii, Idaho, Kentucky, Louisiana, Maine, Massachusetts, Michigan, Minnesota, Nebraska, New Hampshire, New Jersey, New York, North Dakota, Ohio, Oklahoma, Rhode Island, South Carolina, South Dakota, Texas, Utah, Vermont, Virginia, Washington, and Wisconsin to exchange information.

> **COMMENT**
>
> The QETP provides, among other things, increased monitoring of Forms 1099-MISC to ensure compliance. Using an electronic matching system, the IRS can spot businesses issuing Forms 1099-MISC with payments of $25,000 or more to at least five workers who have no other income sources.

> **COMMENT**
>
> "These agreements present a united front for the IRS and its state partners to improve compliance in the employment tax arena," explained Kathy Petronchak, Commissioner of the IRS Small Business/Self-Employed Division. "Combining resources will help the IRS and the states reduce fraudulent filings, uncover employment tax avoidance schemes and ensure proper worker classification."

STUDY QUESTIONS

---

7. Which of the following situations subjects a nonprofit organization to remittance of FICA taxes on behalf of its employees?

   a. The nonprofit is a Section 501(c)(3) organization
   b. An employee of the organization earns $100 during the tax year
   c. The organization and its employee each file exemption requests based on religious reasons
   d. An employee of the nonprofit organization is subject to FUTA for more than one calendar quarter

8. Small employers can claim a temporary tax credit of a maximum of _____ for the difference in a reservist's regular pay and his or her earnings on active duty.

   a. 10 percent or $10,000
   b. 15 percent or $15,000
   c. 20 percent or $20,000
   d. 25 percent or $25,000

CONSEQUENCES OF MISCLASSIFICIATION

There are significant tax consequences when an employer treats an employee as an independent contractor. Because an employer is required to withhold employment taxes from the wages of employees, failure to do so can result in liability for unpaid withholding, FICA, and FUTA taxes as well as penalties for failure to file employment tax returns and failure to withhold. However, the IRS offers some relief—known as *Section 530 relief* or the *Section 530 safe harbor*—to employers that can show, among other justifications, they had a reasonable basis for not treating the workers as employees.

Section 530 Relief

Section 530 relief takes its name from Section 530 of the *Revenue Act of 1978.* Under that section, a firm may qualify for relief if:

- The business has a reasonable basis for not treating the individual as an employee (the reasonable basis justification);
- The business did not treat the individual or any other individual in a similar position as an employee for payroll tax purposes (known as the consistent treatment qualification); and
- The business has timely filed all required federal tax returns, including information returns, in a manner consistent with the individual not being an employee (dubbed consistent reporting).

Section 530 relief is offered for employers and not workers. Consequently, it does not convert a worker from the status of employee to that of independent contractor. Moreover, if the taxpayer does not satisfy the requirements for Section 530 relief, the workers are not automatically employees. Instead, the common law analysis (the IRS factors) of the worker's status is applied.

Reasonable basis. A firm may show reasonable basis by:

- Judicial precedent or published rulings, regardless of whether such authority relates to the particular industry or business in which the taxpayer is engaged; or
- On technical advice, a letter ruling, or a determination letter pertaining to the taxpayer; or
- A past IRS audit (not necessarily for employment tax purposes) of the taxpayer, if the audit entailed no assessment attributable to the taxpayer's employment tax treatment of individuals holding positions substantially similar to the position held by the individual whose status is at issue; however, a taxpayer does not meet this test if, in the conduct of a prior audit, an assessment attributable to the taxpayer's treatment of the individual was offset by other claims asserted by the taxpayer; or
- Long-standing recognized practice of a significant segment of the industry in which the individual was engaged. It is not necessary that the practice be uniform throughout the industry.

EXAMPLE

A small mining company treats its workers as independent contractors. The company provides the tools, equipment, and supplies for blasting, transporting, and milling of silver ore. The miners, and not the company, organize the work to extract the silver from the mine. Nine out of 10 small silver mines in the company's county hire miners as independent contractors. This practice has been common for more than 70 years. Consequently, the company has a reasonable basis under the industry practice safe harbor for treating its workers as independent contractors.

COMMENT

Many courts have held that Congress intended to protect employers that exercised good faith in determining whether their workers were employees or independent contractors. The legislative history of Section 530 indicates that *reasonable basis* is to be "construed liberally in favor of taxpayers."

Consistent treatment. In Rev. Proc. 85-18, the IRS provided guidelines for use in determining whether an employer consistently treated an individual as an employee. One factor to consider is the withholding of income tax or FICA tax from an individual's compensation (other than from a statutory employee), which provides evidence of consistent treatment of the individual as an employee, regardless of whether the tax is actually remitted to the government.

> **CAUTION**
>
> Section 530 relief applies to workers who are employees. It does not cover government workers and certain technical service workers.

As explained earlier, Section 530 relief is intended for employers and not workers. Nevertheless, employees who are misclassified as independent contractors may file Form 8919, *Uncollected Social Security and Medicare Tax on Wages,* to calculate and report their share of uncollected Social Security and Medicare taxes. Additionally, an individual who is unsure whether he or she is an independent contractor may also use Form SS-8, *Determination of Worker Status for Purposes of Federal Employment Taxes and Income Tax Withholding,* to request the IRS to officially determine his or her status.

Notice of Determination of Worker Classification

If the IRS determines that a firm is not entitled to Section 530 relief, the agency cannot assess the proposed tax until it issues a Notice of Determination of Worker Classification (NDWC) and the firm either exhausts its remedies in the U.S. Tax Court or fails to pursue them—or until the firm signs the appropriate waiver of restrictions on assessment. In 2000, Congress gave the Tax Court jurisdiction to decide the correct amounts of employment taxes relating to determinations of worker classification.

The NDWC:

- Informs the business of the opportunity to seek review;
- Includes a schedule of workers classified as employees; and
- Shows the type of employment tax and its adjustment.

The mailing of the NDWC suspends the period of limitations for assessment of taxes attributable to the worker classification issues for a 90-day period. During this time, the business can file a petition with the Tax Court and preclude the IRS from assessing the taxes identified in the NDWC prior to the expiration of the 90 days.

If the IRS erroneously assesses taxes attributable to the worker classification issues without first either issuing an NDWC or obtaining a waiver of restrictions on assessment from the business, the employer is entitled to an automatic abatement of the assessment. However, once the procedural defects are corrected, the IRS may reassess the employment taxes.

PENDING LEGISLATION

Two bills—the Independent Contractor Proper Classification Act of 2007 and the Taxpayer Responsibility, Accountability, and Consistency Act of 2008—have been introduced in Congress to beef-up enforcement of worker classification by the IRS.

The Independent Contractor Proper Classification Act of 2007 (S. 2044) would establish a detailed enforcement scheme shared by several federal administrative agencies, including the IRS and the U.S. Department of Labor (DOL). The IRS and DOL would be required to issue annual reports and exchange information on worker misclassification cases. The bill would prohibit employers from retaliating against workers who petition the IRS for review of their classification. It would also require employers to notify independent contractors of their federal tax obligations, the legal protections that are inapplicable to independent contractors, and their right to seek a determination from the IRS.

The Taxpayer Responsibility, Accountability, and Consistency Act of 2008 (H.R. 5804), would repeal the Section 530 safe harbor and replace it with a new but similar safe harbor.

STUDY QUESTIONS

> **9.** All of the following are functions of the Notice of Determination of Worker Classification (NDWC) *except:*
>
> **a.** Listing the type of employment tax and the adjustment for the proposed tax
> **b.** Informing the business of the opportunity for the employer to seek a review of the proposed assessment
> **c.** Including a schedule of the workers classified as employees
> **d.** All of the above are functions of the NDWC

> **10.** What redress does an employer have if the IRS erroneously assesses taxes based on worker classification issues without issuing an NDWC or obtaining the employer's waiver of restrictions on assessment?
>
> **a.** The employer is entitled to an automatic abatement of the current assessment
> **b.** The employer is permanently pardoned from the assessment
> **c.** The employer may obtain a permanent exemption from withholding for the workers misclassified by the IRS
> **d.** None of the above is an available recourse

CONCLUSION

The misclassification of workers is not a new problem. However, the fact that the issue persists does not minimize its current importance. Misclassification translates into billions of dollars in lost tax revenues for federal and state governments, just at a time when both are aggressively looking to supplement revenue lost to the current economic downturn. Consequently, the IRS and their state tax counterparts will be paying more attention—and seeking new enforcement techniques—as the number of individuals being incorrectly classified as independent contractors steadily increases.

MODULE 3: TAX REPORTING IN TRANSITION — CHAPTER 8
New Preparer Penalty Standards

This chapter explores the recent changes to the Code Sec. 6694 preparer penalty standards, with particular emphasis on the first-tier penalty standard in Code Sec. 6694(a). After Congress revised the preparer penalty standard in 2007, the IRS issued proposed regulations. However, Congress subsequently revised Code Sec. 6694(a) yet again in the *Emergency Economic Stabilization Act of 2008*. This roller coaster of changes has left many practitioners uncertain about the requirements of Code Sec. 6694.

LEARNING OBJECTIVES

Upon completion of this chapter, you will be able to:

- Identify the old Code Sec. 6694 rules;
- Describe the changes made by the *Small Business Work and Opportunity Tax Act of 2007* to Code Sec. 6994;
- Describe the proposed Code Sec. 6694 regs;
- Explain the changes made by the *Emergency Economic Stabilization Act of 2008;*
- Explain the one-preparer per firm rule and how it has change over the past year; and
- Understand tax return preparers' responsibilities under Code Sec. 6694 as they now exist.

INTRODUCTION

In May 2007 Congress passed the *Small Business and Work Opportunity Tax Act of 2007* (P.L. 110-28, the 2007 Small Business Tax Act). At the last minute and with little publicity, Congress voted to change the long-time Code Sec. 6694(a) preparer penalty standard from a *realistic possibility of a tax position being sustained on its merits* to a "reasonable belief that the position would more likely than not be sustained on its merits." The change caught even the IRS off-guard. Then, in October 2008, Congress made more changes to Code Sec. 6694. In the *Emergency Economic Stabilization Act of 2008*, Congress replaced the more likely than not standard in Code Sec. 6694(a) with substantial authority for undisclosed, nonabusive positions. This repeal was retroactive to the 2007 effective date of the original provision in the 2007 Small Business Tax Act.

> **COMMENT**
>
> Although Congress amended the preparer penalty rules yet again in the *Emergency Economic Stabilization Act of 2008*, its changes are limited to the first-tier preparer standard in Code Sec. 6694(a). The *Emergency Economic Stabilization Act of 2008* does not amend the second-tier standard in Code Sec. 6692(b) nor does it affect the scope of Code Sec. 6694. Many portions of the proposed regulations are unaffected or only slightly affected by the changes made in the *Emergency Economic Stabilization Act of 2008*. The IRS could finalize those portions and re-propose other portions impacted by the new law. The first- and second-tier standards are discussed later in this chapter.

OLD STANDARD

Before the changes made by Congress in the 2007 Small Business Tax Act and *Emergency Economic Stabilization Act of 2008*, if an income tax return preparer reported an undisclosed item that caused an understatement and that item had no realistic possibility of being sustained on the merits, and the preparer knew or should have known it, the preparer was subject to a penalty unless the item was disclosed and was not frivolous. Essentially, Code Sec. 6694(a) penalized undisclosed nonfrivolous positions for any entry or a return that did not have a more than one-in-three chance of being sustained on examination by the IRS.

> **COMMENT**
>
> In contrast to the return preparer's standard, the taxpayer's standard is (and remains) *substantial authority*. The substantial authority standard is less stringent than a more likely than not standard (that is, a greater-than-50-percent likelihood of being upheld in litigation) but stricter than a reasonable basis standard (that is, significantly higher than not frivolous or not patently improper). The substantial authority standard is generally understood to mean a 40 percent chance of success.

The IRS generally did not impose an unrealistic position penalty if the position was not frivolous and was adequately disclosed. The unrealistic position penalty was also not imposed if the understatement was due to reasonable cause and the preparer acted in good faith, or relied in good faith on the advice of another preparer.

Unrealistic Position

An *unrealistic position* is one for which there is no realistic possibility of being sustained on its merits. Traditionally, a realistic possibility of success is understood to mean that a position has a one-in-three chance or better of prevailing under an IRS examination.

Disclosed Positions

The threshold for disclosed nonfrivolous positions was even lower. The IRS generally would not impose a penalty with respect to adequately disclosed positions as long as they were nonfrivolous. The IRS would not impose a penalty with respect to adequately disclosed positions as long as they were not frivolous.

Disclosure. Disclosure under the old rules generally was made on Form 8275, *Disclosure Statement,* on Form 8275-R, *Regulation Disclosure Statement,* or on the taxpayer's return. Annually, the IRS issues guidance (Rev. Proc. 2008-14 for 2007 tax forms) identifying circumstances under which the disclosure of a position on a taxpayer's return related to particular issues will be considered adequate disclosure.

Exception for reasonable cause and good faith. Under the old rules, the unrealistic position penalty would not be imposed if the understatement was due to reasonable cause and the preparer acted in good faith. The IRS identified various factors to consider in determining whether an understatement was due to reasonable cause and whether the preparer acted in good faith. These include:

- Nature of the error;
- Frequency of errors;
- Materiality of errors;
- Preparer's normal office practice; and
- Reliance on advice of another preparer.

Income tax return preparers. The old rules applied only to income tax return preparers. An *income tax return preparer* is an individual who prepares for compensation any income tax return or any refund claim. Additionally, an individual who does not physically prepare an income tax return is considered a preparer if that person furnishes to a taxpayer or other preparer sufficient information and advice so that completion of the return or claim for refund is largely a mechanical matter.

However, an income tax return preparer would not include:

- A person who furnishes typing, reproducing, or other mechanical assistance;
- One who prepares a return or refund claim for the employer by whom he or she is regularly and continuously employed;
- A person who prepares as a fiduciary a return or refund claim for any person; and

- One who prepares a refund claim for a taxpayer in response to any notice of deficiency or any waiver of restriction after the commencement of an audit of that taxpayer or another taxpayer, if a determination in such audit of the other taxpayer directly or indirectly affects the tax liability of the taxpayer.

Additionally, the old rules included a *de minimis safe harbor.* A tax return preparer would not be considered to have prepared a *substantial portion* of a return or refund claim if the schedule, entry, or other portion of such return or refund claim involved amounts of gross income, amounts of deductions, or amounts on the basis of which credits were determined that were:

- Less than $2,000; or
- Less than $100,000 and also less than 20 percent on the gross income (or adjusted gross income if the taxpayer is an individual) as shown on the return or refund claim.

Penalties. Different preparer penalties were imposed under the old rules for unrealistic positions and for reckless or intentional disregard of the rules. The penalty was $250 for an unrealistic position. A $1,000 penalty (reduced by the amount of the penalty paid for understatements due to unrealistic positions) was imposed if there was a willful attempt to understate the client's tax liability or a reckless or intentional disregard of rules.

COMMENT

Before releasing the proposed regs, the IRS made available transitional relief, which has generally expired. For income tax returns, amended returns, and refund claims due on or before December 31, 2007 (determined with regard to any extension of time for filing), the pre-2007 Small Business Tax Act standards and the current regulations were applied to determine whether the IRS would impose a penalty under Code Sec. 6694(a). For all other returns, amended returns, and claims for refund, including estate, gift, and generation-skipping transfer tax returns, due on or before December 31, 2007 (determined with regard to any extension of time for filing), employment tax returns and excise tax returns, due on or before January 31, 2008, the "reasonable basis" standard under the current regulations issued under Code Sec. 6662, without regard to the disclosure requirements, is applied to determine whether the IRS will impose a penalty under Code Sec. 6694(a).

STUDY QUESTIONS

---

1. Under the old standard, Code Sec. 6694(a) penalized preparers' undisclosed, nonfrivolous tax positions that did not have more than a ____ of being sustained on its merits upon IRS examination.

   a. Realistic possibility

   b. Substantial likelihood

   c. High degree of certainty

   d. None of the above is the Code Sec. 6694(a) standard

2. The preparer penalty under the old standard for a willful attempt to understate a client's tax liability was:

   a. $250

   b. $1,000

   c. $2,000

   d. 20 percent of the taxpayer's gross income shown on the return or refund claim

---

SMALL BUSINESS AND WORK OPPORTUNITY TAX ACT OF 2007

The *Small Business and Work Opportunity Tax Act of 2007* (2007 Small Business Tax Act), extensively amended Code Sec. 6694 and certain sections of Code Sec. 7701. Not only did Congress extend the scope of return preparer penalties to preparers of all returns (not just income tax returns) and raise the amount of the monetary penalties, lawmakers also heightened the penalty standards.

Under the 2007 Small Business Tax Act:

- The Code Sec. 6694(a) first-tier penalty is imposed in an amount equal to the greater of $1,000 or 50 percent of the income derived—or to be derived—by the tax return preparer from the preparation of the return. The penalty applies when there is an understatement of a client's tax liability that results from an undisclosed position for which the tax return preparer did not have a reasonable belief that the position would more likely than not be sustained on its merits, or is due to a disclosed position for which there is no reasonable basis; and

- The Section 6694(b) second-tier penalty is imposed in an amount equal to the greater of $5,000 or 50 percent of the income derived—or to be derived—by the tax return preparer from preparation of a return that understates a client's tax liability resulting from the preparer's willful attempt to understate the client's tax liability or the preparer's reckless or intentional disregard of rules or regulations.

Effectively, for Code Sec. 6694(a), the 2007 Small Business Tax Act replaced the old "realistic possibility of success" standard for undisclosed, nonabusive positions with "a reasonable belief that the position would more likely than not be sustained on its merits." The new law replaces the old "not frivolous" standard for disclosed, nonabusive positions with "a reasonable basis."

Who Is a Tax Return Preparer?

As amended by the 2007 Small Business Tax Act, Code Sec. 7701(a)(36) defines *tax return preparer* as any person who prepares for compensation a tax return or claim for refund, or a substantial portion of a tax return or claim for refund. The definition of a preparer is no longer limited to persons who prepare income tax returns. It was expanded to include preparers of all types of returns, such as gift tax, estate tax, and employment tax. A preparer may be a signing preparer or a nonsigning preparer. Under the new proposed regulations for Code Sec. 6694, a tax return preparer is subject to penalties only if he or she was "primarily responsible" for the position that gave rise to the understatement.

Signing preparers. The *signing preparer* is generally considered to be primarily responsible for all of the positions on the return. However, another nonsigning individual in the same firm may be considered the person primarily responsible for the return if the signing preparer or another source provides information that shows such nonsigning individual was, in fact, primarily responsible for a position giving rise to an understatement.

EXAMPLE

Franco Dinari and Greta Gemundlich are employed by an accounting firm. They are involved in preparing the Form 990-T, *Exempt Organization Business Income Tax Return,* for a tax-exempt organization. After they complete the return—including the gathering of the necessary information, analyzing the proper application of the tax laws to such information, and the performance of the necessary mathematical computations—Ian McFaber, a supervisory employee of the firm, reviews the return. Ian compares the information the client provided and the application of the tax laws to this information. The mathematical computations and carried-forward amounts are reviewed by Jan Nederwund, an employee of the firm who is not a supervisor. Mary Kay McDoogle, a partner in the firm, finally reviews the return. The scope of Mary Kay's review includes reviewing the information provided, applying her knowledge of the tax-exempt organization's affairs, confirming that the accounting firm's policies and practices have been followed, and making the final determination with respect to the proper application of the tax laws to determine the client's tax liability. Mary Kay is the individual tax return preparer who is primarily responsible for the positions taken in the return, regardless of whether she signed the return.

Nonsigning preparers. If individuals within a firm are nonsigning tax return preparers and there is no signing preparer within that firm, then the individual in the firm with "overall supervisory responsibility" for the position(s) giving rise to the understatement is considered to be the preparer primarily responsible for the position and therefore is the preparer for purposes of Code Sec. 6694.

COMMENT

The IRS created a safe harbor for nonsigning preparers in the proposed regulations. In determining whether an individual is a nonsigning preparer, the proposed regs provide that any time spent on advice given with respect to events that have occurred that is less than 5 percent of the aggregate time incurred by the person with respect to the position(s) giving rise to the understatement will not be taken into account in determining whether an individual prepared a "substantial portion" of the return.

COMMENT

A practitioner who gives advice only in connection with *prospective* tax planning will not be considered a nonsigning preparer under the proposed regulations.

De minimis exception. The proposed regulations also revise the de minimis safe harbor for *nonsigning* tax return preparers. The de minimis exception provides that a nonsigning preparer will not be deemed to have prepared a substantial portion of the return and therefore will not be subject to penalties under Code Sec. 6694, if the item giving rise to the understatement is less than:

- $10,000; or
- $400,000 and is also less than 20 percent of the taxpayer's gross income (or, for an individual, less than 20 percent of the individual's adjusted gross income).

CAUTION

The de minimis exception in the proposed regs does not apply for signing tax return preparers. Additionally, the $10,000 amount refers to the dollar amount of the deduction, credit, or unreported item credit and not to the amount of understated tax. Thus, the de minimis exception is applied equally across the board, no matter what tax bracket applies.

EXAMPLE

Adam Ryan provides advice to his client on the client's income tax return concerning the proper treatment of an item. In preparation for providing that advice, Adam consults with Barry Johnson, who works at the same firm, regarding proper treatment of the item. Adam is the attorney who signs the client's return as a tax return preparer. For the item in question, Barry provides advice on its tax treatment upon which Adam relies. Barry's advice is reflected on client's income tax return. The advice constitutes preparation of a substantial portion of the return within the meaning of Prop. Reg. §301.7701-15(b)(3). The IRS challenges the position taken on the tax return giving rise to an understatement of tax liability. In accordance with the proposed Code Sec. 6694 regs, the IRS initially considers Adam to be the tax return preparer, because he signed the return, and the IRS advises Adam that he may be subject to penalty under Code Sec. 6694. However, based upon information received from Adam or another source, it may be concluded that Barry was primarily responsible for the position taken on the return that gave rise to the understatement because Barry gave advice that was directly relevant to the position giving rise to an understatement, and the signing preparer relied upon that advice.

CAUTION

The IRS has repeatedly cautioned that the examples in the proposed regs, and in earlier preparer penalty guidance, are "just examples." Practitioners should not rely too heavily on the examples or try to plan tax positions based on the examples.

Substantial portion. Only a person who prepares all or a substantial portion of a return or claim for refund is treated as a tax return preparer under the proposed regs. The IRS has identified some factors to take into account in discerning who the preparer is. The factors to consider in determining whether a schedule, entry, or other portion of a return is a substantial portion include but are not limited to the:

- Size and complexity of the item relative to the taxpayer's gross income; and
- Size of the understatement attributable to the item compared to the taxpayer's reported tax liability.

CAUTION

An individual who provides sufficient information and advice so that completion of the return or claim for refund is largely a mechanical or clerical matter is considered a tax return preparer, even though that person does not actually place or review placement of information on the return.

Location. A preparer may be located outside the United States. Under the proposed regs, an individual who prepares a return or refund claim from outside the United States is a tax return preparer, regardless of the person's nationality, residence, or the location of the person's place of business, if the person otherwise satisfies the definition of tax return preparer.

Returns. The IRS has proposed revising the definitions of *return* and *claim for refund* to only include returns and claims for refund that are specifically identified in published guidance. The IRS took a similar approach in the transitional relief issued before the proposed regs (Notice 2008-13) and in subsequent guidance (Notice 2008-56). These notices described the returns and refund claims subject to Code Sec. 6694.

PLANNING POINTER

For an electronically signed tax return, the proposed regs provide that a preparer need not sign the return before presenting a completed copy of the return to his or her client. However, the preparer must provide all of the information that will be transmitted in the electronically signed tax return to the client contemporaneously with Form 8879, *IRS e-file Signature Authorization*, or other similar e-file signature form.

COMMENT

The proposed regs for Code Sec. 7701-15, Tax Return Preparer, also describe persons who are not considered to be preparers. Individuals excluded from classification as tax return preparers include:

- Volunteer income tax return preparers;
- Individuals providing tax assistance as part of a qualified Low Income Taxpayer Clinic;
- General partners of the taxpayer entity;
- Fiduciaries of estates and trusts;
- Individuals preparing claims for refund in response to a notice of deficiency issued to the taxpayer;
- Individuals providing only typing, reproduction, or other mechanical assistance for returns; and
- Individuals preparing returns for their employers.

STUDY QUESTIONS

---

3. The de minimis exception of the proposed regulations under the *Small Business and Work Opportunity Tax Act of 2007* applies only to certain:

    a. Signing tax preparers

    b. Nonsigning tax preparers

    c. Taxpayers

    d. Practitioners who give advice only in connection with prospective tax planning

4. Which of the following would ***not*** be considered a tax return preparer?

    a. A practitioner who prepares and signs a client's U.S. return but is an accountant of Indian citizenship whose business office is located in Calcutta, India

    b. An individual who provides sufficient information and advice to her paralegal assistant, who generates the return, obtains the client's signature, and e-files the return

    c. A nonresident alien who collects and reviews data for a client's return and approves the tax position taken

    d. All of the above would be considered tax return preparers

---

Reliance

Under the proposed regs, a preparer may generally rely in good faith—without independent verification—on information provided by the taxpayer. Similarly, a preparer may rely in good faith and without independent verification on information from:

- Another advisor;
- Another tax return preparer; or
- Another party (including another advisor or tax return preparer at the tax return preparer's firm).

> **CAUTION**
>
> A preparer may not rely on information provided by a taxpayer with respect to legal conclusions on federal tax issues.

A preparer is not required to audit, examine, or review books and records, business operations, or documents or other evidence to independently verify information provided by the taxpayer, advisor, other tax return preparer, or another party. However, a preparer cannot ignore the implications of information furnished to him or her, or information actually known by the preparer. If any information furnished by others appears to be incorrect or incomplete, the preparer must make reasonable inquiries. In addition, the preparer must also comply with other sections of the Internal Revenue Code that require the existence of certain facts and circumstances, or that require certain documentation, such as the substantiation requirements that relate to noncash charitable contributions under Code Sec. 170(f).

EXAMPLE

Fran Franklin's client, Allan Black, told her that he had made a charitable contribution of real estate in the amount of $50,000 during the tax year. In fact, Allan did not make this contribution. Fran did not inquire about the existence of a qualified appraisal nor did she complete a Form 8283, *Non-cash Charitable Contributions,* as required by Code Sec. 170(f)(11). Fran reported a deduction on Allan's federal income tax return for the charitable contribution, which resulted in an understatement of liability for tax, and signed the tax return as the tax return preparer. Fran is liable for a penalty under Code Sec. 6694 because she did not make reasonable inquiries regarding the value of the real estate or complete a Form 8283.

Reasonable Belief/More Likely Than Not Standard

Under the 2007 Small Business Tax Act, a preparer risked being penalized under Code Sec. 6694(a) for an undisclosed, nonabusive position that gives rise to an understatement of tax if, among other factors, he or she did not have a reasonable belief that the position would more likely than not be sustained on its merits. A preparer may reasonably believe that a position would more likely than not be sustained on its merits if:

- The preparer analyzes the pertinent facts and authorities; and
- In reliance upon that analysis, reasonably concludes in good faith that the position has a greater than 50 percent likelihood of being sustained on its merits.

COMMENT

The proposed regulations included provisions on how to make the requisite disclosure under the more likely than not standard in Code Sec. 6694(a). The proposed regulations required preparers to provide disclosure of a return position where the position has a reasonable basis, but the "more likely than not" standard could be satisfied. For a signing return preparer, disclosure could be accomplished in one of five ways, including the use of Form 8275, *Disclosure Statement,* or Form 8275-R, *Regulation Disclosure Statement.* The IRS will likely revisit these proposed disclosure rules to reflect the changes made to Code Sec. 6694 by the *Emergency Economic Stabilization Act of 2008.*

Penalties

The 2007 Small Business Tax Act significantly increased the penalties under Code Sec. 6694:

- The old first-tier $250 penalty in Code Sec. 6694(a) for understatements due to an unreasonable position jumps to the greater of $1,000 or 50 percent of the income derived, or to be derived, by the preparer; and
- The old second-tier $1,000 penalty in Code Sec. 6694(b) for understatements due to willful or reckless conduct increases to the greater of $5,000 or 50 percent of the income derived or to be derived by the preparer.

> **COMMENT**
>
> For purposes of the penalties under Code Sec. 6694, the date that a return is deemed prepared is the date the return is signed by the preparer. If the preparer fails to sign the return, the date the return is filed is deemed the date it was prepared.

Income derived. To determine the amount of income derived by a preparer, all of the compensation the preparer receives or expects to receive in preparing the return or providing tax advice is taken into account. If the preparer is paid by a firm for work done for a client of the firm, income derived would be all compensation that can be reasonably allocated to work done in preparing the return or advising the client on a position giving rise to an understatement. If the firm is subject to penalty under Code Sec. 6694, then all compensation received by the firm would be included as income derived from the transaction.

> **COMMENT**
>
> If both the firm and the preparer are subject to liability under Code Sec. 6694, the income derived from the transaction counts only once. This means that the income received by the firm from the client and paid to the preparer would not be used two times in determining the maximum penalty.

No automatic referral. In good news for practitioners, the IRS announced that a referral by revenue agents to the Service's Office of Professional Responsibility (OPR) will not be automatic when the IRS assesses a penalty under Code Sec. 6694(a) against a preparer who is also a practitioner within the meaning of Circular 230. Circular 230 contains the rules of practice before the IRS for attorneys, CPAs, enrolled agents, and others.

The IRS explained in the proposed regs that "in matters involving non-willful conduct, the IRS will generally look for a pattern of failing to meet the required penalty standards under Code Sec. 6694(a) before making a referral to OPR." However, the IRS cautioned practitioners that egregious conduct may result in a referral to OPR.

> **COMMENT**
>
> The IRS did not describe *egregious conduct.* The final regs may shed some more light on what the IRS would consider to be egregious conduct.

> **COMMENT**
>
> The American Bar Association (ABA) Taxation Section has warned that practitioners may be vulnerable to the stacking of penalties under Code Sec. 6694(a) and Circular 230. The *American Jobs Creation Act of 2004* technically gave the IRS the power to impose monetary penalties for violations of Circular 230. Therefore, practitioners could theoretically be liable for two monetary penalties. However, the IRS has indicated that it will not stack penalties for violations of Code Sec. 6694(a) and Circular 230.

STUDY QUESTION

> **5.** The first-tier penalty under Code Sec. 6694(a) was revised by the *Small Business and Work Opportunity Tax Act of 2007* to impose an understatement penalty for preparers constituting the greater of:
>
> **a.** $5,000 or 100 percent of the preparer's income derived with respect to the return
>
> **b.** $3,000 or 75 percent of the preparer's income derived with respect to the return
>
> **c.** $2,000 or 60 percent of the preparer's income derived with respect to the return
>
> **d.** $1,000 or 50 percent of the preparer's income derived with respect to the return

One Preparer per Firm Rule

The proposed regs make a significant departure from the *one preparer per firm rule* in the old regs. Under the old rules, no more than one individual associated with a firm was treated as a preparer for the same return. If a signing preparer was associated with a firm, that individual, and no other individual associated with the firm, was considered the preparer, for purposes of the Code Sec. 6694 penalties.

If two or more individuals associated with a firm were nonsigning preparers of a return or refund claim, and there were no signing preparers, only one of the individuals was considered the preparer for purposes of the Code Sec. 6694 penalties. Ordinarily, this would have been the individual with overall "supervisory responsibility" for the *advice* given by the firm concerning the return or refund claim.

New approach. The proposed regs revise the one preparer per firm rule. In its place, the proposed regs adopt a framework that focuses on a position-by-position basis. Generally, the preparer signing the return would continue to be held responsible for all of the positions on a return. However, if the IRS determines that another individual had primary responsibility for a *position* giving rise to the understatement, that other individual would be responsible under Code Sec. 6694.

> **COMMENT**
>
> The IRS can determine whether another individual in the firm was primarily responsible for the return or the position at issue, based upon information provided by the signing preparer or from other sources.

Nonsigning preparers. If there are one or more nonsigning tax return preparers at the same firm and no signing preparer, the individual with supervisory responsibility for the position would be responsible for the Code Sec. 6694 penalty.

Firm penalty. Under the proposed regs, a firm would be subject to a penalty when the firm's review procedures are disregarded by the firm through willfulness, recklessness, or gross indifference in the formulation of the advice, or in the preparation of the return or claim for refund that included the position for which the penalty is imposed.

> **EXAMPLE**
>
> Adam Carlson provides advice to his client Corey Snyder about the proper treatment of an item with respect to which all events have occurred. In preparation for providing that advice, Adam seeks advice from Barbara Barton, a supervising attorney in the same firm as Adam. Adam is the preparer who signs Corey's return as a tax return preparer. Barbara provides advice on the tax treatment of the item upon which Adam relies. Barbara's advice is reflected on Corey's income tax return, but no disclosure is made. The advice constitutes preparation of a substantial portion of the return. The IRS challenges the position taken on the tax return, giving rise to an understatement of liability. Adam is initially considered the tax return preparer with respect to Corey's return and the IRS advises Adam that Adam may be subject to the penalty. However, Adam advises the IRS of the information he received from Barbara, and the IRS determines Barbara had primary responsibility for the position taken on the return that gave rise to the understatement because Barbara had overall supervisory responsibility for the position giving rise to an understatement.

Willful/Reckless Conduct: Code Sec. 6694(b)

Code Sec. 6694(b) governs a preparer's willful or reckless conduct. As amended by the 2007 Small Business Tax Act, the penalty under Code Sec. 6694(b) for a preparer's willful attempt to understate a client's tax liability on a return or claim for refund is the greater of $5,000 or 50 percent of the income derived (or to be derived) by the preparer with respect to the return. The penalty also applies to any reckless or intentional disregard of rules or regulations by a preparer. This discussion highlights the Code Sec. 6694(b) penalty under both circumstances.

COMMENT

Rules and regulations include the provisions of the Internal Revenue Code, temporary or final Treasury regulations issued under the Tax Code, and revenue rulings or notices (other than notices of proposed rulemaking) issued by the Internal Revenue Service and published in the *Internal Revenue Bulletin.*

EXAMPLE

Minh Lau provides Alyce Stein, her tax return preparer, with check registers detailing all of her personal and business expenses. One of the expenses was for domestic help. Minh identified this expense as personal on her check register. Alyce knowingly (and without reasonable basis) deducted the expenses of Minh's domestic help as wages paid in the taxpayer's business. Alyce is subject to the penalty under Code Sec. 6694(b).

Exceptions. Generally, a preparer is not considered to have recklessly or intentionally disregarded a rule or regulation if:

- The position has a reasonable basis and is adequately disclosed; and
- If the position represents a good faith challenge to the validity of the regulation and the regulation being challenged is identified.

Additionally, in the case of a position contrary to a revenue ruling or notice (other than an IRS notice of proposed rulemaking), a preparer is not considered to have recklessly or intentionally disregarded the ruling or notice if he or she reasonably believes that the position would more likely than not be sustained on its merits.

Disclosure. With respect to Code Sec. 6694(b), disclosure must be made using Form 8275 or Form 8275-R, in accordance with Prop. Reg. Sec. 1.6694-2(c)(3).

> **CAUTION**
>
> Prop. Reg. Sec. 1.6694-3(c)(2) provides that disclosure merely on the return in accordance with the annual revenue procedure under Reg. §1.6662-4(f)(2) (Rev. Proc. 2008-14 for 2008) is not adequate with respect to the penalty for willful or reckless conduct under Code Sec. 6694(b).

> **EXAMPLE**
>
> In preparing her client's return, Latisha Madison fully deducts certain expenses incurred in the purchase of a business. Final regulations from the IRS provide that such expenses incurred in the purchase of a business must be capitalized. The U.S. Tax Court has expressly invalidated that portion of the regulations in a recent case. The case has been appealed but no decision has yet been announced. Latisha discloses the position using Form 8275. She has a reasonable basis for the position. She will not be subject to a penalty under Code Sec. 6694(b) because the position represents a good faith challenge to the validity of the regulations and is adequately disclosed.

Reduced penalty. The Code Sec. 6694(b) penalty is reduced by any Code Sec. 6694(a) penalty assessed and collected against the preparer for the same return or claim for refund.

Burden of proof. The government has the burden of proof in any proceeding with respect to a Code Sec. 6694(b) penalty on the issue of whether the preparer willfully attempted to understate the liability for tax. The preparer bears the burden of proof on such other issues as whether:

- He or she recklessly or intentionally disregarded a rule or regulation;
- A position contrary to a regulation represents a good faith challenge to the validity of the regulation; and
- Disclosure was adequately made.

> **COMMENT**
>
> If the IRS is unsuccessful in proving willful or reckless conduct under Code Sec. 6694(b), the IRS is not prevented, in the alternative, from imposing the Code Sec. 6694(a) penalty for understatement due to an unreasonable position.

EMERGENCY ECONOMIC STABILIZATION ACT OF 2008

Responding to complaints that the more likely than not standard in Code Sec. 6694(a) and the substantial authority standard in Code Sec. 6662 created a disconnect for preparers and taxpayers, Congress revised

Code Sec. 6694(a) yet again in October 2008. The *Emergency Economic Stabilization Act of 2008* (P.L. 110-343) removes the more likely than not standard from Code Sec. 6694(a) for undisclosed, nonabusive positions and replaces it with substantial authority. Essentially, the new law equalizes the preparer and taxpayer standards at substantial authority. The change is retroactive to the effective date of the *Small Business Work and Opportunity Tax Act of 2007* (May 25, 2007). However, if the position is with respect to a tax shelter, listed transaction, or reportable transaction with significant avoidance or evasion purposes, the changes made by the *Emergency Economic Stabilization Act of 2008* apply to returns prepared after October 3, 2008 (the date of enactment of the *Emergency Economic Stabilization Act of 2008).*

COMMENT

The *Emergency Economic Stabilization Act of 2008* effectively creates three categories for an "unreasonable position." The first category is a general category for undisclosed, nonabusive positions. The second category is for disclosed positions, and the third category is for tax shelters and reportable transactions.

CAUTION

The *Emergency Economic Stabilization Act of 2008* leaves unchanged the increased penalties under Code Sec. 6694 as enacted by the 2007 Small Business Tax Act.

General Category

For undisclosed, nonabusive positions that fall into the general category, the Code Sec. 6694(a) penalty applies unless there is or was substantial authority for the position. This conforms the preparer standard for positions falling within the general category to the Code Sec. 6662(d)(2)(B)(1) taxpayer standard for imposition of the accuracy-related penalty.

Substantial Authority

Substantial authority under the taxpayer standard in Code Sec. 6662 is an objective standard involving an analysis of the law and application of the law to relevant facts. The substantial authority standard is less stringent than a more likely than not standard (that is, a greater-than-50-percent likelihood of being upheld in litigation), but stricter than a reasonable basis standard (that is, significantly higher than not frivolous or not patently improper).

Authorities. In determining whether there is substantial authority, the following are generally considered substantial authority:

- The Tax Code and other statutory provisions;
- Temporary, proposed, and final regulations construing those statutes;
- Court cases;
- Revenue rulings and revenue procedures;
- Tax treaties and regulations and other official explanations of the treaties;
- Congressional intent as reflected in committee reports, joint explanatory statements of managers included in conference committee reports, and floor statements made before enactment by the bill's managers;
- Letter rulings and technical advice memoranda issued after October 31, 1976;
- Actions on decisions and general counsel memoranda issued after March 12, 1981;
- General counsel memoranda published in the pre-1955 volumes of the *Cumulative Bulletin;*
- Information or press releases, notices, announcements and any other similar documents published by the IRS in the *Internal Revenue Bulletin;* and
- General explanations of tax legislation prepared by the Joint Committee on Taxation (the Blue Book).

Substantial authority also exists when the tax treatment of an item is supported by controlling precedent of a U.S. court of appeals to which the taxpayer has a right of appeal as to the item. Otherwise, the applicability of court cases to the taxpayer because of the taxpayer's residence in a particular jurisdiction is not taken into account in determining whether there is substantial authority for the tax treatment of an item.

> **CAUTION**
>
> Court cases do not provide substantial authority if they involve factual situations that differ from the taxpayer's in material ways.

Conclusions reached in treatises, legal periodicals, legal opinions, or opinions rendered by other tax professionals are not authority. However, the authorities underlying these expressions of opinion may give rise to substantial authority for the tax treatment of an item. The advice of hired professionals alone is not substantial authority, even when reasonable under the circumstances and regardless of the form in which it is rendered.

There may be substantial authority for the tax treatment of an item despite the absence of certain types of authority, especially when the taxpayer's situation is novel. Thus, a taxpayer may have substantial authority for a position that is supported only by a well-reasoned construction of the applicable statutory provision. A taxpayer had substantial authority for in correct treatment of income when there were no precedents directly on point, and one case provided partial support for her position.

STUDY QUESTION

6. Which of the following constitutes substantial authority under Code Sec. 6662?

   a. Congressional floor statements made before enactment by the bill's managers
   b. Legal opinions expressed in treatises
   c. Independent auditor's opinions
   d. None of the above is a type of substantial authority

Taxpayer's ruling. There is substantial authority for the taxpayer's treatment of an item if the treatment is supported by the conclusion of a ruling or a determination letter issued to the taxpayer, by the conclusion of a technical advice memorandum in which the taxpayer is named, or by an affirmative statement in a revenue agent's report for a prior tax year of the taxpayer (written determinations). However, this rule does not apply if:

- There was a misstatement or material omission of a material fact, or the facts that subsequently develop are materially different from the facts on which the written determination was based; or
- The written determination was revoked or modified after the date of its issuance by:
  — A notice to the taxpayer to whom the written determination was issued,
  — The enactment of legislation or ratification of a tax treaty,
  — A decision of the U.S. Supreme Court,
  — The issuance of temporary or final regulations, or
  — The issuance of a revenue ruling, revenue procedure, or other statement published in the *Internal Revenue Bulletin*.

The written determination ceases to be authority on the date and to the extent that it is modified or revoked.

Overruled authorities. An authority does not continue to be an authority once it is overruled or modified, implicitly or explicitly, by an authority of the same or higher source. For example, a letter ruling is not an authority if it is revoked, or if it is inconsistent with a subsequent proposed regulation, revenue ruling, or other administrative pronouncement published in the *Internal Revenue Bulletin.* A federal district court opinion is not authority if it is overruled or reversed by the court of appeals for that district. However, a Tax Court opinion is not overruled or modified by a court of appeals to which a taxpayer does not have a right of appeal, unless the Tax Court adopts the holding of the court of appeals.

Disclosed Positions

The standard for disclosed positions under the *Emergency Economic Stabilization Act of 2008* is the reasonable basis standard. Reasonable basis is a relatively high standard; that is, significantly higher than not frivolous or not patently improper.

> **CAUTION**
>
> The reasonable basis standard is not satisfied by a return position that is merely arguable or that is merely a colorable claim.

STUDY QUESTIONS

7. An affirmative statement in a revenue agent's written determination for a prior tax year is not substantial authority if facts subsequently differ materially from those forming the basis of the agent's report. *True or False?*

8. The standard under the *Emergency Economic Stabilization Act of 2008* for disclosed positions is not patently improper. *True or False?*

Tax Shelters, Reportable Transactions, and Listed Transactions

Tax shelters are investments that provide investors with the possibility of reducing their current income taxes through methods sanctioned by the Code, thereby "sheltering" current income from tax. A *material advisor* to a tax shelter transaction is required to file Form 8264, *Application for Registration of a Tax Shelter,* with the IRS describing any "reportable transaction" to which the material advisor was a party. A *reportable transaction* is one identified by the IRS under the Code Sec. 6011 transactions as having the potential for tax evasion or avoidance.

For tax shelters and reportable transactions to which Code Sec. 6662A applies (listed transactions and reportable transactions with significant tax avoidance or evasion purposes), the *Emergency Economic Stabilization Act of 2008* continues the requirement that preparers have a reasonable belief that such transaction would be more likely than not sustained on the merits.

> **COMMENT**
>
> The IRS will likely propose regulations explaining the parameters of what constitutes significant tax avoidance or evasion.

There are two categories of reportable transactions:
- Certain types of transactions identified by the IRS as tax-avoidance transactions; and
- Transactions that warrant further scrutiny because they possess certain identified characteristics that are common in corporate tax shelters.

The IRS has released a listing of specific transactions that are currently designated as *listed transactions*. Each of the transactions on the list has been determined to involve a significant tax-avoidance purpose, and the intended tax benefits of the transactions are subject to disallowance under current law.

> **COMMENT**
>
> Return preparers who are material advisors may also be subject to the reportable transaction requirements of Code Secs. 6111 and 6112. These rules are intended to increase the transparency of certain questionable transactions for the IRS to evaluate the transactions as early as possible.

STUDY QUESTIONS

> **9.** The *Emergency Economic Stabilization Act of 2008*:
> - **a.** Replaces the more likely than not standard in Code Sec. 6694(a) with a realistic possibility of being sustained on its merits standard
> - **b.** Equalizes the preparer and taxpayer penalty standards at more likely than not
> - **c.** Equalizes the preparer and taxpayer penalty standards for undisclosed, positions at substantial authority
> - **d.** Temporarily suspends the effective date of the changes made by the 2007 Small Business Tax Act to Code Sec. 6694(a) until January 1, 2011

10. The *Emergency Economic Stabilization Act of 2008* continues to require preparers to have a reasonable belief that _____ and _____ would be more likely than not sustained on the merits.
  a. Tax shelters; reportable transactions
  b. Transactions with no tax avoidance potential; international transactions
  c. Cross-border transactions; tax positions claiming NOLs
  d. The more likely than not standard has been eliminated for all tax positions

CONCLUSION

Almost no one could have predicted the changes to Code Sec. 6694 created by the *Small Business Work and Opportunity Tax Act of 2007* and one year later by the *Emergency Economic Stabilization Act of 2008*—certainly not the IRS. The traditional rules appeared to work well. However, Code Sec. 6694 has been changed by two major pieces of legislation and practitioners must adapt to the changes. Moreover, practitioners must communicate these important changes to their clients.

CPE NOTE: When you have completed your study and review of chapters 6-8, which comprise Module 3, you may wish to take the Quizzer for this Module.

For your convenience, you can also take this Quizzer online at **www. cchtestingcenter.com.**

TOP FEDERAL TAX ISSUES FOR 2009 CPE COURSE

Answers to Study Questions

MODULE 1 — CHAPTER 1

1. b. Correct. As long as recipients of Railroad Retirement or VA benefits filed federal tax returns for 2007 and their income did not exceed the maximum of $75,000 ($150,000 for joint-filing couples), these taxpayers received stimulus payments.
a. Incorrect. If the taxpayer owed back taxes or other debts, the amount of the payment would be offset by the amount owed.
c. Incorrect. To receive the stimulus payments, nonbusiness taxpayers were required to have Social Security numbers. An exception was allowed in the HEART Act for a couple in which at least one spouse was a member of the U.S. military.
d. Incorrect. Congress prohibited the IRS from issuing payments to taxpayers filing returns using ITINs.

2. a. Correct. The depreciation for passenger automobiles previously capped at $3,060 was raised by $8,000 for a total first-year depreciation limit of $11,060.
b. Incorrect. The caps are greater under the act. The $4,600 limit applied in the past, when 30-percent depreciation was available.
c. Incorrect. Each of the first-year depreciation maximum amounts is greater for 2008. The $7,650 limit applied when 50-percent depreciation was available.
d. Incorrect. The previous first-year depreciation for luxury automobiles was raised by the act.

3. a. Correct. With few exceptions, taxpayers must make equal installments over 15 years to repay the tax credit amount.
b. Incorrect. The credit is not required to be claimed on amended returns.
c. Incorrect. The claim for the tax credit is not made in installments.
d. Incorrect. The credit is subject to income phaseouts.

4. d. Correct. All three choices are tax-relief initiatives of the *Housing and Economic Recovery Act of 2008*.
a. Incorrect. The Housing Act increases the amount of and simplifies the rules for claiming the credit.
b. Incorrect. The Housing Act temporarily expands the program to allow borrowers to refinance existing subprime mortgages.

c. Incorrect. The Housing Act bans the practice of seller funded down payment assistance programs.

5. a. Correct. For 2008, individuals who do not itemize their deductions on their federal income tax returns may claim an additional standard deduction for state and local real property taxes, up to $500 ($1,000 for joint returns).
b. Incorrect. The temporary additional standard deduction does not apply to business entertainment expenses.
c. Incorrect. The temporary additional standard deduction does not apply to medical expenses of individuals or employers' health plans.
d. Incorrect. The temporary additional standard deduction does not create an additional deduction for individuals or businesses making charitable contributions.

6. b. Correct. HOPE for Homeowners was created to enable homeowners to obtain new mortgages if the homeowners' debt-to-income ratio was greater than 31 percent as of March 31, 2008.
a. Incorrect. The program created has another title but was created under the *Mortgage Forgiveness Debt Relief Act of 2007* to help homeowners obtain new mortgages through FHA-approved lenders.
c. Incorrect. The program has another title but enables mortgage workouts by offering new mortgages for borrowers having a debt-to-income ratio greater than 31 percent.
d. Incorrect. The program carries a different title but offers new mortgages for distressed homeowners through FHA-approved lenders.

7. b. Correct. The HEART Act raises the minimum penalty for failure to file a federal tax return within 60 days of the due date (with extensions) to the lesser of $135 or 100 percent of the net amount of tax due.
a. Incorrect. Under the HEART Act, the minimum penalty for failure to file a federal tax return within 60 days of the due date (with extensions) is increased higher than $100 or 50 percent of the net amount of tax due.
c. Incorrect. The HEART Act changed the minimum penalty for failure to file a federal tax return within 60 days of the due date (with extensions) to a different amount and percentage of the net amount of tax due.
d. Incorrect. Under the HEART Act, the minimum penalty for failure to file a federal tax return within 60 days of the due date (with extensions) is increased, but to a lower amount or percentage of the net amount of tax due.

8. d. Correct. Through 2009, farmers and ranchers may claim up to 100 percent of their contribution base for charitable donations of conservation property.

a. _Incorrect._ The PPA raised the existing 20 percent limitation for the deduction of the contribution base.

b. _Incorrect._ The percentage was raised to 50 percent of the contribution base by the PPA but has since been changed.

c. _Incorrect._ The deduction has not been set at 75 percent, either by the Farm Act or previously by the PPA.

9. a. _Correct._ Many so-called extenders (popular but temporary tax breaks) expired at the end of 2007 and others will expire in 2008 and beyond. Also, the AMT exemption amounts approved for the 2007 tax year will revert to lower floors (subjecting taxpayers with lower incomes to the tax). The _Emergency Economic Stabilization Act of 2008_ extends many of the temporary tax incentives and also creates an AMT patch for 2008. **b. _Incorrect._** The HEART Act has already been enacted and targets tax relief for military families.

c. _Incorrect._ The _Economic Stimulus Act of 2008_ has already supplemented the first-year $3,060 depreciation on luxury automobiles by $8,000, for total allowance of up to $11,060.

d. _Incorrect._ Just one of the choices reflects some of the tax incentives in the _Emergency Economic Stabilization Act of 2008_.

10. False. _Correct._ The AMT patch passed in October 2008 applies retroactively to the 2008 tax year only.

True. _Incorrect._ The AMT patch enacted in 2008 applies only to that tax year.

MODULE 1 — CHAPTER 2

1. b. _Correct._ Code Sec. 121 requires ownership and use of the property, for an aggregate of two years out of the five-year period preceding the sale in order to qualify for the exclusion of gain from the property from taxable income. Although hardship exceptions are available to allow a partial exclusion if the time periods are only partially satisfied, that exclusion is not automatically granted in foreclosure situations but must be proved to the satisfaction of the IRS, usually through its letter ruling process.

a. _Incorrect._ Gain exclusions applying only to a homeowner's principal residence under Code Sec. 121 enable homeowners to exclude gain of up to $250,000 (single filers) or $500,000 (joint filers) from the foreclosure action.

c. _Incorrect._ When mortgaged property is classified as the principal residence, all or some debt forgiveness amounts may be excluded from taxable income.

d. _Incorrect._ One of the choices is not a form of tax relief for homeowners facing foreclosure sale of their principal residence.

2. d. Correct. All three choices are factors usable in determining a homeowner's principal residence fox tax purposes.
a. Incorrect. The taxpayer's place of employment is but one of the factors that may be considered in determining his or her principal residence.
b. Incorrect. Where the homeowner's religious organizations and recreational clubs are located is but one of the factors that may be considered in determining his or her principal residence.
c. Incorrect. The address listed for his or her tax returns, driver's license, automobile registrations, and voter registration are but some of the factors that may determine the homeowner's principal residence.

3. b. Correct. Code Sec. 108(a)(1)(A) through (E) list specific circumstances for exclusion from gross income of amounts in discharges of indebtedness.
a. Incorrect. Code Sec. 61(a) focuses on defining items includible in gross income with a general exclusion of income from discharge of indebtedness.
c. Incorrect. Code Sec. 1082(a)(2) describes basis adjustments of corporations.
d. Incorrect. One of the choices is the section of the Internal Revenue Code operative in determining exclusions from income recognition in discharges of indebtedness.

4. True. Correct. The tax benefit rule generally applies to forgiving past deductible interest, which is usually a part of any forgiven mortgage debt.
False. Incorrect. The common law principle of the tax benefit rule generally applies to forgiving past deductible interest due.

5. True. Correct. The fees may not be considered income.
False. Incorrect. Because they were not owed under law, the fees may not be income when reversed.

6. a. Correct. The basis is reduced (but not below zero) by the amount of forgiven qualified principal residence debt excluded from income.
b. Incorrect. Gain does not determine the effect on basis of excluding discharged indebtedness.
c. Incorrect. The basis in the property is affected by the exclusion of the discharged indebtedness.
d. Incorrect. One of the choices describes the effect on basis of the exclusion.

7. a. Correct. The exclusion is the legal insolvency, limited to the amount of liabilities exceeding the fair market value of all of the taxpayer's assets.
b. Incorrect. The Code Sec. 108 legal insolvency is not identical to functional insolvency.

c. Incorrect. Acquisition indebtedness is not the measure of insolvency under Code Sec. 108.

d. Incorrect. The amount of the borrower's mortgage loan is not the determinant of his or her insolvency under Code Sec. 108. The exclusion also applies to credit card and other unsecured debt that is forgiven.

8. a. Correct. The bankruptcy exclusion takes precedence over the insolvency exclusion, and both take precedence over the farm indebtedness exclusion. The effect of the ordering is that if a taxpayer is both in bankruptcy and insolvent, the exclusion amount is not limited to the amount of insolvency.

b. Incorrect. The insolvency exclusion does not have the highest precedence in exclusions of income from discharges of debt.

c. Incorrect. The other types of exclusion both take precedence over the farm indebtedness exclusion.

d. Incorrect. All three exclusion types have different precedence levels.

9. b. Correct. Any amount in excess of the $500,000 exclusion amount for joint filers on the sale of a principal residence is taxed at capital gains rates.

a. Incorrect. The gain exceeding the $500,000 exclusion is not taxed as ordinary income but at the lower, capital gain rate.

c. Incorrect. The basis reduction within the bankruptcy indebtedness exclusion occurs at the start of the *next* tax year and the gain on subsequent sale attributable to the exclusion amount is recaptured as ordinary income.

d. Incorrect. The excess gain to the extent of basis reduction for use of the principal residence exclusion, unlike the other exclusions under Code Sec. 108, is not recaptured as ordinary income to any extent.

10. b. Correct. Forgiveness of indebtedness income is generated only to the fair market value of the property for federal tax purposes because only the property is reachable to satisfy the mortgage debt.

a. Incorrect. Treatment is not the same for recourse and nonrecourse mortgages since the extent of a homeowner's liability in a recourse mortgage situation extends beyond the value of the property securing the mortgage.

c. Incorrect. More forgiveness of debt income is not created by nonrecourse mortgages; in many situations in a falling real estate market, it creates less.

d. Incorrect. One of the choices reflects the treatment of forgiveness of indebtedness income for nonrecourse mortgages.

11. True. *Correct.* Home equity loans not put back into home improvements (also known as cashout refinancing) do not qualify for the principal residence exclusion of forgiven debt under Section 108 no matter how laudable the purpose; nor do they increase basis for purposes of determining gain under Section 121.

False. *Incorrect.* These uses of refinancing in excess of the acquisition indebtedness, which is not used for improvement of the principal residence, always give rise to potential forgiveness of indebtedness income.

12. a. *Correct.* In a strict foreclosure the court orders conveyance of a property's deed to the lender to satisfy the mortgage debt fully.

b. *Incorrect.* There is no type of foreclosure process termed *nonnegotiable.* Especially under the terms of the *Mortgage Forgiveness Debt Relief Act of 2007,* mortgage renegotiations and workouts are sought.

c. *Incorrect.* A bid in at a foreclosure sale occurs when the mortgagee lenders purchase the mortgaged property at a foreclosure sale.

d. *Incorrect.* Curing a default occurs in the notification process that a property will have a foreclosure date set if payment and costs for the default are not paid within a time specified.

13. c. *Correct.* The deed in lieu of foreclosure option eliminates the need for an immediate sale to determine debt forgiveness income.

a. *Incorrect.* No temporary transfer is made in this alternative to foreclosure.

b. *Incorrect.* This circumstance is the short sale.

d. *Incorrect.* The deed in lieu of foreclosure is a separate alternative to foreclosure from bankruptcy.

14. a. *Correct.* Tax consequences benefit the former owner, especially when the property is a vacation home not eligible for the Code Sec. 108 exclusion or gain exclusion for principal residence sale.

b. *Incorrect.* The impact on the homeowner's credit rating of the sale of the residence does not depend directly on the valuation of the property sold.

c. *Incorrect.* A *vacation home* is personal use property, and losses from its sale cannot be netted against investment gains. Losing a home to a lender may create a greater psychological loss to the homeowner if it worth more when it is foreclosed upon, but will in fact create less ordinary debt forgiveness income, assuming that the value of the home cannot cover the amount of the mortgage in any event.

d. Incorrect. Although the vacation homeowner ends up without a vacation home whether it is valued high or low when a deed in lieu of foreclosure is transferred, the tax consequences will vary. Only in situations in which a principal residence is involved and the principal residence exclusions prevent any tax liability being recognized is valuation not an issue for the homeowner.

15. a. Correct. The IRS considers the sale portion of the foreclosure sale separate from income from the cancellation of indebtedness portion.

b. Incorrect. The loss is not considered an investment loss subject to the capital gains and losses tax structure.

c. Incorrect. Although typically the year of purchase and subsequent sale of the property are different, timing differences do not drive the IRS rule prohibiting deduction of the loss.

d. Incorrect. The loss is nondeductible, just as an excess of mortgage debt over home value is forgiveness of indebtedness income.

MODULE 1 — CHAPTER 3

1. a. Correct. The gross receipts of the final 2 months must total at least 25 percent of the total gross receipts of the requested period during the past 3 years.

b. Incorrect. The test is not based on a single tax year's gross receipts.

c. Incorrect. The taxpayer may not select 2 out of 5 years' gross receipts to support a change in tax year under the test.

d. Incorrect. One of the choices describes the qualifications for tax years considered under the gross receipts test.

2. b. Correct. Both cash and accrual basis taxpayers may not currently deduct prepaid expenses that create an asset or right to services with a useful life substantially beyond the end of the current tax year.

a. Incorrect. Both cash and accrual basis taxpayers who pay in advance for services may not deduct the expense until the services related to that expense are rendered or received.

c. Incorrect. Expenses that relate only to a single year are not amortized.

d. Incorrect. A cash basis taxpayer does not lose the right to an eventual deduction simply because an expense is prepaid.

3. a. Correct. Accelerating and deferring income recognition and deduction claims may even out taxable income and therefore keep the taxpayer in the lowest tax rate bracket overall for the two years under consideration.

b. Incorrect. Accelerating deductions for property purchases or delaying recognition of income may lower the business's overall tax liability over two years but not because it allows for some taxable income to go unreported.

c. Incorrect. Tax liability is not increased by proper use of deferral or acceleration. Total taxable income may be the same, but the planning of offsetting deductions can lower tax liability between the two years; expenses, too, may remain the same but their effective use in offsetting income can vary depending upon the year in which they are used.

d. Incorrect. The 50-percent bonus depreciation available only for 2008 is not phased out dependent on a company's profit level or income, so businesses may claim the deduction regardless of their income or deductions. Bonus depreciation does not generate more depreciation, merely front-loads it. The higher deduction for 2008 returns reduces the amount of depreciation available for the property in subsequent tax years.

4. d. Correct. The estimated cost of the property must exceed $1 million to claim bonus depreciation when a placed-in-service date occurs in 2009.

a. Incorrect. The required estimated value for property placed in service during 2009 is higher for claims of 50-percent bonus depreciation.

b. Incorrect. The required estimated value for property placed in service during 2009 is not $250,000 for bonus depreciation.

c. Incorrect. The *Economic Stimulus Act of 2008* mandates a different minimum estimated cost for property placed in during 2009 in order to claim 50-percent bonus depreciation.

5. c. Correct. The investment limit is $800,000 for the 2008 tax year, above which the dollar amount of the deduction phases out dollar for dollar.

a. Incorrect. The $125,000 amount is the dollar amount of the expense deduction for 2009 and 2010 (subject to an inflation adjustment).

b. Incorrect. The dollar amount of the expense deduction begins to phase out dollar-for-dollar at $500,000 when the expensing cap is $125,000 in 2009 and 2010 (subject to an inflation adjustment).

d. Incorrect. The investment ceiling for 2008 purchases is $800,000, so that the dollar amount of the expense deduction is reduced to zero under the phaseout schedule at $1.05 million.

6. b. Correct. The Code Sec. 179 limits, although still subject to the same limits on the annual deduction ceiling, investment ceiling, and taxable income, are increased by any carryovers.

a. Incorrect. The limits are not decreased by carryovers.

c. Incorrect. The limits are not independent of deductions carried over from prior tax years.

d. Incorrect. The tax credits do not increase the ceiling for Code Sec. 179 expensing.

7. a. Correct. The difference does not become part of the creditor's basis but rather a gain or loss in relation to the creditor's basis for the debt.
b. Incorrect. Accrued interest is included in the basis of the debt if the creditor included the interest in income in prior tax periods.
c. Incorrect. The creditor's basis is the fair market value of the property, if ascertainable, plus certain other components.
d. Incorrect. One of the choices is not a component of the creditor's basis.

8. b. Correct. The cancelled business debt of the bankrupt borrower is not included in income, and the taxpayer must reduce its tax attributes accordingly.
a. Incorrect. Cancelled debt of a bankrupt business taxpayer is not considered to be ordinary income to the borrower.
c. Incorrect. The cancelled debt of an insolvent business borrower is not treated as long-term capital gain for the debtor.
d. Incorrect. One of the choices is the outcome when debt is cancelled for a bankrupt business taxpayer.

9. d. Correct. An individual may include in NOLs losses due to work as an employee, casualty and theft, moving expenses, and rental property in addition to any business losses.
a. Incorrect. Moving expenses not reimbursed or associated with business ownership may be included in NOL computations by individuals.
b. Incorrect. Employees' work expenses may be included for purposes of computing an NOL.
c. Incorrect. Losses incurred from rental property are includible in NOL computations.

10. c. Correct. The current carryforward period for NOLs is 20 years, after which the loss expires.
a. Incorrect. The 2 years is the carryback period in which amended returns can claim NOLs as offsetting prior years' income.
b. Incorrect. The NOL carryforward period is not 5 years nor are unused NOLs applied against passive activity income.
d. Incorrect. One of the choices is the treatment of NOLs outlasting their carryforward period.

MODULE 2 — CHAPTER 4

1. d. Correct. The LLC business entity affords passthrough tax treatment of income and losses, limits personal liability of its members, is able to hold nonbusiness assets, and may make disproportionate distributions.

a. Incorrect. An LLC combines the positive corporate characteristic of limited liability, which is afforded to all LLC members, with the passthrough tax treatment of partnerships, subject to a single level of taxation.

b. Incorrect. LLCs may hold nonbusiness assets, such as investments. The income and expenses associated with such investment assets are also reported on members' individual income tax returns

c. Incorrect. LLCs are allowed to make disproportionate distributions to members. An example is income tax deductions for depreciation expenses, which may be allocated among members in proportion to their capital contributions.

2. d. Correct. All three choices are items usually included in the operating agreements. The agreements typically also specify how profits and losses will be shared, types of membership interest, how members are to be admitted or withdrawn, distribution rights, and other management rights.

a. Incorrect. Operating agreements usually include rules governing the LLC's capital account.

b. Incorrect. Transfer rights for membership interests are items specified in the operating agreement.

c. Incorrect. Voting rights are discussed in the LLC's operating agreement in most cases.

3. d. Correct. Schedule C of the owner's individual income tax return (Form 1040) lists the income and expense items for the SMLLC classified as a disregarded entity (sole proprietorship). All profits and losses of the SMLLC flow through to its owner.

a. Incorrect. Form 1065, *U.S. Return of Partnership Income*, is the return used by an LLC taxed as a partnership, not by an SMLLC treated as a disregarded entity.

b. Incorrect. Schedule K-1 of Form 1065 is the IRS schedule used to report each partner's distributive share of passthrough income and expenses of an entity taxed as a partnership.

c. Incorrect. Form 8832, *Entity Classification Election*, is the form used to make the election to be considered a disregarded entity, corporation, or partnership. It does not report income and expenses of the entity.

4. a. Correct. The judgment creditor obtains an economic interest in LLC distributions; however, the entity is not required to make distributions to its members.

b. Incorrect. The charging order cannot require the LLC to make distributions.

c. Incorrect. The debtor-member is not required to sell his or her LLC interest in order to cover financial liabilities under a charging order.

d. Incorrect. Only one of the choices reflects the result of the charging order.

5. b. Correct. Both the LLC and S corporation feature the passthrough taxation benefit. S corporations are not taxed at both the entity and shareholder levels.
a. Incorrect. S corporations are limited to having no more than 100 shareholders, whereas the LLC may have an unlimited number of members.
c. Incorrect. These types of LLC members are not allowed to be S corporation shareholders; the shareholders must be individuals, estates, certain trusts, or certain charities.
d. Incorrect. The tax treatment of appreciated or debt-encumbered property contributions is an advantage of the LLC compared with the S corporation.

6. a. Correct. All LLC members may be active participants in managing the company and maintain limited liability for the liabilities of the company, but limited partners are generally not allowed to actively participate in the business's management, or they risk the loss of their limited liability.
b. Incorrect. Both entity types are subject to Subchapter K rules.
c. Incorrect. Both the LLC taxed as a partnership and limited partnership are passthrough entities for federal tax purposes.
d. Incorrect. One of the choices reflects an advantage of the LLC as an entity preferable to the limited partnership.

7. a. Correct. Conversion into an LLC taxed as a partnership is treated as a taxable event (a deemed liquidation of the corporation).
b. Incorrect. Stock is exchanged for an interest in the LLC, so basis is not an issue.
c. Incorrect. All LLCs may create more than a single class of ownership interests.
d. Incorrect. One of the choices is a major disadvantage of converting from a C corporation into an LLC.

8. c. Correct. The transaction is treated as a nontaxable contribution in exchange for a partnership interest.
a. Incorrect. The existing member of the SMLLC is not taxed on the transaction.
b. Incorrect. The converted entity is not a corporation, but rather a partnership, for federal tax purposes.
d. Incorrect. One of the choices describes the outcome of the conversion of the SMLLC.

9. a. Correct. Under the IRS's proposed regs and in conjunction with Code Sec. 1402(a)(13), self-employment tax would apply to guaranteed payments that an LLC member receives for services he or she provided to the business.

b. Incorrect. Under the proposed regs, an LLC member who is not personally liable for the LLC's debts and obligations would not be required to pay self-employment tax.

c. Incorrect. An LLC member who does not have the authority to contract on the LLC's behalf would not be subject to self-employment tax under the proposed regs.

d. Incorrect. One of the choices describes the application of self-employment tax to LLC members.

10. d. Correct. After January 1, 2009, a disregarded SMLLC is to be treated as a corporation for employment tax purposes and is responsible for collecting, reporting, and paying over employment taxes. It continues to be disregarded for other federal tax purposes.

a. Incorrect. The SMLLC has been treated as a sole proprietorship for federal tax purposes under prior regulations.

b. Incorrect. These are not the changes imposed for tax treatment under the final regulations.

c. Incorrect. Under the final regulations taking effect January 1, 2009, a disregarded SMLLC is not to be treated as an S corporation passthrough entity.

MODULE 2 — CHAPTER 5

1. d. Correct. Because they are not as tax-advantaged as qualified plans, nonqualified plans are not as heavily regulated and generally have lower administrative costs.

a. Incorrect. Under Code Sec. 409A, income tax is deferred on the amounts of deferred compensation contributed by the employer to a nonqualified plan, only if there is a substantial risk that the employee may forfeit his or her rights to the funds, because payment is contingent upon the employee providing substantial future services or reaching a specific performance goal. Employees cannot deduct their own contributions to nonqualified plans.

b. Incorrect. Employers sponsoring nonqualified plans are not entitled to deduct contributions to the plans until the employees receive distributions.

c. Incorrect. Just the opposite is true. Highly compensated employees may receive a higher percentage of benefits than rank-and-file employees from nonqualified plans designed to reward key employees. Qualified plans are required to offer benefits to rank-and-file employees, on a nondiscriminatory basis with respect to salary level.

2. d. Correct. All three choices are benefits prior to retiring for employees participating in a qualified plan.
a. Incorrect. Savings in defined contribution plans are portable. If an employee changes jobs, he or she may transfer plan funds to the new employer's account without tax penalty.
b. Incorrect. Employees may often reduce their pretax salary by the amount of their qualified plan contributions or deduct annual contributions from their federal income tax.
c. Incorrect. Lower-income contributors may claim a saver's credit on federal income tax returns.

3. a. Correct. Employers not only are prohibited by Code Sec. 401(a)(4) from discriminating against coverage of rank-and-file employees but also, under the top-heavy requirement, may reserve no more than 60 percent of total account benefits for key employees.
b. Incorrect. A qualified plan is required to pay vested benefits to employees terminating their employment, but that payment benefit is not tied to reserving plan benefits for highly compensated employees.
c. Incorrect. Assets of qualified plans are generally protected from creditors of both the employer and employee under bankruptcy laws, but that protection covers all employees not just highly compensated employees.
d. Incorrect. Qualified plans are held to vesting rules for employer contributions, but these are not specific to highly compensated employees. Qualified plan features are applied to key and rank-and-file employees without discrimination.

4. b. Correct. Plan benefits are to be paid within 60 days after the close of the plan year in which the latest of the following occurs—the date that the employee reaches age 65, marks his or her 10-year anniversary of plan participation, or leaves the organization's employ.
a. Incorrect. The fifth employment anniversary does not trigger availability of benefits under Code Sec. 401(a)(14).
c. Incorrect. The starting date of employment is irrelevant to the availability of plan benefits.
d. Incorrect. One of the choices is a requirement of Code Sec. 401(a)(14).

5. a. Correct. An IRS-approved master plan is used by employers that do not tailor a plan for their specific organizations.
b. Incorrect. A prototype plan provides standardized terms and conditions that employers tailor to their organizations.
c. Incorrect. An individual written plan is designed for a specific employer's requirements and conditions.
d. Incorrect. There is no plan type referred to as *default.*

6. d. Correct. The IRS issues determination letters to review a plan's tax-exempt status, to retroactively review a new plan after adoption, and to review an amendment to an existing plan.

a. Incorrect. The IRS will issue a determination letter regarding the qualified plan trust's tax-exempt status.

b. Incorrect. An administrator may obtain a determination letter regarding retroactive qualification for a new plan after it is adopted.

c. Incorrect. The plan administrator may obtain a determination letter from the IRS when an existing plan is amended.

7. a. Correct. The plan administrator under the Self-Correction Program corrects the plan's operations without involving the IRS, avoiding fees and sanctions.

b. Incorrect. This is not the name of an EPCRS program.

c. Incorrect. The Audit Closing Agreement Program is the most costly and formal option for correcting plan failures.

d. Incorrect. A plan administrator may obtain IRS approval to correct all types of plan errors under this program but may be required to pay a fee. Requests must be made before the IRS initiates an audit.

8. c. Correct. The IRS will abate, credit, or refund the entire 100 percent excise tax if the prohibited transaction is corrected during grace period.

a. Incorrect. The IRS allows 90 days after the day it mails a notice of deficiency for the correcting the transaction without imposition of the 100 percent excise tax.

b. Incorrect. An extension of the correction period may be granted if the employer petitions the U.S. Tax Court for assistance or the IRS grants the extension.

d. Incorrect. One of the choices is not an allowance described in IRS Publication 560 for addressing prohibited transactions by a disqualified person.

9. b. Correct. "Excess" earnings may not be distributed to benefit recipients or withdrawn by the employer-sponsor.

a. Incorrect. Such "extra" earnings are not spread among the distributions to benefit recipients.

c. Incorrect. Earnings of a defined benefit plan are not commingled with corporate stock or distributed as dividends.

d. Incorrect. A defined benefit plan sponsor is not permitted to withdraw "surplus" earnings from plan investments.

10. d. Correct. A profit-sharing plan is a type of defined contribution plan that has a formula for *allocation* of employer contributions among each participant's accounts (bond funds, international funds, etc.), but no formula is mandated for the *amount* of business profits that must be contributed.

a. Incorrect. The focus of a defined benefit plan is attaining and maintaining a certain guaranteed amount of benefits to distribute to retirees, not the amount of employer revenues.

b. Incorrect. Money purchase plans mandate fixed, determinable employer contributions to participants' accounts regardless of current company profits.

c. Incorrect. This is not the name of a type of qualified retirement plan.

11. d. Correct. Designated Roth contributions are elective contributions includible in gross income at the time of contribution but excludable from the employee's taxable income upon distribution. Separate accounting and maintenance of designated Roth accounts is required.

a. Incorrect. SIMPLE 401(k) contributions (up to certain limits) are deductible for the employer and employee.

b. Incorrect. Contributions to traditional 401(k) accounts (up to certain limits) are excluded from the employee's taxable income and are deductible by the employer; they are taxed as ordinary income when funds are distributed subsequently.

c. Incorrect. This is another name for traditional Code Sec. 401(k) plans and is not a form of contribution or distribution mechanism.

12. b. Correct. This combination defined benefit/defined contribution plan mandated by the *Pension Protection Act of 2006* will become available starting January 1, 2010.

a. Incorrect. The Roth 401(k) is not a hybrid plan that guarantees a retirement benefit level along with offering the typical 401(k) plan's flexibility of contributions and asset allocations.

c. Incorrect. The safe harbor 401(k) is a traditional 401(k) that enables plans to fulfill the nondiscrimination requirements of the ADP test.

d. Incorrect. One of the choices names the type of qualified plan that combines a minimum guaranteed benefit like that of a defined benefit plan with flexibility of contributions and simple administration akin to those of defined contribution plans.

13. a. Correct. As long as the employer establishes a separate SEP account for each participant, the company can have an unlimited number of employees. Sponsors of SIMPLE IRAs may have a maximum of only 100 employees.

b. *Incorrect.* Just the opposite is true. Under Code Sec. 408(p)(2)(A)(iii), employers are required to make matching contributions to SIMPLE plans. Employers sponsoring SEP IRA plans are not required to make contributions every year under Reg. §1.408-7(c).

c. *Incorrect.* Unlike 401(k) plan contributions, all IRA contributions are immediately 100 percent vested.

d. *Incorrect.* One of the choices describes a true difference between the two types of IRA.

14. d. *Correct.* Although contributions to a Roth IRA account are not currently deductible, qualified distributions of earnings and contributions are tax-free. Unlike traditional IRAs, the owner of a Roth IRA can make contributions from earned income after age 70½ but is not required to receive distributions at all during his or her lifetime.

a. *Incorrect.* The owner of the Roth IRA may receive qualified distributions without federal income taxation on the original amount contributed (contribution was made after-tax) and on the earnings from his or her investment.

b. *Incorrect.* Owners of traditional IRAs may not contribute to their accounts once the owners reach age 70½, but Roth IRA owners have no maximum age for making contributions as long as they have current compensation.

c. *Incorrect.* Unlike traditional IRAs, Roth IRA accounts have no rules for required minimum distributions. Thus, Roth IRA accounts may serve as a vehicle for passing on wealth that builds from tax-free earnings.

15. b. *Correct.* The taxpayer may not convert a traditional IRA account to a Roth plan if he or she submits income tax returns using the married filing separately filing status.

a. *Incorrect.* The maximum AGI for the year of conversion is $100,000, not $15,000.

c. *Incorrect.* There is no conversion restriction based on the taxpayer's other qualified plans.

d. *Incorrect.* Only one of the choices reflects a restriction on traditional-to-Roth IRA rollovers before the revised rules take effect in 2010.

MODULE 3 — CHAPTER 6

1. b. *Correct.* Organizations grown casual in complying with the rules for tax exemption are concerned about becoming compliant with the requirements of the new form.

a. *Incorrect.* The IRS issued complete instructions providing line-by-line guidance to the core form and schedules for the revised form on August 19, 2008.

c. Incorrect. The IRS provided a glossary of key terms containing 176 definitions.

d. Incorrect. The IRS provided a compensation table to help organizations determine where and how to report types of compensation.

2. True. Correct. Although no penalty will be imposed if an e-Postcard is not filed timely, loss of exempt status is automatic for organizations that fail to file returns for three consecutive years.

False. Incorrect. The IRS will send reminders to small organizations that do not file an e-Postcard timely, but failure to file the required Form 990-N for three consecutive years automatically rescinds the organizations' tax-exempt status.

3. a. Correct. The caps for gross receipts and assets are highest for 2008, then decline for 2009, 2010 and later years.

b. Incorrect. These ceilings apply to gross receipts and total assets for the filing year 2009.

c. Incorrect. These are the thresholds for reporting gross receipts and total assets that will apply for 2010 reporting.

d. Incorrect. The $25,000 amount of gross receipts is the maximum for filing the e-Postcard for 2008 and 2009. Neither amount applies to filing Form 990-EZ.

4. d. Correct. All three forms must remain available under the public disclosure rule for three years after filing.

a. Incorrect. Code Sec. 527 political organizations and private foundations must disclose contributors on Schedule B for the previous three reporting years.

b. Incorrect. Charities must reveal unrelated business income tax (UBIT) for the previous three years using Form 990-T.

c. Incorrect. The three-year disclosure rule for public scrutiny applies to private foundations that submit Form 990-PF.

5. b. Correct. The Statement of Program Service Accomplishments composes Part III of the core form of Form 990. That part records the new, ongoing, and discontinued exempt-purpose accomplishments of the tax-exempt organization during the 2008 reporting period. Part I of the core form, the Summary, may also reveal a general view of the organization's activities.

a. Incorrect. Part II of the core form is the Signature Block, which divulges which officer and paid preparer were involved in the return preparation.

c. Incorrect. Part IV of the core form is the Checklist of Required Schedules, intended mainly to help reporting organizations to discern which schedules they must prepare and submit for the reporting period.

d. Incorrect. Part V of the core form solicits IRS filings and compliance information from the reporting organization.

6. False. Correct. Organizations may no longer file freeform attachments; schedules are to be used instead to ensure compliance by all tax-exempt organizations.
True. Incorrect. Freeform attachments to Form 990 or Form 990-EZ are no longer permitted for use by any tax-exempt organization, regardless of size. Schedules are to be completed and submitted with the returns.

7. b. Correct. Organizations are to use Schedule G to list the 10 highest-paid individuals or entities to which the organizations paid a minimum of $5,000 for the reporting period for professional fundraising services.
a. Incorrect. The thresholds for the number of paid fundraisers and amount of remuneration are higher for 2008.
c. Incorrect. These are not the thresholds for reporting on Schedule G for the 2008 reporting period.
d. Incorrect. Reporting thresholds for 2008 are lower for reporting both the number of paid fundraisers and the amount each was paid for those services.

8. False. Correct. The IRS has eliminated advance rulings and Form 8734. The organization may qualify as a public charity for its first five years if it can demonstrate a charitable purpose and that it expects to meet the public support test.
True. Incorrect. This was the previous route by which an organization earned public charity status and proved its public support. Currently, the organization is to use Schedule A to prove qualification for its public charity status if the organization can show that it expects to meet the public support test.

9. b. Correct. Setting the 25-percent threshold for reporting dispositions of net assets eliminates inconsistent reporting of *significant disposition* of assets under the previous form's rules.
a. Incorrect. A higher threshold has been mandated for reporting on Schedule N of the new Form 990.
c. Incorrect. The reporting rule for Schedule N of the revised form does not set the threshold at 50 percent.
d. Incorrect. The threshold for reporting disposition of net assets by a nonprofit organization is lower than 75 percent.

10. b. Correct. Part III core form items generally were requested on the 2007 form. This part now appears on page 2 of the 2008 Form 990.

a. *Incorrect.* Part III of Schedule D is new, created to report assets and revenues of art and treasure that are held for public exhibition, education, or research.

c. *Incorrect.* A new requirement for organizations receiving more than $25,000 in noncash contributions, or any contributions of art, historical treasures, or qualified conservation items in 2008 is completion of Schedule M.

d. *Incorrect.* One choice is not a new tool for the 2008 form.

11. a. *Correct.* Schedule M, Non-Cash Contributions, calls for listing both qualified and nonqualified conservation easements, but the latter are recorded as "other property."

b. *Incorrect.* Qualified and nonqualified conservation easements are not reported together.

c. *Incorrect.* Schedule D, Part VIII, is completed to report program-related investments.

d. *Incorrect.* One of the choices states where nonqualified easements are reported.

12. d. *Correct.* Awards, fellowships, and research grants also constitute grants for reporting on Schedule F.

a. *Incorrect.* Grants include noncash assistance for reporting foreign activities on Schedule F.

b. *Incorrect.* Scholarships are considered grants for Schedule F reporting.

c. *Incorrect.* Stipends are included as grants for reporting purposes of foreign activities on Schedule F.

13. b. *Correct.* The floor for completing the new Schedule M, Non-Cash Contributions, is receipt of more than $25,000 in noncash contributions during the 2008 reporting year.

a. *Incorrect.* Cash contributions are not associated with the requirements for completing Schedule M of Form 990 for 2008.

c. *Incorrect.* UBIT is reported using Form 990-T, not Schedule M of Form 990.

d. *Incorrect.* Only one of the choices is the trigger for requiring completion of Schedule M of Form 990 for 2008.

14. d. *Correct.* Key employees are among the 20 highest paid non-HCEs, and they meet the criteria of the responsibility and compensation tests for Form 990 reporting purposes.

a. *Incorrect.* Key employees are among the organization's 20 highest paid persons other than HCEs.

b. Incorrect. Key employees are individuals having powers or responsibilities in the organization similar to those of officers or directors, or employees managing 10-percent or more of the organization's activities, assets, income, or expenses, or employees who control or determine at least 10 percent or the capital, operating budget, or employee compensation.

c. Incorrect. Under the compensation test, key employees are those receiving reportable, W-2 compensation from the organization and related organizations exceeding $150,000 during the calendar year.

15. d. Correct. Completing all parts of Schedule K will be required for 2009. However, only Part I, which lists bond issues, is required for the 2008 reporting period.

a. Incorrect. Completing Private Business Use is not required on Schedule K until the 2009 reporting period.

b. Incorrect. Completion of Schedule O, which permits an organization to provide additional information about bond issues, is only required for 2008 if the tax-exempt organization uses a different reporting period for different bond issues or the issue price is not identical on Schedule K and Form 8038.

c. Incorrect. Tax-exempt organizations are not required to complete Proceeds, Part II of Schedule K, for the 2008 reporting period.

MODULE 3 — CHAPTER 7

1. a. Correct. The key test of which workers qualify as employees is whether the employer has the right to control and direct the individuals' services.

b. Incorrect. Employees' classifications do not necessarily depend on their work schedules; following an employer-set schedule may be but one factor indicative of an employer–employee relationship.

c. Incorrect. Although employees may be subject to company dress codes and required to use cellular telephones on the job, costs related to these expenses are not necessarily considered employer reimbursed or tax deductible, nor do they establish employee status.

d. Incorrect. Statutory employees are not necessarily restricted in distributing other products or services incidental to those for handling the specific responsibilities of the employer, and many workers classified as employees hold jobs for multiple employers (i.e., "moonlighting," "freelancing," or other part-time additional employment).

2. b. Correct. Even if the insurer provides office equipment and supplies, the salesperson is a statutory employee if he works for just one company.

a. Incorrect. Any individual whose primary business activity consists of soliciting annuity contracts for just one insurance company is not classified as a common law employee or independent contractor.

c. *Incorrect.* Salespersons are not independent contractors, although they may appear to be because their income is not a steady, flat rate of pay and they do not work primarily in an office within their companies' premises.
d. *Incorrect.* This is not the IRS classification of a life insurance or annuity salesperson.

3. d. *Correct.* A worker who delivers newspapers or shopping news is classified as a direct seller, which is one of the categories of workers treated as statutory nonemployees.
a. *Incorrect.* The seamstress is classified as a homeworker, a type of statutory employee.
b. *Incorrect.* The truck driver is an agent-driver and thus a type of statutory employee.
c. *Incorrect.* A salesperson who travels (despite having a home-based office) and obtains wholesale orders is considered a statutory employee.

4. b. *Correct.* Direct sellers perform their services under contracts that specify their classification as nonemployees for employment tax purposes.
a. *Incorrect.* Federal tax law classifies direct sellers (as well as real estate agents) as statutory nonemployees, which are self-employed individuals to whom payments are not subject to employment tax.
c. *Incorrect.* The consumer products sold by direct sellers include tangible goods as well as intangible services.
d. *Incorrect.* Direct sellers provide consumer products wholesale to resellers as well as nonwholesale goods such as newspapers or salespapers to home consumers.

5. d. *Correct.* Collaboration with other workers, submission of work reports, and limitations on customers or clients are factors that favor the employer–employee relationship between an employer and an individual.
a. *Incorrect.* Requiring a worker to perform services with an experienced employee and requiring the worker to attend meetings indicate training requirements in an employer–employee relationship.
b. *Incorrect.* Submission by a worker of regular reports, oral or written, suggests an employer–employee relationship.
c. *Incorrect.* If the individual is limited under terms of employment from offering services to other employers, the individual is likely to be considered an employee.

6. a. *Correct.* Liability to the worker for terminating the relationship without cause may indicate an independent contractor relationship.
b. *Incorrect.* A lack of liability or penalty for terminating a worker without cause generally indicates an employer–employee relationship.

c. Incorrect. A worker is not classified as either a customer or supplier by the IRS.

d. Incorrect. One of the choices is indicated when an employer terminates the relationship without cause or for reasons not permitted by an employment agreement.

7. b. Correct. FICA taxes must be remitted if an employee of a nonprofit organization earns $100 or more during the calendar year.

a. Incorrect. Nonprofit 501(c)(3) organizations are exempt from federal income taxes and FUTA taxes.

c. Incorrect. If both a 501(c)(3) organization and its employee file objections to FICA tax for religious reasons, the FICA tax may not apply.

d. Incorrect. An employee of a nonprofit organization other than a 501(c)(3) organization is subject to FUTA if he or she earns more than the $50 maximum wage exemption in a quarter.

8. c. Correct. The maximum allowed under the temporary credit is 20 percent or a maximum of $20,000.

a. Incorrect. The credit is greater than 10 percent or a maximum of $10,000.

b. Incorrect. This is not the maximum allowable under the temporary credit.

d. Incorrect. The maximum percentage or amount of the temporary credit is lower.

9. d. Correct. The notice lists the proposed tax, informs the employer of its review opportunity, and provides a schedule of workers that the IRS is classifying as employees.

a. Incorrect. The NDWC shows the type of employment tax and the IRS adjustment sought.

b. Incorrect. The NDWC informs the employer of the right to seek a review of the proposed assessment and worker classification.

c. Incorrect. The NDWC gives a schedule of the workers that the IRS is classifying as employees.

10. a. Correct. The taxpayer is entitled to an automatic abatement of the assessment. However, the IRS may reassess the employer once the procedural defects are corrected.

b. Incorrect. The IRS may reassess the same taxes against the employer at a later date.

c. Incorrect. The IRS does not issue permanent exemptions based on its procedural errors.

d. Incorrect. One of the choices reflects the recourse available to an employer.

MODULE 3 — CHAPTER 8

1. a. Correct. Prior to enactment of the 2007 Small Business Tax Act, preparers were held to a standard of reporting entries or tax positions that had a realistic possibility of being sustained on the merits. The 2007 Small Business Tax Act holds preparers to the stricter more likely than not standard.
b. Incorrect. A 40 percent chance is generally considered as the substantial authority standard to which *taxpayers* are subject.
c. Incorrect. The preparer penalty standards have never required a high degree of certainty.
d. Incorrect. One of the choices is the threshold under the old standard for avoiding a preparer penalty under Code Sec. 6694(a).

2. b. Correct. The $1,000 penalty applied to a preparer who willfully attempted to understate a client's tax liability or who recklessly or intentionally disregarded reporting rules.
a. Incorrect. The $250 penalty applied to a preparer who took an unrealistic position but did not willfully understate the client's tax liability.
c. Incorrect. The $2,000 amount applied to the de minimis safe harbor, with respect to the substantial portion requirement.
d. Incorrect. The 20 percent of gross income applied to the de minimis safe harbor, with respect to the substantial portion requirement.

3. b. Correct. The exception applies only to nonsigning preparers when the item (not the understatement) is less than $10,000 or $400,000 for an item of less than 20 percent of the taxpayer's gross income.
a. Incorrect. Signing tax preparers are not eligible to use the de minimis safe harbor.
c. Incorrect. Taxpayers are not eligible for the de minimis exception, which protects certain preparers.
d. Incorrect. Individuals who give advice about prospective tax planning are not subject to the Code Sec. 6694 preparer penalty because they do not prepare the clients' returns.

4. d. Correct. Preparers are held responsible under the proposed regulations regardless of their nationality, residence, or business location, if they prepared at least a substantial portion of the clients' returns or refund claims.
a. Incorrect. The preparer may be a non-U.S. citizen whose business is located outside of the United States.
b. Incorrect. An individual who provides sufficient information and advice so that completing the return or refund claim is largely a clerical matter is considered the signing preparer, even if the individual does not actually place or review the information on the paper or electronic document.
c. Incorrect. A nonresident alien may be a preparer.

5. d. Correct. The first-tier preparer penalty was increased from a flat amount of $250 to the greater of $1,000 or 50 percent of the preparer's income derived or to be derived from preparing the return or refund claim.
a. Incorrect. The first-tier preparer penalty still has a lower maximum under revised Code Sec. 6694(a). However, the second-tier penalty of Code Sec. 6694(b) has been increased to the greater of $5,000 or 50 percent of the preparer's income derived or to be derived from preparing the return.
b. Incorrect. The first-tier preparer penalty under revised Code Sec. 6694(a) is neither $3,000 nor 75 percent of the preparer's income from preparing the return.
c. Incorrect. The first-tier preparer penalty amount is neither the greater of $2,000 or 60 percent of the preparer's income derived or to be derived from preparing the return.

6. a. Correct. Substantial authority includes congressional intent as reflected in committee reports, joint explanatory statements of managers included in conference committee reports, as well as floor statements made before enactment by the bill's managers.
b. Incorrect. Conclusions reached in treatises, legal periodicals, and legal opinions are not substantial authority under Code Sec. 6662.
c. Incorrect. Auditors' opinions are not substantial authority under the Code Sec. 6662 taxpayer standard.
d. **Incorrect.** One of the choices describes substantial authority for the Code Sec. 6662 taxpayer standard.

7. True. Correct. The written determination is not substantial authority if the tax position reflects a misstatement or material omission of a material fact, or the facts that subsequently develop are materially different from the facts on which the written determination was based.
False. Incorrect. The agent's written determination is not substantial authority if subsequent facts are materially different from those on which the report was based.

8. False. Correct. The reasonable basis standard applies under the *Emergency Economic Stabilization Act of 2008.*
True. Incorrect. The *Emergency Economic Stabilization Act of 2008* uses the reasonable basis standard, which is significantly higher than not patently improper.

9. c. Correct. The *Emergency Economic Stabilization Act of 2008* equalizes the preparer and taxpayer penalty standards for undisclosed, positions at substantial authority.

a. Incorrect. The *Emergency Economic Stabilization Act of 2008* does not replace the more likely than not standard in Code Sec. 6694(a) with a realistic possibility standard.

b. Incorrect. The *Emergency Economic Stabilization Act of 2008* equalizes the preparer and taxpayer penalty standards differently.

d. Incorrect. The *Emergency Economic Stabilization Act of 2008* changes the Code Sec. 6694(a) standard for undisclosed, nonabusive positions. It does not temporarily suspend the changes made by the 2007 Small Business Tax Act until January 1, 2011.

10. a. Correct. The *Emergency Economic Stabilization Act of 2008* continues the requirement that a preparer have a reasonable belief that tax shelters and reportable transactions with significant avoidance or evasion purposes have a reasonable belief that the transaction will be sustained on the merits.

b. Incorrect. Transactions with no tax avoidance potential and international transactions per se are not held to the more likely than not standard.

c. Incorrect. Cross-border transactions and tax positions claiming NOLs do not generally have tax avoidance or evasion purposes that are held to the more likely than not standard.

d. Incorrect. One of the choices reflects two types of transactions to which the more likely than not standard still applies.

Index

T

U

TOP FEDERAL TAX ISSUES FOR 2009 CPE COURSE

CPE Quizzer Instructions

The CPE Quizzer is divided into three Modules. There is a processing fee for each Quizzer Module submitted for grading. Successful completion of Module 1 is recommended for **7 CPE Credits.*** Successful completion of Module 2 is recommended for **5 CPE Credits.*** Successful completion of Module 3 is recommended for **7 CPE Credits.*** You can complete and submit one Module at a time or all Modules at once for a total of **19 CPE Credits.***

To obtain CPE credit, return your completed Answer Sheet for each Quizzer Module to **CCH Continuing Education Department, 4025 W. Peterson Ave., Chicago, IL 60646**, or fax it to (773) 866-3084. Each Quizzer Answer Sheet will be graded and a CPE Certificate of Completion awarded for achieving a grade of 70 percent or greater. The Quizzer Answer Sheets are located after the Quizzer questions for this Course.

Express Grading: Processing time for your Answer Sheet is generally 8-12 business days. If you are trying to meet a reporting deadline, our Express Grading Service is available for an additional $19 per Module. To use this service, please check the "Express Grading" box on your Answer Sheet and provide your CCH account or credit card number **and your fax number.** CCH will fax your results and a Certificate of Completion (upon achieving a passing grade) to you by 5:00 p.m. the business day following our receipt of your Answer Sheet. **If you mail your Answer Sheet for Express Grading, please write "ATTN: CPE OVERNIGHT" on the envelope.** NOTE: CCH will not Federal Express Quizzer results under any circumstances.

NEW ONLINE GRADING gives you immediate 24/7 grading with instant results and no Express Grading Fee.

The **CCH Testing Center** website gives you and others in your firm easy, free access to CCH print Courses and allows you to complete your CPE Quizzers online for immediate results. Plus, the **My Courses** feature provides convenient storage for your CPE Course Certificates and completed Quizzers.

Go to **www.cchtestingcenter.com** to complete your Quizzer online.

---

* Recommended CPE credit is based on a 50-minute hour. Participants earning credits for states that require self-study to be based on a 100-minute hour will receive ½ the CPE credits for successful completion of this course. Because CPE requirements vary from state to state and among different licensing agencies, please contact your CPE governing body for information on your CPE requirements and the applicability of a particular course for your requirements.

Date of Completion: The date of completion on your Certificate will be the date that you put on your Answer Sheet. However, you must submit your Answer Sheet to CCH for grading within two weeks of completing it.

Expiration Date: December 31, 2009

Evaluation: To help us provide you with the best possible products, please take a moment to fill out the Course Evaluation located at the back of this Course and return it with your Quizzer Answer Sheets.

CCH is registered with the National Association of State Boards of Accountancy (NASBA) as a sponsor of continuing professional education on the National Registry of CPE Sponsors. State boards of accountancy have final authority on the acceptance of individual courses for CPE credit. Complaints regarding registered sponsors may be addressed to the National Registry of CPE Sponsors, 150 Fourth Avenue North, Suite 700, Nashville, TN 37219-2417. Web site: www.nasba.org.

CCH is registered with the National Association of State Boards of Accountancy (NASBA) as a Quality Assurance Service (QAS) sponsor of continuing professional education. State boards of accountancy have final authority on the acceptance of individual courses for CPE credit. Complaints regarding registered sponsors may be addressed to NASBA, 150 Fourth Avenue North, Suite 700, Nashville, TN 37219-2417. Web site: www.nasba.org.

CCH has been approved by the California Tax Education Council to offer courses that provide federal and state credit towards the annual "continuing education" requirement imposed by the State of California. A listing of additional requirements to register as a tax preparer may be obtained by contacting CTEC at P.O. Box 2890, Sacramento, CA, 95812-2890, toll-free by phone at (877) 850-2832, or on the Internet at www.ctec.org.

Processing Fee:	**Recommended CPE:**	
$84.00 for Module 1	7 hours for Module 1	
$60.00 for Module 2	5 hours for Module 2	
$84.00 for Module 3	7 hours for Module 3	
$228.00 for all Modules	19 hours for all Modules	
CTEC Course Number:	**CTEC Federal Hours:**	**CTEC California Hours:**
1075-CE-7153 for Module 1	3 hours for Module 1	N/A for Module 1
1075-CE-7163 for Module 2	2 hours for Module 2	N/A for Module 2
1075-CE-7173 for Module 3	3 hours for Module 3	N/A for Module 3
	8 hours for all Modules	N/A for all Modules

One **complimentary copy** of this Course is provided with certain copies of CCH Federal Taxation publications. Additional copies of this Course may be ordered for $31.00 each by calling 1-800-248-3248 (ask for product 0-0982-200).

Quizzer Questions: Module 1

Answer the True/False questions by marking a "T" or "F" on the Quizzer Answer Sheet. Answer Multiple Choice questions by indicating the appropriate letter on the Answer Sheet.

---

1. Congress authorized child payments of $_____ per qualifying child as part of the *Economic Stimulus Act of 2008*.

   a. $100
   b. $150
   c. $250
   d. $300

2. The *Economic Stimulus Act of 2008* temporarily raised the maximum deduction for Code Sec. 179 expensing for qualifying property to:

   a. $125,000
   b. $175,000
   c. $225,000
   d. $250,000

3. Bonus depreciation under the *Economic Stimulus Act of 2008* temporarily enables taxpayers to deduct _____ of the adjusted basis for qualified property against their alternative minimum tax liability.

   a. 25 percent
   b. 50 percent
   c. 75 percent
   d. 100 percent

4. The *Housing and Economic Recovery Act of 2008* creates a _____ first-time homebuyer tax credit that generally must be repaid over ____ years:

   a. Temporary; 15
   b. Permanent; 15
   c. Temporary; 20
   d. Permanent; 5

5. Under the *Mortgage Forgiveness Debt Relief Act of 2007*, a married couple filing jointly may be able to exclude up to _____ in qualifying discharge of indebtedness on their primary residence of:

    a. $400,000
    b. $500,000
    c. $1.5 million
    d. $2 million

6. Under the *Heartland, Habitat, Harvest, and Horticulture Act* (Farm Act), taxpayers receiving certain government farming subsidies may claim maximum losses on Schedule F of the greater of _____ or the taxpayers' net farm income for the prior five tax years.

    a. $100,000
    b. $200,000
    c. $300,000
    d. $500,000

7. The child tax credit is refundable to the extent of 15 percent of the taxpayer's earned income in excess of a $10,000 floor ($12,050 as adjusted for inflation for 2008). The *Emergency Economic Stabilization Act of 2008* reduces the floor to $____.

    a. Zero
    b. $1,000
    c. $8,500
    d. Make no changes to the child tax credit

8. The *Emergency Economic Stabilization Act of 2008* extends disaster relief to all of the following **except:**

    a. Taxpayers in 10 Midwest states (the Midwestern Disaster Area)
    b. Taxpayers recovering from Hurricane Ike (the Hurricane Ike Disaster Area)
    c. Victims of all federally declared disasters nationwide
    d. All of the above are provided disaster relief

9. The first-time homebuyer credit is available to a same-sex couple in a civil union as well as to unmarried taxpayers. **True or False?**

10. Under the HEART Act, small businesses having fewer than 50 employees can claim a temporary tax credit equal to 20 percent of differential wages paid to qualified workers who are called up for active military duty. **True or False?**

11. Forgiveness of indebtedness such as that in a mortgage workout or short sale creates income under:

a. Code Sec. 108
b. Code Sec. 121
c. Code Sec. 1017
d. None of the above creates income

12. A joint filing couple who have owned and used their principal residence for at least two years of a five-year period may exclude up to _____ of gain from the sale of their principal residence

a. $100,000
b. $250,000
c. $350,000
d. $500,000

13. To claim the full exclusion of gain on the sale of his or her principal residence, the homeowner must have lived in the home as a principal residence since acquisition, for at least two years of the five years preceding the sale under the:

a. Use test
b. Code Sec. 108 debt forgiveness requirements
c. Code Sec. 61 discharge of indebtedness rules
d. None of the above qualifies a homeowner for the full exclusion

14. The *Mortgage Forgiveness Debt Relief Act of 2007* added Code Sec. 108(a)(1)(E), and the *Emergency Economic Stabilization Act of 2008* extended it, to exclude from gross income principal residence indebtedness forgiven from:

a. January 1, 2006, through December 31, 2008
b. January 1, 2007, through December 31, 2012
c. January 1, 2008, through December 31, 2010
d. January 1, 2009, through December 31, 2011

15. Under the *Mortgage Forgiveness Debt Relief Act of 2007*, and as extended by the *Emergency Economic Stabilization Act of 2008,* what is the maximum acquisition indebtedness that may qualify for consideration under the principal-residence gross income exclusion?

   a. $500,000
   b. $1 million
   c. $1.5 million
   d. $2 million

16. Cancelled credit card debt may be excluded from taxation as forgiveness of indebtedness income if:

   a. Purchases made with the card fund capital improvements for the principal residence
   b. The debt is incurred to cover an initial down payment on the home purchase
   c. It was treated by the homeowner as an open line of credit
   d. Forgiveness of credit card debt always gives rise to recognized forgiveness of indebtedness income (although the insolvency or bankruptcy exceptions may still be available)

17. Which alternative to a straight foreclosure may create a problem in determining the correct amount of potential debt forgiveness income and gain on the sale of the property?

   a. Short sale
   b. Chapter 7 bankruptcy
   c. Sale to an escrow agent for the lender
   d. Deed in lieu of foreclosure

18. When is there recognition of debt forgiveness in a walk-away situation?

   a. When the homeowner abandons the property
   b. When the homeowner fails to make the fourth sequential required mortgage payment
   c. When the homeowner files for Chapter 7 bankruptcy protection
   d. When the lender abandons further collection on recourse debt and pursues foreclosure

19. What is the threshold amount of discharged indebtedness triggering filing of Form 1099-C by lenders or mortgage servicers?

   a. $400
   b. $500
   c. $600
   d. $1,000

20. Which of the following results when a lender reports a discharge of indebtedness using Form 1099-C?

   a. The filing completes the processing a discharge of debt by the lender
   b. The IRS initiates a meeting with both lender and borrower to resolve the discharge amount and tax year in which the forgiveness is recognized
   c. The borrower must be prepared to rebut an IRS assumption that the amount and tax year reported are correct
   d. The borrower receives a copy of the form to attach to his or her individual Form 1040 to substantiate the forgiveness terms

21. Which of the following generally increases a homeowner's basis in his or her residence?

   a. Rollover of gain into purchasing the property from sale of residence prior to May 7, 1997
   b. Capital improvements
   c. Depreciation
   d. None of the above increases basis

22. A *full* $250,000/$500,000 exclusion of gain on the sale or exchange of principal residence may be used:

   a. One time only during the homebuyers' lifetimes
   b. Once every two years
   c. Once every five years
   d. Upon each sale of the homebuyers' principal residence, regardless of timing

23. The tax benefit rule is generally applied to mortgage debt in forgiving past interest due. *True or False?*

24. Home equity loans may not be considered in the borrower's principal residence exclusion for discharged indebtedness even if the loan amounts are applied to construction or improvement projects for the residence. ***True or False?***

25. Code Sec. 108 uses the same criteria as do the bankruptcy court and state laws to determine a taxpayer's insolvency for the principal residence exclusion. ***True or False?***

26. The type of tax year that an S corporation or partnership uses regularly is the:

   a. Short year
   b. Required year
   c. Fiscal year
   d. Seasonal year

27. The effect of depreciation is to _____ deduction of the cost of an asset to better match the periods over which the asset is expected to help generate income.

   a. Defer
   b. Accelerate
   c. Eliminate
   d. Enhance

28. General bonus depreciation for depreciable business purchases in the 2008 tax year is computed:

   a. Only if the business forgoes Code Sec. 179 expensing of other property purchased during the 2008 tax year
   b. By netting depreciation deductions already taken on property purchased in the 2007 tax year
   c. In lieu of Code Sec. 179 expensing on the depreciable purchases
   d. Before regular depreciation is taken, but after any property receives any Code Sec. 179 expensing available to it

29. For which of the following types of property can a business claim bonus depreciation on 2008 business tax returns?

   a. Inventory
   b. Property obtained from the original purchaser
   c. Property held for the production of income
   d. None of the above is eligible for bonus depreciation

30. The general Code Sec. 179 maximum writeoff for 2008 (exclusive of any special treatment for designated disaster areas) is:

    a. $25,000
    b. $100,000
    c. $125,000
    d. $250,000

31. The amount of bad debt that is deductible is:

    a. The taxpayer's basis in the debt
    b. The face value of the debt
    c. The fair market value of the debt
    d. Exclusive of unpaid interest, wages, fees, or rents that have been included in income

32. A foreclosure or repossession of property having secured debt is treated as:

    a. An abandonment of the property
    b. A sale resulting in gain or loss
    c. A cancellation of whatever mortgage debt is secured by the property
    d. A reduction of basis in the property for the lender

33. For forgiven business real property debt, which is the first to have basis reduced?

    a. Inventory and receivables
    b. Personal property used in the business and securing the debt
    c. Real property used in the business and securing the debt
    d. Other property except for inventory and receivables

34. Congress and the IRS oppose _____ of net operating losses (NOLs).

    a. Claims by exempt organizations having taxable unrelated income
    b. Trafficking
    c. Carryforwards
    d. Claims by acquiring corporations

35. Bonus depreciation is not phased out as a business's investment in qualifying property increases, making it less advantageous to larger companies. *True or False?*

Quizzer Questions: Module 2

Answer the True/False questions by marking a "T" or "F" on the Quizzer Answer Sheet. Answer Multiple Choice questions by indicating the appropriate letter on the Answer Sheet.

---

36. Under the laws of some states, which of the following business types cannot elect to be an LLC?

- **a.** One-person S corporation
- **b.** Insurance company
- **c.** Sole proprietor
- **d.** C corporation

37. LLCs are formed by filing:

- **a.** Form 8832
- **b.** Form 1065
- **c.** Service partnership agreement
- **d.** Articles of organization or certificate of formation

38. The default status for an entity wholly owned by one individual when the owner fails to make an affirmative election under the check-the-box regulations is:

- **a.** S corporation taxed under corporate tax regulations
- **b.** Disregarded entity taxed as a sole proprietorship
- **c.** C corporation taxed under corporate tax rules
- **d.** Disregarded entity taxed under corporate tax regulations

39. An LLC cannot change its elected classification under the check-the-box regulations for _____ without obtaining a waiver by the IRS.

- **a.** Two years
- **b.** Three years
- **c.** Four years
- **d.** Five years

40. Distributions of loan proceeds of a single-member LLC:

    a. Are not included in the owner's income

    b. Are treated as ordinary business income on the member's Schedule C of Form 1040

    c. May be used to offset current losses or carried over for up five tax years

    d. None of the above is the treatment of loan proceeds of an SMLLC

41. A potential financial disadvantage of the LLC as an entity choice is:

    a. An LLC's debt generally does not create at-risk basis for LLC members making it difficult for members to deduct losses in excess of their actual investment in the company

    b. Double taxation at the entity and individual level for SMLLCs

    c. Immediate recognition of income at the individual level for contributions of appreciated property to the LLC

    d. Inability to issue more than a single class of stock

42. Conversion of a partnership to an LLC taxed as a partnership for federal income tax purposes:

    a. Closes the partnership's tax year

    b. Is considered a sale, exchange, or liquidation of each partner's interest

    c. Does not change the proportionate interest of each partner/member unless the shares of liabilities change

    d. Triggers a new holding period for determination of short- versus long-term capital gains from sale of interests in the resulting LLC

43. If a multimember LLC taxed as a partnership shrinks to having just one member, the entity automatically:

    a. Becomes a disregarded entity whose single owner and seller(s) may have taxable gain

    b. Converts to an SMLLC in a nontaxable event

    c. Triggers gain or loss on the sale of the partnership interests of the sellers with no taxable event for the new single owner

    d. None of the above is an automatic result of the conversion

44. A single businessperson operating a personal holding company can elect to be taxed as a single-member LLC. *True or False?*

45. Unless an LLC elects S corporation status for federal tax purposes, in most states the entity has no limitation on the number of members it may admit, and other LLCs, partnerships, corporations, and foreign entities may be LLC members. *True or False?*

46. Which general employee benefit technique maximizes tax advantages under the Internal Revenue Code?

   a. Supplemental unemployment benefits
   b. Qualified retirement plans
   c. Annual increases in employee salaries
   d. Employee welfare benefit plans

47. The portability feature of a qualified plan means that:

   a. The employee's account is housed at the employee's savings institution regardless of business relocations
   b. The plan's funds may be transferred to the new employer's plan without taxation if the employee changes employers, and if completed in accordance with the distribution and rollover rules
   c. The employee is guaranteed the ability to switch among mutual fund allocations at any time
   d. The plan's assets are convertible to a Roth IRA without income recognition and taxation

48. The written plan for an employer's qualified retirement plan must be adopted by the:

   a. First day of the next fiscal quarter after the employer documents the plan
   b. Last day of the tax year in which the employer initiates the plan
   c. Last day of the calendar month in which the plan first enrolls participants
   d. First day that the employer initiates contributions to fund the plan

49. An employer may request a _____ for advance qualification of a new qualified retirement plan.

   a. Preemptive ruling by the Tax Court
   b. Private letter ruling by the IRS
   c. Revenue ruling by the IRS
   d. Determination letter from the IRS

50. Which of the following is **not** one of the Employee Plans Compliance Resolution System programs?

    a. Retirement Plan Revision Program
    b. Audit Closing Agreement Program
    c. Self-Correction Program
    d. All of the above are EPCRS programs

51. Under the EPCRS program, which of the following enables an employer to address a plan administrator's diversion of assets from the plan?

    a. Audit Closing Agreement Program
    b. Self-Correction Program
    c. Voluntary Correction Program
    d. None of the above may be used to address diversion of plan assets by an administrator

52. Code Sec. 4975 imposes a _____ excise tax as a penalty for uncorrected, prohibited transactions of a plan involving a disqualified person.

    a. 50 percent
    b. 60 percent
    c. 75 percent
    d. 100 percent

53. ERISA requires the plan administrator to provide each employee-participant in a qualified retirement plan with a:

    a. Summary annual report of benefits
    b. Form 5500, *Annual Return/Report of Employee Benefit Plan*
    c. Form 5300, *Application for Determination for Employee Benefit Plan*
    d. None of the above is a document required for distribution to the plan's participants

54. A *defined contribution plan* is defined in Code Sec. 414(i) as a qualified plan:

    a. To which the employer makes discretionary contributions to accounts of employee participants
    b. Offering a guaranteed amount of annual or monthly benefits to all employee participants
    c. Constituting a SIMPLE-IRA
    d. That guarantees a fixed benefit from fixed employer and employee levels of contributions

55. The maximum annual amount that employees older than age 50 may defer from salary using a 401(k) retirement plan for 2008 is:

   a. $5,000
   b. $15,500
   c. $20,500
   d. $25,500

56. To meet nondiscrimination requirements, 401(k) plans limit the percentage of deferred wages for highly compensated employees to satisfy the:

   a. Actuarial assumptions test
   b. Actual deferral percentage test
   c. Summary plan formula
   d. Weighted contributions test

57. What is a disadvantage for employers of sponsoring a SIMPLE IRA versus a SEP IRA as an employee retirement plan?

   a. SIMPLE plans are more complex to administer because SEP IRAs are not subject to nondiscrimination rules
   b. SIMPLE plans may be used by employers having no more than 100 employees; SEP sponsors have no size limitations
   c. Employers sponsoring SIMPLE plans may not also sponsor a Roth IRA plan, but Roth plans are allowed for SEP IRA sponsors
   d. SIMPLE plans require employer funding to be completed each year at an earlier date than do SEP plans

58. Under the *Tax Increase Prevention and Reconciliation Act of 2005,* after 2009 taxpayers can avoid the income limitations for contributing to Roth IRAs by:

   a. Opening the Roth IRA in a family member's name
   b. Contributing to the Roth IRA through an employer's qualified retirement account
   c. Contributing to a traditional IRA that is subsequently converted to a Roth account
   d. Creating the account as a safe harbor 401(k) plan

59. When new federal legislation necessitates updates to a qualified plan, the administrator has a remedial period in which to revise the written agreement but should begin immediately to operate the plan in accordance with the new law. *True or False?*

60. An advantage to some employers of sponsoring a defined benefit plan is that it requires no minimum number of employees to participate. *True or False?*

Quizzer Questions: Module 3

61. All of the following are features of the instructions for Form 990 that were released on August 19, 2008, *except:*

  a. Resources for computer system updates to capture information necessary to complete returns for 2008
  b. A sequencing list matched to the order of the Form 990 information requests
  c. A compensation table organizations may use to determine when and how to report types of compensation
  d. A change in the definition of key employee for reporting purposes

62. Small tax-exempt organizations are allowed to file the e-Postcard if their 2008 gross receipts are:

  a. $10,000 or less
  b. $12,000 or less
  c. $20,000 or less
  d. $25,000 or less

63. Organizations eligible to file e-Postcards include:

  a. Code Sec. 509(a)(3) supporting organizations
  b. Tax-exempt organizations having gross receipts less than $25,000
  c. Code Sec. 527 (political) organizations
  d. Private foundations

64. All of the following are differences between old and revised Form 990 revenue reporting requirements *except:*

  a. Revenues are split in different ways on the revised form
  b. Contributions are divided into various types on the revised Part VIII
  c. The types of revenue reported are different on the revised form
  d. All of the above are differences between revenue reporting on the old and new form and schedules

65. Lobbying and promotion expenses of nonprofit organizations must be reported for 2008 using:

   a. Part IX of the revised Form 990 core form
   b. Schedule D of revised Form 990
   c. Part VII of the revised Form 990 core form
   d. These expenses are not required on information returns of nonprofit organizations for 2008

66. When an exempt organization goes out of existence, it must provide information about asset distributions, transaction expenses, and valuations on _____.

   a. Schedule A, Public Charity Status and Public Support
   b. Schedule B, Schedule of Contributors
   c. Schedule D, Supplemental Financial Statements
   d. Schedule N, Liquidation, Termination, Dissolution or Significant Disposition of Assets

67. Which of the following is *not* considered to be an ODTKE whose compensation is reported using Part VII of the Form 990 core form?

   a. Key employees
   b. Advisory board members having no governing powers
   c. Trustees
   d. Appointed officers

68. Which of the following is a required filing for tax-exempt organizations having excess benefit transactions with disqualified persons?

   a. Submission of Form 1065 by the organization
   b. Completion of Schedule L of new Form 990
   c. Listing the disqualified persons on Schedule I of the Form 990
   d. None of the above is required for tax-exempt organizations

69. A facility recognized as a hospital is required to complete _____ of Form 990, Schedule H, for the 2008 reporting period. Other parts are optional for the 2008 year but required in 2009.

   a. Part I, Charity Care and Certain Other Community Benefits at Cost
   b. Part II, Community Building Activities
   c. Part IV, Management Companies and Joint Ventures
   d. Part V, Facility Information

70. The new Schedule K, Supplemental Information for Tax-Exempt Bonds, replaces _____ explaining the purpose and amount of issue, unexpended bond proceeds, and whether a third party uses a bond-financed facility.

    a. Schedule P of the previous Form 990
    b. A freeform attachment
    c. Schedule L, Part I, of the previous Form 990
    d. Schedule I of Form 4720

71. The information on Part I of Schedule K to Form 990 should be consistent in issuer name and price with:

    a. Form 8038, *Information Return for Tax-Exempt Private Activity Bond Issues*
    b. Schedule O, Supplemental Information to Form 990
    c. Schedule A describing the exempt status and public support of the organization
    d. None of the above has overlapping descriptions with Part I of Schedule K

72. Tax-exempt organizations that participate in political campaigning or lobbying do have to use Schedule C, Political Campaign and Lobbying Activities, of Form 990 to report:

    a. Indirect political campaign activities
    b. Total number of volunteers' hours for Code Sec. 527 exempt function activities
    c. Segregated funds created for exempt function activities
    d. All of the above are required

73. Tax-exempt organizations whose gross receipts totaled less than $25,000 were not required to file annual information with the IRS prior to the enactment of the *Pension Protection Act of 2006*. *True or False?*

74. Completion and submission of the entire 11-part core form is required for small tax-exempt organizations and private foundations for the 2008 reporting period. *True or False?*

75. Although the IRS has expressed interest in determining the method of accounting used by filers of the updated Form 990, the IRS disclosures do not require nonprofit organizations to state whether preparers of their financial statements compiled, reviewed, or audited them. *True or False?*

76. Workers who may appear to be independent contractors but are employees under codified law for IRS purposes are classified as:

   a. Freelance employees
   b. Statutory employees
   c. Contract employees
   d. Directed employees

77. All of the following are differences between workers classified as independent contractors and those classified as homeworkers *except:*

   a. Independent contractors are responsible for payment of all their own taxes; companies using homeworkers must withhold Social Security and Medicare taxes from workers' wages
   b. Independent contractors are unreimbursed for delivery of work materials or goods; employers pay for the transport of work for homeworkers
   c. Independent contractors may supply their own materials; homeworkers' materials or goods are supplied by their employers
   d. Independent contractors may hire employees or subcontractors to perform the actual work; homeworkers perform services personally

78. Which of the following is classified by the IRS as a statutory nonemployee?

   a. A tradesperson subcontracting for a home construction firm
   b. A medical transcriptionist working in her apartment who is paid per the number of words transcribed
   c. A freelance magazine writer
   d. A qualified real estate agent

79. Which of the following shows financial control of an employee for purposes of worker classification?

   a. Making services available to the relevant market
   b. Determining which workers to hire to assist with the work
   c. Where to purchase supplies
   d. Business instruction regarding the timing of work and tools required

80. Jessie Johnson, an independent plumbing contractor, loses income on a project due to overbuying supplies and scheduling overlapping jobs. This loss is an example of:

    a. Behavioral control risk
    b. Entrepreneurial risk
    c. Jobbing risk
    d. Performance risk

81. According to the IRS's list of 20 factors, payment of workers based on invoices submitted is indicative that the worker is a(n):

    a. Direct seller
    b. Statutory nonemployee
    c. Statutory employee
    d. Independent contractor

82. A child performing domestic work for his or her parents is not subject to Social Security and Medicare taxes until he or she reaches age:

    a. 21
    b. 18
    c. 16
    d. Domestic workers of any age are exempt from Social Security and Medicare taxes

83. In all of the following situations an employer is required to furnish Form W-2 to an employee for the previous calendar year **except:**

    a. The employer withheld income or Social Security taxes
    b. The employer paid total wages or other compensation with both totaling $600 or more
    c. The employer paid the employee for services performed
    d. All of the above require the employer to provide a Form W-2 to the employee

84. Except for some religious workers, employees of not-for-profit employers are subject to the worker classification rules. **True or False?**

85. Factors indicating the nature of the employment relationship that have been identified by the U.S. Tax Court include consideration of the relationship that the parties believe they are creating. **True or False?**

86. The *Small Business and Work Opportunity Act of 2007* changed the preparer penalty standard under Code Sec. 6694(a) from:

    a. Substantial authority to realistic possibility

    b. Realistic possibility to reasonable belief that the position would more likely than not be sustained on its merits

    c. More likely than not to a high degree of certainty

    d. Reasonable basis to substantial authority

87. Prior to enactment of the 2007 Small Business Tax Act, the IRS generally would impose a preparer penalty for a tax position adequately disclosed on Form 8275, Form 8275-R, or on the tax return only if the position:

    a. Did not have a more likely than not chance of being sustained in litigation

    b. Was taken on a refund claim

    c. Resulted in issuance of a notice of deficiency for tax liability exceeding $5,000

    d. Was frivolous

88. Under the 2007 Small Business Tax Act, a second-tier Code Sec. 6694(b) penalty of the greater of _____ applies if a tax preparer willfully understates a client's tax liability or recklessly or intentionally disregards the rules or regulations.

    a. $250 or 20 percent of income the preparer derives with respect to the return

    b. $1,000 or 30 percent of income the preparer derives with respect to the return

    c. $3,000 or 40 percent of income the preparer derives with respect to the return

    d. $5,000 or 50 percent of income the preparer derives with respect to the return

89. The taxpayer standard for undisclosed, nonabusive positions is substantial authority, which generally means a ___ chance of being sustained on its merits.

    a. 10 percent

    b. 30 percent

    c. 40 percent

    d. More than 51 percent

90. As a safe harbor for nonsigning preparers, time spent on advice given with respect to events that have occurred that is less than _____ of the aggregate time incurred by the person with respect to the position(s) giving rise to the understatement will not be taken into account in determining whether an individual prepared a "substantial portion" of the return.

    a. 5 percent
    b. 10 percent
    c. 25 percent
    d. None of the above is the floor percentage

91. When there are one or more nonsigning preparers at a firm and no signing preparer, who may be subject to a preparer penalty?

    a. All of the nonsigning preparers may be penalized equally
    b. The individual with overall supervisory responsibility for the position
    c. The firm becomes subject to a whole-firm penalty
    d. The nonsigning preparer(s), supervisor, and the firm as a whole may each be penalized separately

92. For which of the following does the government bear the burden of proof in a proceeding to impose a preparer penalty under Code Sec. 6694(b)?

    a. Willful attempt to understate the tax liability
    b. Reckless or intentional disregard of a rule or regulation
    c. Adequate disclosure of the position
    d. All of the above are issues for which the government bears the burden of proof

93. What change to the preparer penalty rules of Code Sec. 6694(a) applies under the *Emergency Economic Stabilization Act of 2008*?

    a. The more likely than not standard is replaced with the substantial authority standard, equalizing the preparer and taxpayer standards for undisclosed, nonabusive positions
    b. The realistic possibility standard is replaced with a reasonable basis standard
    c. A high degree of certainty standard is substituted for the realistic possibility standard
    d. There is no change to Code Sec. 6694(a)

94. An individual who prepares a claim for refund for a taxpayer in response to an IRS notice of deficiency is not considered a return preparer under either the old standard or the proposed regulations for purposes of Code Sec. 6694. *True or False?*

95. Although the preparer is not required to verify information provided by the taxpayer, under the proposed regulations the preparer must make reasonable inquiries to ascertain the correctness of the taxpayer's position if information appears to be incorrect. *True or False?*

TOP FEDERAL TAX ISSUES FOR 2009 CPE COURSE   (0715-3)

Module 1: Answer Sheet

NAME _____

COMPANY NAME _____

STREET _____

CITY, STATE, & ZIP CODE _____

BUSINESS PHONE NUMBER _____

E-MAIL ADDRESS _____

DATE OF COMPLETION _____

CRTP ID (for CTEC Credit only) _____(CTEC Course # 1075-CE-7153)

On the next page, please answer the Multiple Choice questions by indicating the appropriate letter next to the corresponding number. Please answer the True/False questions by marking "T" or "F" next to the corresponding number.

A $84.00 processing fee wil be charged for each user submitting Module 1 for grading.

Please remove both pages of the Answer Sheet from this book and return them with your completed Evaluation Form to CCH at the address below. You may also fax your Answer Sheet to CCH at 773-866-3084.

You may also go to **www.cchtestingcenter.com** to complete your Quizzer online.

METHOD OF PAYMENT:

☐ Check Enclosed ☐ Visa ☐ Master Card ☐ AmEx

☐ Discover ☐ CCH Account* _____

Card No. _____ Exp. Date _____

Signature _____

* Must provide CCH account number for this payment option

EXPRESS GRADING: Please fax my Course results to me by 5:00 p.m. the business day following your receipt of this Answer Sheet. By checking this box I authorize CCH to charge $19.00 for this service.

☐ Express Grading $19.00   Fax No. _____

Mail or fax to:
CCH Continuing Education Department
4025 W. Peterson Ave.
Chicago, IL 60646-6085
1-800-248-3248
Fax: 773-866-3084

®.CCH
a Wolters Kluwer business

TOP FEDERAL TAX ISSUES FOR 2009 CPE COURSE   (0715-3)

Module 1: Answer Sheet

Please answer the Multiple Choice questions by indicating the appropriate letter next to the corresponding number. Please answer the True/False questions by marking "T" or "F" next to the corresponding number.

1. ___	11. ___	21. ___	31. ___
2. ___	12. ___	22. ___	32. ___
3. ___	13. ___	23. ___	33. ___
4. ___	14. ___	24. ___	34. ___
5. ___	15. ___	25. ___	35. ___
6. ___	16. ___	26. ___	
7. ___	17. ___	27. ___	
8. ___	18. ___	28. ___	
9. ___	19. ___	29. ___	
10. ___	20. ___	30. ___	

Please complete the Evaluation Form (located after the Module 3 Answer Sheet) and return it with this Quizzer Answer Sheet to CCH at the address on the previous page. Thank you.

TOP FEDERAL TAX ISSUES FOR 2009 CPE COURSE   (0716-3)

Module 2: Answer Sheet

NAME _____

COMPANY NAME _____

STREET _____

CITY, STATE, & ZIP CODE _____

BUSINESS PHONE NUMBER _____

E-MAIL ADDRESS _____

DATE OF COMPLETION _____

CRTP ID (for CTEC Credit only) _____ (CTEC Course # 1075-CE-7163)

On the next page, please answer the Multiple Choice questions by indicating the appropriate letter next to the corresponding number. Please answer the True/False questions by marking "T" or "F" next to the corresponding number.

A $60.00 processing fee wil be charged for each user submitting Module 2 for grading.

Please remove both pages of the Answer Sheet from this book and return them with your completed Evaluation Form to CCH at the address below. You may also fax your Answer Sheet to CCH at 773-866-3084.

You may also go to **www.cchtestingcenter.com** to complete your Quizzer online.

METHOD OF PAYMENT:

☐ Check Enclosed   ☐ Visa   ☐ Master Card   ☐ AmEx

☐ Discover   ☐ CCH Account* _____

Card No. _____ Exp. Date _____

Signature _____

* Must provide CCH account number for this payment option

EXPRESS GRADING: Please fax my Course results to me by 5:00 p.m. the business day following your receipt of this Answer Sheet. By checking this box I authorize CCH to charge $19.00 for this service.

☐ Express Grading $19.00   Fax No. _____

Mail or fax to:

CCH Continuing Education Department
4025 W. Peterson Ave.
Chicago, IL 60646-6085
1-800-248-3248
Fax: 773-866-3084

TOP FEDERAL TAX ISSUES FOR 2009 CPE COURSE   (0716-3)

Module 2: Answer Sheet

Please answer the Multiple Choice questions by indicating the appropriate letter next to the corresponding number. Please answer the True/False questions by marking "T" or "F" next to the corresponding number.

36. ___	42. ___	48. ___	54. ___
37. ___	43. ___	49. ___	55. ___
38. ___	44. ___	50. ___	56. ___
39. ___	45. ___	51. ___	57. ___
40. ___	46. ___	52. ___	58. ___
41. ___	47. ___	53. ___	59. ___
			60. ___

Please complete the Evaluation Form (located after the Module 3 Answer Sheet) and return it with this Quizzer Answer Sheet to CCH at the address on the previous page. Thank you.

TOP FEDERAL TAX ISSUES FOR 2009 CPE COURSE   (0717-3))

Module 3: Answer Sheet

NAME _____

COMPANY NAME _____

STREET _____

CITY, STATE, & ZIP CODE _____

BUSINESS PHONE NUMBER _____

E-MAIL ADDRESS _____

DATE OF COMPLETION _____

CRTP ID (for CTEC Credit only) _____ (CTEC Course # 1075-CE-7173)

On the next page, please answer the Multiple Choice questions by indicating the appropriate letter next to the corresponding number. Please answer the True/False questions by marking "T" or "F" next to the corresponding number.

A $84.00 processing fee wil be charged for each user submitting Module 3 for grading.

Please remove both pages of the Answer Sheet from this book and return them with your completed Evaluation Form to CCH at the address below. You may also fax your Answer Sheet to CCH at 773-866-3084.

You may also go to **www.cchtestingcenter.com** to complete your Quizzer online.

METHOD OF PAYMENT:

☐ Check Enclosed   ☐ Visa   ☐ Master Card   ☐ AmEx

☐ Discover   ☐ CCH Account* _____

Card No. _____ Exp. Date _____

Signature _____

* Must provide CCH account number for this payment option

EXPRESS GRADING: Please fax my Course results to me by 5:00 p.m. the business day following your receipt of this Answer Sheet. By checking this box I authorize CCH to charge $19.00 for this service.

☐ Express Grading $19.00   Fax No. _____

Mail or fax to:

a Wolters Kluwer business

CCH Continuing Education Department
4025 W. Peterson Ave.
Chicago, IL 60646-6085
1-800-248-3248
Fax: 773-866-3084

TOP FEDERAL TAX ISSUES FOR 2009 CPE COURSE   (0717-3)

Module 3: Answer Sheet

Please answer the Multiple Choice questions by indicating the appropriate letter next to the corresponding number. Please answer the True/False questions by marking "T" or "F" next to the corresponding number.

61. ___	70. ___	79. ___	88. ___
62. ___	71. ___	80. ___	89. ___
63. ___	72. ___	81. ___	90. ___
64. ___	73. ___	82. ___	91. ___
65. ___	74. ___	83. ___	92. ___
66. ___	75. ___	84. ___	93. ___
67. ___	76. ___	85. ___	94. ___
68. ___	77. ___	86. ___	95. ___
69. ___	78. ___	87. ___	

Please complete the Evaluation Form (located after the Module 3 Answer Sheet) and return it with this Quizzer Answer Sheet to CCH at the address on the previous page. Thank you.

TOP FEDERAL TAX ISSUES FOR 2009 CPE COURSE   (0982-2)

Evaluation Form

Please take a few moments to fill out and mail or fax this evaluation to CCH so that we can better provide you with the type of self-study programs you want and need. Thank you.

About This Program

1. Please circle the number that best reflects the extent of your agreement with the following statements:

	Strongly Agree				Strongly Disagree
a. The Course objectives were met.	5	4	3	2	1
b. This Course was comprehensive and organized.	5	4	3	2	1
c. The content was current and technically accurate.	5	4	3	2	1
d. This Course was timely and relevant.	5	4	3	2	1
e. The prerequisite requirements were appropriate.	5	4	3	2	1
f. This Course was a valuable learning experience.	5	4	3	2	1
g. The Course completion time was appropriate.	5	4	3	2	1

2. This Course was most valuable to me because of:

_____ Continuing Education credit   _____ Convenience of format
_____ Relevance to my practice/   _____ Timeliness of subject matter
      employment   _____ Reputation of author
_____ Price
_____ Other (please specify) _____

3. How long did it take to complete this Course? (Please include the total time spent reading or studying reference materials and completing CPE Quizzer).

Module 1 _____   Module 2 _____   Module 3 _____

4. What do you consider to be the strong points of this Course?

5. What improvements can we make to this Course?

TOP FEDERAL TAX ISSUES FOR 2009 CPE COURSE   (0982-2)

Evaluation Form *cont'd*

General Interests

1. Preferred method of self-study instruction:
    _____ Text   _____ Audio   _____ Computer-based/Multimedia   _____ Video

2. What specific topics would you like CCH to develop as self-study CPE programs? _____
    _____
    _____
    _____

3. Please list other topics of interest to you _____
    _____
    _____

About You

1. Your profession:

    _____ CPA   _____ Enrolled Agent
    _____ Attorney   _____ Tax Preparer
    _____ Financial Planner   _____ Other (please specify)
                                 _____

2. Your employment:

    _____ Self-employed   _____ Public Accounting Firm
    _____ Service Industry   _____ Non-Service Industry
    _____ Banking/Finance   _____ Government
    _____ Education   _____ Other _____

3. Size of firm/corporation:

    _____ 1   _____ 2-5   _____ 6-10   _____ 11-20   _____ 21-50   _____ 51+

4. Your Name _____
    _Firm/Company Name _____
    Address _____
    City, State, Zip Code _____
    E-mail Address _____

THANK YOU FOR TAKING THE TIME TO COMPLETE THIS SURVEY!

NOTES